Legal Advocacy

Legal Advocacy

Lawyers and Nonlawyers at Work

Herbert M. Kritzer

Ann Arbor
THE UNIVERSITY OF MICHIGAN PRESS

Copyright © by the University of Michigan 1998
All rights reserved
Published in the United States of America by
The University of Michigan Press
Manufactured in the United States of America
⊗ Printed on acid-free paper

2001   2000   1999   1998   4   3   2   1

A CIP catalog record for this book is available from the British Library.

Library of Congress Cataloging-in-Publication Data

Kritzer, Herbert M., 1947–
    Legal advocacy : lawyers and nonlawyers at work / Herbert M.
Kritzer.
        p.   cm.
    Includes bibliographical references and index.
    ISBN 0-472-10935-9 (cloth : acid-free paper)
    1. Practice of law—United States.   I. Title.
KF300   .K75   1998
340'.023'73—dc21   98-19708
                                                             CIP

To my teachers at
Colonel White High School
Dayton, Ohio

and most particularly
Stanley L. Blum, social studies
Robert O. Nunemacher, chemistry
Willis Bing Davis, art

Contents

Figures

Tables

Acknowledgments

The research reported in this book was supported by grants from the National Science Foundation (Grant No. SES-9212756), the Robert M. La Follette Institute of Public Affairs, the Research Committee of the University of Wisconsin Graduate School, and the Glenn B. and Cleone Orr Hawkins Endowment to the University of Wisconsin Department of Political Science.

I have received significant research assistance from a number of graduate students over the years that the project has been under way: Charles Epp, Matt Bosworth, Laura Olson, Tracy Wahl, Moses Price, Laila Van Eyck, Greg Jolivette, Andrew Diefenthaler, Jill Carnahan, and Jay Krishnan. I have also benefited from the opportunity to discuss my research with many practitioners and participants in the venues I studied; I would particularly like to thank Jane Buffett, Freg Berg, Diana Weiss, Tom Bush, John Kaiser, Louise Trubek, Mitch Hagopian, Larry Smith, Linda Roth, and Donn Lind. Many of these people have provided valuable comments on draft chapters, as have a number of other persons including Arlen Christenson, Carol Ottenstein, Mark Musolf, Arthur Thexton, William Whitford, Joseph Mettner, Neil Vidmar, Carroll Seron, and Richard Block. Carrie Menkel-Meadow, Neil Vidmar, and Amelia Howe Kritzer read and commented on the entire draft, both substantively and editorially.

The National Organization of Social Security Claimants' Representatives, and particularly its president, Nancy Shor, provided assistance in contacting Social Security practitioners and in locating data on representation patterns. The Bureau of Legal Affairs of the Division of Unemployment Compensation of the Wisconsin Department of Industry, Labor, and Human Relations granted me access to its administrative data base in order to compile data for analysis and to sample respondents and representatives for a participant survey (particular thanks to Mary Stevens and Sandra Stull for their help). The staff of the Wisconsin Employment Relations Commission facilitated my use of the commission's files for compiling data. Administrative staff at the Wisconsin Tax Appeals Commission, particularly Joe Ziesel and Darlene Skolaski, put up with what at times must have seemed like daily calls to find out if a hearing was still going to happen.

I benefited from having the opportunity to present parts of my research to a faculty Law and Society seminar at Indiana University, to an Unemployment Compensation Law Seminar conducted by the State of Wisconsin's Labor and Industry Review Commission, and at a faculty colloquium at the Georgetown Law Center.

CHAPTER 1

Does It Really Take a Lawyer?

What difference does a lawyer make? That is the central question of this book. Usually, this question is posed as the choice between turning some matter or dispute over to a lawyer and handling it on your own. This need not be the case. Consider the following scenarios.

> *It is a beautiful spring Sunday, and you take a drive out into the country. Some idiot makes a left turn across your path. You suffer a broken leg. The idiot is insured by State Farm. You have the following options.*

Doing nothing ("lumping it")[1]
Negotiating a settlement directly with State Farm
Hiring a lawyer, who will most likely request a fee of one-third of the recovery plus his or her expenses[2]

What if you had the option of hiring a "public insurance adjuster" to estimate your damages and negotiate on your behalf with State Farm, paying a commission of only 15 to 20 percent rather than what amounts to a commission of 33 percent? After all, insurance companies use nonlawyer adjusters; why can't you? Perhaps the public adjuster has spent twenty years working for State Farm before going into independent operation.

Or, what about the following situation?

> *It's Friday afternoon. You've been out for a few drinks with your friends after work. You're stopped by a police officer and arrested for driving while intoxicated (DWI). In this case you have two options.*

Pleading guilty and facing the music
Hiring a lawyer and fighting (or negotiating), paying a fee of $100 or more per hour

What if you had the alternative of hiring an experienced "paralegal" who specializes in defending DWI cases, and who charges $50 per hour? Perhaps this person is a retired highway patrol officer who has appeared as a witness in hundreds of traffic cases including many involving DWI.

If you want help with a drunk driving case or a personal injury case or another matter that might lead to having to appear in court, your only choice in the United States is, with some very specific exceptions, to hire a lawyer.[3]

Over much of American history there has been a cyclical debate over the question of whether, or to what degree, nonlawyers should be prevented from providing services in competition with lawyers.[4] The debate has again become loud and contentious at the end of the century. A number of states have conducted, or are in the process of conducting, inquiries into the question of allowing nonlawyers to provide routine legal assistance in specific limited circumstances. In 1992 the American Bar Association created a Commission on Nonlawyer Practice to examine these issues from a nationwide perspective. The commission's final report,[5] issued in 1995, never came before the ABA's House of Delegates for discussion or endorsement. For all purposes, the report was buried, presumably with the hope in the ABA that it would quickly be forgotten.

All of this is happening as the legal profession finds itself under public attack. While criticism of lawyers has a long history, the profession has seldom been used as a major political target, as it was in the Republican Party's 1995 "Contract with America." As part of the contract, the U.S. House of Representatives passed "The Attorney Accountability Act of 1995" (H.R. 988). This proposal, as with most of the contract's provisions, died in the U.S. Senate. The love/hate relationship between the public and lawyers has long been reflected in jokes about lawyers, but other factors suggest that lawyers' public image in the late twentieth century may really have fallen to a low point, with law graduates even being booed at university commencement ceremonies.[6]

The American legal profession is clearly worried about both its image and its prerogatives. It is probably right, particularly about the latter. The profession has generally been extremely successful in securing and protecting limitations on potential competitors. The two previous scenarios represent situations for which alternatives to representation by lawyers are available in one or more common law countries. In England, nonlawyers are free to represent injured persons up to the stage of filing an action in court, although there have been efforts to allow assistance in the lower courts that approaches representation.[7] In Ontario, nonlawyers routinely provide representation in traffic court (as well as in other lower court proceedings), and in settings such as workers' compensation boards.[8]

In fact, lawyers in England possess a monopoly only on representation and advocacy in the courts of law.[9] Nonlawyers may provide legal advice and legal advocacy for matters outside the court context, including personal injury claims which might eventually develop into court cases.[10] Many of the types of tasks routinely handled by lawyers in the United States are handled by nonlawyers in England.

While the solicitors' branch of the English legal profession dominates in the handling of personal injury claims, "loss assessors" are available to individuals who would prefer to pay a representative on a percentage basis to negotiate a settlement with an insurer.[11] The clear attraction of loss assessors is their fee structure—solicitors are not permitted to charge individuals in this way.[12] Little is known about the background or qualifications of loss assessors, although at least some of them worked as "claims inspectors" representing insurance companies before switching to representing claimants.[13] The Law Society, the professional organization of solicitors, regularly warns against the loss assessors,[14] arguing that assessors lack the potential leverage of threatening court action. The Law Society also points out that disgruntled clients of solicitors have means of recourse that are not available to clients of loss assessors. Interestingly, I know of no evidence that shows widespread (if any) dissatisfaction with the services provided by loss assessors. Furthermore, British insurance officials have told me that assessors typically have solicitors to whom they can turn for backup should the need arise.

England uses an extensive set of "administrative tribunals" to deal with issues such as social security (broadly defined) benefits, workplace disputes, housing issues, immigration, and the like. Because these tribunals are not courts, the legal profession must compete with other potential providers of advocacy. In the late 1980s, an empirical study compared the effectiveness of representation before tribunals by lawyers to that by various types of lay advocates of various types. The researchers found no evidence that one type of advocate was consistently more effective than another. In some of the tribunals examined, lay specialists had more impact than either barristers or solicitors; in other tribunals law-trained advocates had more impact, and in others certain lay specialists had impacts more or less equal to that of law-trained advocates.[15] When the researchers asked members of the tribunals (i.e., those who decided the cases) what seemed to be associated with effective representation, the members generally reported that it was not legal training but specialized backgrounds and experience that led to effective representation.[16]

Ontario permits "paralegals" (i.e., nonlawyers) to appear as advocates in the same types of administrative tribunals as does England. In addition, paralegals can represent parties in the lower-level courts—those hearing traffic offenses, minor criminal matters, and small claims.[17] The best information available shows little difference between the lawyers and nonlawyers within specific venues. Clients of paralegals found paralegals more responsive and attentive to their problems, and they believed that the fees charged by paralegals were lower than those they would have had to pay a lawyer for the same work.[18] Adjudicators before whom the paralegals appeared reported occasional problems with such advocates, but tempered these concerns with statements such as the following.

"It should be noted that the Board also sees poor quality representation by lawyers and not just paralegals."

"It has been our experience that for the most part, an experienced non-legal representative does a better job than the lawyer who may not have a background or experience in Workers' Compensation."

"The level of competence tends to vary for all groups. There is good and bad in both. [I have] often seen a lawyer who is completely out of his/her field do a very poor job and the same goes for a paralegal. On the other hand, [I have] seen a paralegal who is used to dealing in court do an outstanding job."[19]

A small survey of clients of one of the best-known companies providing nonlawyer representation in traffic cases found that 96 percent rated the person who represented them as excellent (81 percent) or good (15 percent), and 93 percent would use the company's services again.[20] In contrast, a 1993 U.S. survey of persons who had hired a lawyer in the preceding five years found that only 75 percent would use the same lawyer again.[21] Another 1993 survey found that only 67 percent were satisfied or very satisfied with a lawyer they had used during the preceding ten years.[22] A third survey found that 79 percent of respondents who had used a lawyer in the last five years were satisfied or somewhat satisfied with the lawyer's performance.[23] This limited comparison suggests that nonlawyers are capable of providing services to the satisfaction of their clients.

As it turns out, the United States may not be as different as the last few pages imply. In its 1995 final report, the ABA Commission on Nonlawyer Practice noted that "commission members were genuinely surprised to learn of the extent of nonlawyer practice, both in terms of that which is already lawful and also with regard to new and expanding forms of activity by nonlawyers."[24] Nonlawyers regularly appear as advocates before a variety of administrative and private dispute processing venues, sometimes directly competing with lawyers for clients, and sometimes directly confronting lawyers representing an opposing party. Nonlawyers are generally barred from appearing in court, and the organized legal profession has worked hard, often successfully, but sometimes not, to exclude nonlawyers from even the venues where they currently appear.[25]

The American legal profession makes a number of arguments in justifying why you should not have the option of hiring a nonlawyer.

> The legal professional will put the client's interest first.
> The legal professional is trained in advocacy and legal thinking.
> The legal professional has the knowledge, training, and experience to recognize subtle and important issues and linkages.
> The legal professional can pursue a case "all the way" through the legal system if needed.
> The client has recourse to the legal profession's disciplinary bodies if dissatisfied with the services provided by a lawyer.

These arguments are closely identified with the literature on professionalism and the defining features of professions: formal expertise, other-regardingness, and disciplinary options.[26]

In recent years both interest groups and scholars have challenged the legal profession's ongoing success in excluding nonlawyers from providing representation. The most vocal critic is an organization now called HALT (originally an acronym for Help Abolish Legal Tyranny). HALT presents itself as an organization of consumers of legal services; it argues that Americans should be free to choose the type of representative they need and want, and that the current restrictions on legal practice serve largely to "protect [lawyers'] pocket books at the expense of consumer access."[27]

Richard L. Abel, in the conclusion of his detailed examination of the development and structure of the American legal profession, argues that the profession must "eliminat[e] every restrictive practice unsupported by convincing evidence that it is necessary to protect against incompetence, fraud, or other abuse. . . . The profession should encourage other occupations to advise, negotiate, draft, and represent, offering the supervision of lawyers but not requiring it."[28]

In my own study of the work of lawyers in perhaps the most jealously guarded of venues, civil litigation, I come to the conclusion that paraprofessionals, whom I refer to as "legal brokers," might be as effective and less expensive than legal professionals in handling routine cases of personal and property injury or routine contract disputes. I argue that the nature of the lawyer's work in routine litigation provides little basis to argue that such work should be the exclusive realm of lawyers. I note that, particularly from the side of businesses, it is common for nonlawyers to handle work that, when performed for an individual, is restricted to lawyers (e.g., negotiating the settlement of injury claims).[29] In moments of candor, American lawyers will admit that paralegals can do many, if not most, of the tasks that a lawyer does in certain types of practices. In her study of solo and small-firm lawyers in the New York City area, Carroll Seron quotes a practitioner she calls Robert Rothman: "A good paralegal can do just about everything I can, everything except go to court and meet the client on the initial—you know, selling of the client."[30]

We commonly decry the American "I'll be suing you" culture—our reputed tendency to turn every complaint or problem into a court case. While much of the rhetoric about the litigious American and our disease of "hyperlexis" is overdrawn,[31] there may be a connection between our inclination to use the courts for a wide range of issues and problems,[32] and our granting to the legal profession purview over a variety of activities that in other countries involve a range of service providers. One can look outside the United States for evidence that there may be some connection between the use of courts and the legal profession's control over access to legal advice and advocacy.

For example, the Netherlands and the neighboring German state of Northrhine-Westphalia share most of the social and economic characteristics often said to be associated with litigiousness. Nonetheless, these two areas differ sharply on a variety of indicators of court use. At least part of the reason is probably the larger role assigned to the legal profession in Germany than in the Netherlands. As do American lawyers, German lawyers possess a monopoly on giving legal advice; in contrast, in the Netherlands (as in England) anyone can give legal advice, and many alternative sources of such advice are available.[33]

Asserting Control: How the Legal Monopoly Came to Be

The practice of excluding nonlawyers from providing law-related services is actually a twentieth-century phenomenon, largely a product of the efforts of the bar associations during the 1920s and 1930s. How did the exclusion of nonlawyers from many types of activities come to be? A number of authors have related the general story of the development of the American legal profession and its efforts to secure a monopoly.[34] The success of the "unauthorized practice of law" movement is important for the analysis I present in the chapters that follow. Because state law has governed the practice of law, the specific history of efforts to impose restrictions varies from state to state. However, the general pattern of the organized bar taking the lead is common across states. To illustrate the historical process that brought us to the restrictive situation that dominates in the 1990s, I draw upon (and supplement) a detailed, unpublished history of the California bar's efforts to eliminate nonlawyers from a variety of areas of practice.[35]

In 1872, California enacted a Code of Civil Procedure that explicitly permitted nonlawyers to perform all legal functions other than appearing in court on behalf of fee-paying clients: "Any person may engage in the profession of law. The *profession* is open to all, and it is simply the right to *practice* in Court which is not permitted except to those duly qualified."[36] The result was a plethora of legal service providers. Banks advertised free legal services such as drafting wills and trust agreements to attract customers; these same banks provided legal advice and employed lay agents to handle tasks in probate court on behalf of customers. Various groups involved in the sale of real estate routinely handled legal tasks associated with such sales (and even drafted legal documents unrelated to these tasks). Nonlawyers routinely handled injury and damage claims, with the insurance company's own adjuster dealing with independent claims adjusters representing accident victims. Automobile clubs provided legal services to members on a variety of minor matters. Collection agencies advertised legal services and handled their own cases, without lawyers, in the courts. Accountants provided legal advice on a range of financial issues (tax, receiverships, estates, trusts, etc.), and both the U.S. Treasury Department and the federal Tax Court explicitly permitted accountants to appear as advocates in various proceedings. Under the Code of Civil Procedure of 1872, anyone could practice law in the Justice of the Peace Court and the Police Court. The result was that only in the higher courts of California did the legal profession possess a monopoly—actually a near monopoly because lay employees of collection agencies could appear on behalf of their employers in the higher courts.

Starting early in the twentieth century, the California Bar Association—then a small group with little political influence—unsuccessfully sought to get bills passed by the legislature excluding competitors from engaging in what the CBA viewed as the practice of law. When the CBA did succeed in getting a bill passed in 1921 restricting the activities of powerful competitors such as the banks, those competitors got a referendum on the ballot the following year that overwhelmingly repealed the 1921 law. After the humiliating defeat on the referendum, it was the California Supreme Court that came to the bar's rescue by handing down a decision which adopted a broad definition of the practice of law.

> The practice of law is the doing and performing services in a court of justice in any matter depending therein throughout its various stages

and in conformity with the adopted rules of procedure. But in a larger sense it includes legal advice and counsel and the preparation of legal instruments and contracts by which legal rights are secured although such matter may or may not be depending in court.[37]

The Supreme Court thus opened the door to the CBA to move against a range of competitors. The State Bar Act of 1927 made it a misdemeanor for an unlicensed person to advertise a readiness to "practice law"; the act left undefined what it was to "practice law," simply relying on the Supreme Court's broad definition. By the late 1930s, case law clearly established that giving legal advice for a fee constituted the practice of law.

The bar did not limit its efforts to remove competitors to the development of case law. It pursued two other tactics: using disciplinary procedures against lawyers who worked with the politically weaker competitors and negotiating boundary agreements with the politically more powerful competitors. For some competitors subject to regulation, the bar also sought to work through the competitors' regulatory bodies to limit the competitors' activities.

Because lawyers had always retained exclusive rights to represent injured parties in the higher courts, the successful independent claims adjusters—operating under names like the General Claims Bureau of Southern California, Golden State Adjustment Organization, Royal Adjustment Company, or the West Coast Claims Bureau—relied upon lawyers to handle the cases the adjusters were unable to resolve. Starting in 1930, the bar sought to discipline these attorneys, getting one after another suspended from practice. The end result was to put the independent adjusters out of business.[38]

With the most powerful groups—automobile clubs, banks, title companies, and insurance companies—the bar tried to negotiate agreements limiting what these groups could do in the way of legal work.[39] The auto clubs agreed to restrict their handling of members' legal work to matters "involving sums of money so small that the Club member cannot afford to employ counsel."[40] The bar persuaded the land title companies to limit their legal work to filling in blanks or retyping standard forms.[41] Real estate brokers similarly limited their legal work, and the real estate commissioner of the state agreed to eliminate some of the less standard legal forms that had been included in the real estate handbook.

The banks were very resistant to having limits placed on their legal service activities, which had become an important method of attracting large depositors. In 1933, the state bar filed suit against two of the state's most powerful banks. While the suit was pending, committees from the bar and the California Bankers Association met to try, unsuccessfully, to reach an agreement. In the wake of the failure to reach an agreement, the banks prepared a referendum initiative to secure their (and all laypersons') right to give gratuitous legal advice related to lawful business activities.[42] The vehemence of the bar's negative reaction to the proposed referendum led to its withdrawal and propelled the negotiators to reach an agreement in 1935. The banks agreed that they would not prepare wills, appear in court except through an attorney, or advertise that they gave legal advice. Instead, banks were to encourage their customers to seek the advice of an independent attorney.

The bar failed in its attempt to reach agreements with the insurance industry to end the industry's use of in-house adjusters to negotiate third-party settlements. The bar argued that adjusters could certainly investigate claims on behalf of their employers, but that when it came to negotiating a settlement with a party injured by the company's client, the matter should be turned over to an attorney. The response of the insurance companies was that this was none of the bar's business, and that what their adjusters did was perfectly legal.

The bar won the battle but lost the war in its conflict with the accountancy profession over where to draw the line between what was legitimately the work of one versus the other profession. The fight did not really start until mid-century, after World War II. The bar wanted accountants to refrain from giving legal advice beyond that involved in preparing tax returns. CPAs were unwilling to cease doing the work that they had done for years. The bar made little progress until a judge of the Appellate Department for the Los Angeles Superior Court ruled against an accountant who was suing to collect an unpaid fee. After the accountant testified about the many hours he had spent in the law library doing legal research as part of his work for the client, the judge ruled that this legal research constituted the unauthorized practice of law, and that an accountant could collect a fee only for accounting services and not for giving advice on a difficult point of law.[43]

The American Institute of Accountants and the California Society of Certified Public Accountants considered an appeal to the U.S. Supreme Court (the Superior Court decision was not appealable to the California Supreme Court) but decided not to for three reasons. First, it seemed unlikely that the Supreme Court would agree to hear the decision. Second, the Secretary of the Treasury issued an interpretation of Treasury Department regulations concerning tax practice by accountants that reaffirmed the right of accountants to perform many of the tasks that the bar claimed were the exclusive domain of the legal profession. Third, bar leaders from around the country, including the dean of the Harvard Law School, Erwin Griswold, made public statements urging an accommodation between the two professions.[44] Accountants learned not to describe their consulting of court cases as "legal research," and several years later a California court found that an accountant who had referred to cases for the purposes of determining appropriate accounting principles (rather than as "legal research") had not engaged in the unauthorized practice of law.[45]

Clearly, the California Bar was not completely successful in its efforts to eliminate competitors.[46] Interestingly, the greatest success came in eliminating competition for the business of individuals (e.g., personal injuries, wills and estates, and the like). When it came to the specialized services of large corporations, particularly claims resolution and accountancy, the bar was unable to secure its monopoly. It was able to eliminate some aspects of the competition, but professionals and paraprofessionals continued to perform many or most of the tasks they had done throughout the twentieth century.

We can turn back to the national picture to see how the bar enforced the restrictions it obtained. Most state bars established committees on unauthorized practice. These committees collected reports and initiated legal action. Through the middle of the century (1934 to 1977), the ABA's Special Committee on the Unauthorized Practice of the Law published a newsletter, *Unauthorized Practice News,* which kept the various state committees informed of developments around the country.[47]

As of 1979, state bars continued actively to enforce rules regarding unauthorized practice. The California Bar's Unauthorized Practice Department handled 201 complaints that year. Nationally, enforcement officials handled between 1,600 and 2,000 complaints, investigations, or inquiries.[48] During the period from 1970 to 1980, there were 84 reported cases. Few bar officials were willing to state that unauthorized practice actually threatened lawyers (only 3 of 41 respondents to a survey conducted by Deborah Rhode) while most (23 of 39) asserted that such practice posed a threat to the public.[49] In fact, few of the complaints received by officials came from the consuming public or involved injury to that public: of 1,188 complaints and inquiries, only 27 came from or directly involved the consuming public. Of the 84 reported cases referred to previously, only 9 (11 percent) involved allegations of injury to clients, and 4 of those dealt with individuals who falsely claimed to their clients that they were attorneys.[50]

Nonlawyer Advocates Today

The legal profession has been most successful in excluding nonlawyers from tasks that routinely involve the courts—for example, third-party damage (tort) claims, matters related to probate (drafting and processing wills), dissolution of marriage, criminal and traffic cases. In the administrative arenas where adjudicatory bodies often closely resemble courts in process and function and courts provide largely appellate review, nonlawyers are often regular players. Prominent in this group are the previously mentioned tax specialists, both those who are members of the accountancy profession (CPAs) and nonaccountants who are permitted by both state and federal tax authorities to practice before them in revenue department proceedings, the U.S. Tax Court, and various state equivalents.[51] (At the federal level, authorities have formally recognized non-CPA practitioners by establishing a paraprofession called "enrolled agents.") The Administrative Procedures Act allows federal agencies to determine who is qualified to appear as advocates,[52] and nonlawyers are very common in proceedings before agencies such as the Patent Office,[53] the Immigration and Naturalization Service,[54] and the Social Security Administration.[55] In fact, by one count, as of 1994, nonlawyers can appear as advocates before thirty-eight federal agencies.[56]

Nonlawyers have had a somewhat rougher time in gaining rights to appear before state agencies, because state bar associations have been more inclined to put up a fight. While the bar association's allies on the state courts can do little to help regarding federal agencies, they can be crucial for excluding nonlawyers from appearing before state agencies. Still, the situation is mixed. Every state has an agency to decide contested workers' compensation claims, and twenty of the fifty states permit nonlawyer advocates.[57] Only seventeen states completely exclude nonlawyers from appearing before public utility commissions (PUCs), although twenty-two of the other states limit such appearances to corporate officers or corporate agents[58]—that is, citizens' organizations desiring to appear before the PUCs must be represented by a lawyer.[59] Nonlawyers also appear in appeal hearings associated with the payment of unemployment compensation, zoning variances, eviction from public housing,[60] and a variety of welfare benefits.[61]

One nonpublic venue in which nonlawyers routinely serve as advocates is in labor grievance arbitration, with nonlawyers appearing for both employers and unions. For the latter, nonlawyers are most often inside staff members, but there are nonlawyer labor consultants who appear for employers.

As I mentioned at the beginning of this chapter, the question of what nonlawyers should be permitted to do, and how they should be regulated, has become an increasingly important topic of debate within the legal profession. To return to the example of California, in 1987 the State Bar established a Committee on Public Protection to determine whether public harm was likely to result from the providing of legal services by those who are not members of the bar; whether such harm is substantial enough to warrant regulation; what form any such regulation might take; what entity or entities would be charged with the responsibility for such regulation; how the expense of such regulation could be funded; and what would be an appropriate timetable for consideration of the aforementioned issues.[62]

Much to the surprise of those who called for the creation of the Committee on Public Protection, the committee found that "legal technicians" (as the report referred to them) provide services that are unavailable or unaffordable from lawyers, and that the quality of work of many of the technicians was high. The committee called for replacing the unauthorized practice of law statute with legislation that would simply prohibit someone "who is not an active member of the State Bar from claiming to be an attorney," and requiring that legal technicians register, disclose to clients that they are not attorneys, and become subject to civil and criminal remedies for nonfeasance and malfeasance.

In the wake of the controversy created by the Committee on Public Protection's *Report,* the State Bar of California created a second body, a Commission on Legal Technicians, to develop guidelines for the practice of such technicians. The commission developed recommendations that would have licensed legal technicians in three areas (family law, landlord-tenant law, and bankruptcy), with other areas (government benefits, adoption, etc.) to be considered in the future. The state's Consumer Affairs Department would regulate the legal technicians and provide a source of redress for dissatisfied clients.[63] Nothing has ever come of either this proposal or a companion proposal to start a pilot program for technicians handling landlord-tenant matters; the former stalled in the state legislature, and the latter was voted down by the State Bar's Board of Governors.[64] A 1993 survey of lawyers in California showed that a clear majority opposed permitting nonlawyer legal technicians to provide paid legal assistance to clients (58 percent oppose, 25 percent allow, 17 percent unsure), although a majority expected that this would happen in the future (56 percent it will happen, 15 percent it won't, 29 percent unsure).[65]

In recent years, at least a dozen states have considered measures to reform traditional prohibitions on unauthorized practice of law by permitting at least some forms of nonlawyer practice in a variety of areas that the bar has called its own for most of the twentieth century.[66] In 1993, the American Bar Association's Commission on Nonlawyer Practice conducted hearings around the country.[67] The following year, the commission issued a "Discussion Draft" of its factual findings, based on those hearings plus background research on the status of nonlawyer practice in the states. The commission's final report extended the discussion about the current state of nonlawyer practice, by advancing a series of recommendations reflecting its collective judgment that such practice

was here to stay;
provided a valuable service to the public; and, if anything,
should be expanded rather than restricted.

The commission's recommendation also recognized the need to come to grips with the issue of regulating the activities of nonlawyer practitioners in ways that genuinely protected the public without denying to the public the services such practitioners could provide. Confronted by intense lobbying by some state bar leaders, the commission did not go so far as to argue that the ABA should urge the individual states to make specific changes;[68] instead it merely urged states to "allow nonlawyer representation in state administrative agency proceedings" and to weigh carefully the costs and benefits of permitting a wide range of other nonlawyer activities.[69] As noted previously, the ABA leadership essentially buried these recommendations when they were presented to the ABA Board of Governors. The commission's report was referred to various committees for further consideration and discussion. Neither the commission's report nor its recommendations have, at least as this book goes to press almost two years later, ever emerged back onto the ABA's agenda. Nonetheless, by the summer of 1997, the legislatures of at least fourteen states were considering bills dealing with provision of legal services by nonlawyers.[70]

Despite this current interest in nonlawyer practice, and the fact that lawyers and nonlawyers regularly compete for clients and confront each other as advocates in a variety of venues, there is almost no research that directly compares the performance of lawyer and nonlawyer advocates in those venues.[71] The groups debating the future of nonlawyer practice have made no effort to commission empirical research that would provide such comparisons. The extant research, most of it from fifteen to twenty years ago, fails to find the kinds of differences that either the rhetoric of professionalism or the rhetoric of the profession would lead one to expect.[72]

A study of the Social Security Administration's (SSA) hearing system in the mid-1970s[73] by Mashaw et al. reported a significant amount of dissatisfaction with the quality of "much of the legal representation" at SSA hearings. This was attributed to attorneys' failing to invest the time necessary to become familiar with either the particular facts of a case or the governing law.[74] In contrast, the authors reported the impression that nonlawyers knowledgeable about the system (typically persons who previously worked in or as consultants to the system) "provide excellent representation."[75]

The only other area in which there is been systematic comparison of lawyer and nonlawyer advocacy in the United States concerns disputes over the payment of veterans' benefits.[76] (Generally, because of extreme statutory restrictions on fees that may be charged, lawyers have not provided representation to veterans denied benefits by the Veterans' Administration, now the Department of Veterans' Affairs.) The results of those analyses have been mixed. One comparison of paid lawyer representation versus volunteer representatives from veterans' service organizations in discharge upgrade proceedings showed substantially higher success rates for lawyers: 72.73 percent versus 48.28 percent.[77] In contrast, in the more broadly defined arena of veterans' benefits, the difference in success for lawyer representatives versus service organization representatives is only one or two percentage points: 16 to 17 percent versus 18 percent.[78]

Thinking about Why Legal Training Might Matter

We now come back to the core question: Does it really matter whether an advocate has formal legal training? The traditional argument that it does matter revolves around the professional ideology of the bar. A better starting point, however, is to think through a variety of dimensions that might be relevant to understanding the practice of representation. As it will turn out, I will focus on only a limited subset of the possible factors, effectively controlling for the others.

What are the core dimensions that serve to differentiate among representatives? I have identified three general dimensions—expertise, representative–client relationships, and accountability and control—and within each of those a series of three subdimensions (which are listed in table 1).[79] While all of the general dimensions are relevant for a complete comparison of lawyer and nonlawyer advocacy, not all of the subdimensions are equally important. Let me explicate each of the elements of this typology.[80]

Expertise

The three subdimensions of expertise are:

> *Formal training vs. insider knowledge*
>> Should expertise be defined in terms of formal training and credentials (e.g., a law degree or a license as a certified public accountant), or should it be defined in terms of knowledge,

particularly people knowledge, gained from day-to-day practice and experience dealing with particular types of issues in a
specific setting?

Generalist vs. specialist
Should expertise be defined in terms of a broad base of knowledge that recognizes the possible interrelationships among a
wide range of issues (e.g., an unemployment compensation
dispute over what constitutes grounds for discharge for misconduct may be directly relevant to a pending criminal charge
or to a discrimination claim), or should it focus on detailed
knowledge of the rules and regulations governing one specific
area (e.g., unemployment compensation)?

Substantive vs. process
Does the core expertise consist of the substance of law, regulations, and so on, governing decisions in a specific forum (or a
specific type of case), or does it consist of the hearing/advocacy
process itself?

In the public discourse, expertise is the primary dimension in the
debates over who should and should not be permitted to provide representation. Each of the subdimensions is relevant to the expertise issue, but the
relative balance among them varies depending upon the specific context.
For example, the conflict between the two English legal professions over
rights of audience in court revolves heavily around process-related expertise: barristers claim to have the skills necessary to be effective oral advocates in court, while solicitors argue that they too have such expertise,

TABLE 1.   Dimensions of Advocacy Representation

1. Nature of expertise
   a. Formal training vs. insider knowledge
   b. Generalist vs. specialist
   c. Substantive vs. process

2. Representative–Client Relationship
   a. Pre-existing vs. ad hoc
   b. Broker vs. alter ego
   c. Agency vs. fiduciary (delegate vs. trustee)

3. Accountability and control
   a. Shareholder vs. nonshareholder
   b. Regulated vs. unregulated
   c. Client-centered vs. forum-centered

pointing to their regular appearance in lower courts.[81] In Ontario, as discussed above, independent paralegals regularly provide representation for traffic offenders in the traffic courts; these representatives' effectiveness comes from their intimate knowledge of the process that derives from their prior experience as traffic officers prosecuting such cases in the same forums where they now appear as advocates for offenders.

In my previous research and writing on lawyers in ordinary civil litigation, I dealt extensively with the issue of formal training versus insider knowledge as applied to routine litigation in the United States.[82] Other studies of those involved in the resolution of routine injury claims also emphasize knowing the other players, knowing what cases are worth, and being able to process cases through a routinized system.[83] A study of lawyers and clients in divorce cases emphasized not the broad precepts of the law governing divorce but the lawyers' explanations to their clients of what to expect from the judges and opposing lawyers. Thus, the divorce lawyers emphasized and relied more on their "people knowledge" than on their formal legal skill or training.[84]

The final expertise subdimension is the generalist vs. specialist dimension. As noted in the introduction, part of the bar's defense of its monopoly has rested upon the need to be able to see beyond the specific aspects of a particular claim or issue. However, what is the relevant broader perspective? In a tax claim, there may be accounting issues implicit in the tax matter, and the specialized knowledge of a tax accountant may be more relevant than the generalized knowledge of an attorney.[85] For example, Clog Away, a small plumbing company, might have a small law firm, Smith & Smith, that regularly handles its legal work. It is likely that each of the lawyers at Smith & Smith who does work for companies like Clog Away has a general business practice, rather than that the firm is organized around a series of specialties such as tax. If a tax dispute came up, Clog Away's accountant might be better able to represent the company than would a lawyer at Smith & Smith.

Representative–Client Relationship

The three subdimensions of representative–client relations are:

Preexisting vs. ad hoc
> Are representatives retained on a one-shot, issue-specific basis, or does the representation extend across cases and issues, and include structuring predispute activities to avoid problems or to position the client for favorable outcomes (i.e., is the representation anticipatory or simply responsive)?

Broker vs. alter ego

> Are representatives there solely to reflect the interest of the client, or are they recognized as having interests of their own that may not be entirely consistent with those of the client (e.g., the outside, retained representative who is concerned with earning a fee versus the inside representative whose future is directly tied to the future of the party represented)?

Agency vs. fiduciary (delegate vs. trustee)

> Are representatives expected simply to act on behalf of the interest of the client as the client defines that interest, or are representatives expected to exercise independent judgment as to what is and is not in the client's interest?[86]

My hypothetical plumber with the tax problem provides an excellent example of the question of choosing between a representative that has been involved in the issues or process that led to the need for advocacy versus retaining a representative on a case-specific basis. Beyond the question of start-up costs (i.e., the one-shot representative must devote substantial energies to understanding the specifics and background of the case), the ongoing representative is more likely to see the broader picture into which the current dispute fits. The accountant knows the accounting structure used by the plumber and knows the implications of various outcomes for the continuation of that structure. Furthermore, the accountant combines this ongoing connection with specialized knowledge relevant for the resolution of the dispute.

This combination of an ongoing relationship with specialized knowledge may be common. This can be further illustrated by an unemployment compensation example. Presume that Clog Away has retained the firm UC Inc. to manage its unemployment compensation affairs (a number of national, regional, and local firms provide such services).[87] UC Inc. has assisted Clog Away in establishing a series of procedures to conform to the regulations surrounding eligibility for unemployment compensation. Clog Away fires an employee for habitual tardiness, and the employee appeals his denial of unemployment compensation benefits. Clog Away could hire its law firm, Smith & Smith, to represent it at the hearing concerning benefits for its former employee, but Smith & Smith knows nothing about Clog Away's personnel practices and charges $130 per hour (it is also unlikely that anyone at Smith & Smith has extensive experience appearing before the Unemployment Compensation Appeal Board). On the other hand, UC Inc. is thoroughly familiar with the relevant personnel procedures, knows what the administrative law judge will be looking for, and charges only $75 per hour. *No one at UC Inc. has a law degree.*

The potential for conflicts of interest between lawyers and clients is well known.[88] While the ethical ideal of the legal profession is that the lawyer acts without regard to his or her own interest, serving purely as the client's "alter ego," lawyers and law firms do have their own interests, which may not always be the same as those of their clients. I label the relevant subdimension of representation as "broker vs. alter ego" with the former indicating the relevance of the representative's own interest and the latter indicating that the representative serves solely as the client's alter ego.[89]

The traditional analysis of conflicts of interest between lawyer and client focuses on the incentives structured by methods of compensation.[90] Under certain circumstances, the hourly-fee lawyer has an incentive to devote substantial time to a matter. The fixed-fee lawyer has an incentive to minimize the time devoted to a matter, and the contingent-fee lawyer has an incentive to avoid activities that require substantial amounts of time and effort even if those activities will increase the benefit to the client. These problems do not necessarily occur, either because of the lawyer's ethical commitment or because the economic circumstances of the lawyer or the case work against them, but the potential is present. Clients can avoid problems by close involvement with the lawyer,[91] but many clients have neither the time nor the knowledge to provide the oversight needed.

The issue of self vs. client interest can be viewed more broadly. For example, for larger businesses there is the distinction between inside and outside representation. Particularly in administrative proceedings with relatively low stakes, an organizational party may choose to have an internal specialist who is not a direct party to the dispute in question serve as its representative (e.g., in a hearing before the Unemployment Compensation Appeals Board, a staff attorney from the General Counsel's office may serve as the representative, calling and questioning witnesses but offering no testimony of his or her own). The inside representative may be a lawyer, a paralegal, or a specialist of some other type (e.g., a personnel manager or fringe benefits manager).

The third subdimension of representative–client relations, agency vs. fiduciary, concerns the kind of role the representative plays in reflecting the interests of the client. One approach to representation is that the representative serves as an agent or delegate, simply carrying out the instructions of the client with a minimal exercise of discretion. Alternately, the representative may function as a fiduciary or trustee using discretion to advance the client's interest even if the specific act or decision is not what the client would have chosen to do acting on his or her own.[92] In some ways, this last dimension is most relevant to the professional/nonprofessional distinction. One aspect of the "ideology of the professional" is the application of independent knowledge based upon expertise acquired and certified through formal processes. As a consequence, one would expect professionals to prefer the fiduciary approach over the agency approach; however, this expectation is tempered by norms that require the professional to obtain approval from the client for key decisions and actions.

This subdimension is related to the substantive vs. process subdimensions of expertise. One might distinguish between the substance of action and the process of action. A representative might take a delegate approach in regard to the substance of the representation (i.e., in regard to the goals the representation is intended to serve). At the same time, the representative may have more discretion regarding the means (i.e., the process), serving more as a trustee in terms of deciding how to achieve the goals of the client.

Accountability and Control

There are three subdimensions of accountability and control.

Regulated vs. unregulated
> Is the representative answerable to some licensing or disciplinary authority?

Client-centered vs. forum-centered
> Is the representative's allegiance primarily to specific clients, or is it to the forum in which the representative appears on a regular basis?

"Shareholder" vs. nonshareholder
> Does control flow in part from the representative's having a direct stake in the outcome (i.e., the contingent-fee lawyer who will receive a share of the winnings, or the civil rights attorney who will receive a fee award set by the court), or is the representative's interest not directly related to the outcome of the specific case?

One standard issue raised by the legal profession in opposing infringements by nonlawyers on what the profession claims as its turf is that the dissatisfied client of the nonlawyer has little or no recourse. Of course, this blanket charge must be more carefully specified because some types of representatives (e.g., accountants, real estate brokers, etc.) are subject to licensing and disciplinary procedures of licensing boards. Even with this modification, many actual and potential representatives are not subject to formal discipline. As I discussed previously, few complaints about lay representatives come from dissatisfied clients; almost all complaints come from lawyers concerned about threats to their livelihood. While the small number of client complaints may reflect general satisfaction with nonlawyer representatives, it might also be that such complaints would rise substantially if fee-for-service paraprofessionals became a prominent alternative.

While regulation and formal discipline are the most often cited forms of control, there are at least two other mechanisms through which to constrain representatives. The first of these is informal group control. For example, in the criminal arena, we know that the "courtroom workgroup" exercises considerable control over the defense attorneys who are regular players,[93] and we know that clients of these attorneys—particularly clients of public defenders—perceive themselves as having little or no control over their attorneys.[94] In contrast, there is no evidence that the control of lawyers handling white-collar defense is forum-centered.[95] While there is little or no evidence that American lawyers handling civil trial work look to the court as their primary locus of loyalty and control,[96] the British barrister, removed from his or her client by the two-stage structure of representation, may focus more on the expectations of the court than those of the client.[97] In contrast, the elite of the American legal profession is so dependent on a narrow range of clientele that it is often willing to bend to the demands of the client.[98]

A third form of control flows from economic incentives. Compensation through a commission payment system—as exists for real estate brokers, contingent-fee lawyers, and English loss assessors—creates a shareholder interest in the outcome. This interest is not necessarily identical to that of the client, but by manipulating the nature and condition of the shareholder interest one can control the actions of the representative in a variety of ways. At the extreme, one may effectively limit the availability of representation—Wisconsin's statutory limit of ten percent on representatives' fees for unemployment compensation claimants has led to little interest in such work from the legal profession.[99] Share holding affects not only the availability of representation, but also the content of representation, and possibly the results achieved as well. Lawyers who will receive a percentage of a recovery have an incentive to concentrate on the monetary aspects of dispute resolution rather than seeking alternative forms of problem resolution.[100] However, in cases where the potential outcome is fixed rather than negotiable, a lawyer working on a "no win, no pay" basis has more of an incentive to succeed for the client than does a lawyer with no direct stake in the outcome.

Comparing Advocates

The bottom-line question in comparing advocates is whether there is a difference in the results achieved. Of course, even the most effective advocate will not win every case; sometimes the facts and/or the law are not favorable.[101] Thus, one needs aggregate statistics to make this bottom-line assessment. However, such statistics tell us little about why differences do or do not exist. To understand the basis of the patterns in outcomes, we need to combine the dimensions described above with a broader notion of advocate effectiveness that considers performance as well as results. Advocate effectiveness in this broader sense involves a set of interrelated elements.[102]

> Recognition of the core questions at issue
> Quality of questioning of witnesses
> Relationship between evidence presented and issue to be decided
> Nature of the resources employed
> Preparation of the client for the hearing
> Ability to counter and/or respond to issues raised by the opposing
> side or by the third party (adjudicator, mediator, etc.)

I did not seek to formalize these elements of effectiveness but rather used them as observational and analytic guides.

Research Design

Because of the various dimensions described above, drawing conclusions about nonlawyer advocates from a single setting is not possible (except with regard to that setting). Furthermore, the complexity of the possible combinations of dimensions makes impractical a research design that covers all of those combinations. My approach was to select sites using a "replication logic" so that the venues I examined varied along key dimensions.[103] In each of these venues I employed a mixed research strategy that combined statistical assessment of outcomes with observation of processes.

I looked at four very different settings (all located in Wisconsin, but some embedded in national systems):[104] appeals of unemployment compensation claims, state tax appeals before the Wisconsin Tax Appeal Commission, appeals of denials of social security disability claims, and labor grievance arbitrations before arbitrators from the Wisconsin Employment Relations Commission. For each venue, I first observed hearings (spread over a period of 18 to 36 months, depending on the venue); based on these observations, I formed tentative conclusions about the effectiveness of lawyers and nonlawyers. I then looked at quantitative indicators of outcome, using either institutional reports or data I collected or processed from institutional records. Had I done this the other way around (looked first at outcomes and then observed), my observations might have been biased by what I knew from the quantitative analysis (i.e., if nonlawyers were less effective than lawyers, I would be looking for reasons why this was the case).[105] For all four venues, my statistical results were consistent with my observational conclusions. I supplemented these two primary sources of data with information obtained from surveys of participants, informal conversations with advocates and adjudicators, and, for one venue, a small-scale experiment.

In the first two of the settings (unemployment compensation appeals and state tax appeals), I included unrepresented parties in the observation and the statistical analysis. They provide a useful baseline for comparison. In the Social Security appeals, I observed only represented parties because of the necessity of getting advance permission to be present (I had a list of advocates from various sources, and through them I could obtain both the time and date of the hearings and permission from their clients to be present).[106] There was no practical way to obtain in advance lists of unrepresented claimants (the relevant files of the Social Security Administration are confidential). In labor grievance arbitrations, both sides almost always have some type of advocate, although the line between an advocate and a party can be very fuzzy.

Plan of the Book

In the following four chapters, I look in detail at each of the four venues. I will describe the kinds of issues involved in the cases and processing of those cases. In each chapter, I provide sufficient detail for one or more exemplary cases to give a good picture of the nature of the hearings. Because of the differences in process, advocates, and cases, I cannot provide a single, integrated analysis, either of the quantitative indicators or of the observational material.

As will quickly become evident, the pattern I found is complex. One cannot make simple statements that lawyers are better than nonlawyers, or that nonlawyers are just as good (or better) than lawyers. The framework described previously does provide a way of understanding the patterns.

The implications of my analysis for the legal profession and for the availability of legal advocacy are potentially profound. In the concluding chapter I will argue that this study shows both the need to make available alternative types of representation and the need to rethink some aspects of legal training and practice.

CHAPTER 2

Unemployment Compensation Appeals

The system of unemployment compensation used in the United States was established as part of the New Deal in the 1930s. The first state to create a program was Wisconsin (the legislature passed the statute in 1932, with first benefits coming about five years later).[1] The Social Security Act of 1935 contained provisions to extend the system nationwide. The structure of the Wisconsin program, as modified by the 1935 federal statute, continues to provide the basis of unemployment compensation in the United States.[2]

The designers of the system closely tied benefits to prior employment. The system pays benefits as a function of prior wages (rather than providing a uniform benefit rate for all recipients as do employment security systems in many other countries). Furthermore, employers fund the system by paying taxes based on the size of their work forces and their prior claims experience. In part, the purpose of this design was to encourage employers to create work structures that minimized unemployment by creating disincentives for employers to lay off workers. Ironically, this provision may have served to increase the level of conflict in the system: employers have incentives to contest claims of former employees, because by lowering the number of claims paid, the employer reduces the taxes it must pay.[3]

The goal of the system is to provide transitional income for those who lose their jobs through no fault of their own. The system is not intended to provide compensation to all persons whose employment ends. Persons ineligible for compensation include those whose former employment is not covered (e.g., self-employed, employment while a full-time student), those who voluntarily leave employment (with specific exceptions), those whose employment is terminated for misconduct (broadly construed), those who have not worked long enough to establish eligibility, and those who have exhausted their eligibility for unemployment benefits. Furthermore, to receive compensation, a person must be available for work and, in theory, actively seek a job while receiving benefits.

These limitations on eligibility for unemployment compensation lead to large numbers of disputes between claimants and their former employers, or between claimants and officials of the agency administering the unemployment compensation program. The conflict between claimants and former employers arises because employers pay unemployment taxes based upon compensation claims filed by former employees;[4] employers can minimize their liability for unemployment taxes by avoiding having claims filed by former employees. Sophisticated employers go to significant lengths to minimize the unemployment compensation taxes that they pay.

A person who finds him- or herself unemployed must file a claim with the unemployment compensation bureau (UCB), providing the UCB with information on employment over the last 18 months, including dates and employers, and the circumstances leading to the end of the employment relationship. Many claims are noncontroversial: for example, a seasonal layoff, the end of a construction project, or layoffs because of surplus inventory or low demand. In cases where there is any question about eligibility, a "claims deputy" investigates the circumstances, which often simply involves interviewing the claimant and/or the employer. In Wisconsin in 1993, of the approximately 164,000 such "determinations" concerning individuals who were monetarily eligible for compensation,[5] 53 percent (about 87,000) were denied. The majority of these denials (64 percent) involved issues unrelated to the end of employment (i.e., some failure to comply with the UC regulations such as timely filing of claim cards, failure to engage in a work search, etc.).[6] These denials led to about 20,000 appeals in 1993.[7]

In all states appeals of initial determinations must be decided by an "impartial tribunal." In Wisconsin this unit is called the Bureau of Legal Affairs (BOLA). Administrative law judges[8] employed by BOLA conduct hearings for all appeals of initial determinations of unemployment claims.[9] In Wisconsin, all of these judges are lawyers; in some states, there is no requirement that "referees" (the more generic title used to refer to persons deciding these cases) have law degrees.[10] Each state sets the rules governing the appeals process, following standards imposed by the federal government.[11] Some of the federal mandates have significant influence on the hearing process.

A party dissatisfied with the judge's decision has the right to appeal that decision up the administrative ladder.[12] In Wisconsin that second level appeal goes to the Labor and Industry Review Commission (LIRC).[13] In 1994, LIRC affirmed the administrative law judge's decision in 93 percent of the cases it reviewed.[14] A party who is still dissatisfied may appeal the second-level decision to state court.

Representation in Unemployment Compensation Appeals

Throughout the appeals process, parties can employ the services of an advocate, who need not be an attorney. Wisconsin requires no explicit qualifications for nonattorney "agents" appearing in UC cases.[15] While one might argue that such representation would fall under laws governing the practice of law, the bar has not sought to apply the statutes governing the unauthorized practice of law to UC representation. This laissez-faire view does not hold for all states;[16] for example, the Michigan bar went to the state supreme court (unsuccessfully) in an effort to eliminate non-lawyer advocates in contested UC cases.[17] In other states, the bar had more success in blocking nonlawyer advocates from appearing as advocates, even when state law appears to have permitted representation by "authorized agents."[18]

On the claimant's side, advocates appear in only a small fraction of cases; during calendar year 1991, 13,273 claimants appeared at hearings.[19] Of these, only 9.2 percent had an advocate, about three-quarters of whom were lawyers. The nonlawyers included union officials, law students, and other advocates. The absence of representatives is at least in part due to limitations on fees that a representative might earn. Under Wisconsin law, attorneys (and nonattorney agents) representing claimants may receive no more than 10 percent of the benefits at issue;[20] given a maximum benefit period of 26 weeks and a maximum benefit of around $200 per week,[21] this creates a fee-cap of about $500.

Characterizing representation on the employer side is more complex, because the distinction between the employer and the representative is often ambiguous. For example, a large employer may have staff in the personnel department who have experience as advocates in UC appeals, or the employer may have inside legal staff. In some cases, these staff may appear solely as advocates, not having been involved in the events leading to the end of the claimant's employment. In other cases, these staff may have been involved in the decision to terminate employment and will appear at the appeal both as an advocate and as a witness. Of the 10,740 employers who appeared at UC appeals hearings in 1991, lawyers or corporate counsel appeared on behalf of 1,790, nonlawyer agents appeared on behalf of 847, and "inside" staff (other than corporate counsel) appeared for 8,434. Those referred to as "agents" are persons working for specialized firms that provide a variety of services related to managing unemployment compensation matters to businesses; the backgrounds and expertise of these agents vary widely.

The presence of these agents who specialize in UC matters suggests one of the key asymmetries between claimants and employers. Claimants tend to be one-shot players, concerned primarily about their immediate financial needs. Employers, on the other hand, typically have concerns well beyond the individual claim: they seek to establish and enforce procedures that minimize their liability for UC taxes. Furthermore, while claimant representatives are strictly limited in the fees they can charge, there are no limits on what employer representatives can charge. However, firms providing UC management services typically provide those services as a bundle and do not bill separately for appearing at UC appeals hearings.[22]

The Hearing Process

Three factors combine to structure the style of hearings: the lack of representation for the vast majority of claimants, the types of issues raised, and the need to dispose of large numbers of cases very quickly. While a national commission that reviewed the unemployment compensation system concluded that "parties involved in disputed [unemployment compensation] claims should have representation,"[23] the reality is that few hearings involve persons who themselves are not party to the disputed issues. The absence of representation, particularly for the "one-shot" claimant,[24] creates a need for someone other than the parties or their representatives to take on the primary responsibility to identify the issue for determination under the UC regulations and to extract the evidence and testimony relevant for arriving at a just determination. This burden falls on the administrative law judges.

While UC appeals can raise a number of issues, one dimension is centrally important: does the dispute relate to employment separation, or is the issue about other aspects of the eligibility equation (e.g., did a claimant have "good cause" for failing to attend a workshop on how to find a job?). The former usually involves a conflict between the claimant and the employer; the latter usually involves a dispute between the claimant and those who administer the compensation program. When the issue does not concern job separation, it is rare for the employer to appear at the hearing, and the UCB does not as a matter of practice appear as an adverse party at those hearings. Moreover, while most UC claimants appear unrepresented at appeals, representation is more likely at separation appeals (10.3 percent of those who appear have representatives) than at nonseparation appeals (6.7 percent have representatives).

The UC judges work under a great deal of time pressure. Given that the purpose of unemployment compensation is to provide a short-term financial cushion for individuals who find themselves unemployed, it is important to provide a quick avenue of redress for individuals who believe that the system has incorrectly denied them benefits. Furthermore, federal mandates require that 60 percent of appeals be heard and decided within thirty days of filing and 80 percent within forty-five days.[25] These expectations force judges to handle hearings expeditiously—some would say hurriedly—getting to the core issue as quickly as possible. As a result of (1) nonadversarial cases involving nonseparation issues, (2) the lack of representation for most claimants, and (3) the pressures to handle hearings quickly, administrative law judges depart significantly from the American style of adversarial presentation of cases. There are two archetypes for case presentation. The common-law approach is termed adversarial because the burden is placed on the parties to a dispute to identify and present evidence. In the pure adversarial model, the decision maker—whether it be a single professional adjudicator (e.g., a judge), a panel of professional adjudicators, or a panel of lay adjudicators (a jury)—functions as a passive receiver of information, intervening only to resolve procedural disputes and maintain decorum (in the case of professional adjudicators).

The civil-law system generally rejects the adversarial approach and uses in its place what is technically referred to as an inquisitorial model. While the term *inquisitorial* harks back to such sinister events as the Spanish Inquisition, in law it simply refers to a system in which the adjudicator is responsible for obtaining the evidence needed to make his or her decision. In a pure inquisitorial model, the adjudicator would not rely upon the parties to identify relevant evidence; they would be present to respond to the questions and requests of the adjudicator. In practice, most civil-law countries do not rely upon a pure inquisitorial model. Judges often rely upon the parties to inform them of relevant evidence and questions to ask. In many countries one judge is responsible for assembling the evidence, and another will review this evidence (and perhaps hear arguments by the parties) to decide the case. The degree to which a proceeding may be characterized as inquisitorial varies, with Germany typically recognized as being more inquisitorial and other countries being more "dispositive," employing a process in which the parties determine what issues to raise, what evidence to introduce, and what arguments to make.[26]

In practice, a continuum exists between the adversarial approach, in which the adjudicator is a passive recipient of evidence provided by the parties and their advocates, and the inquisitorial approach, in which the adjudicator has the responsibility to obtain the facts needed to reach a decision. Rather than thinking about the pure models, it is more productive to contrast an "advocate-centered" system (i.e., one falling toward the adversarial end of the continuum) and an "adjudicator-centered" system (one falling more toward the inquisitorial end). Unemployment compensation appeal hearings in Wisconsin are adjudicator-centered.

A Typical Hearing

While one must be cautious in describing a "typical hearing," there does seem to be a clear structure to the hearing. In this section, I provide a sense of what such a hearing is like, first by outlining the process and then by providing a brief synopsis of an actual hearing. For purposes of illustration, I will assume the appeal involves a separation issue, and that neither party is represented by a professional or paraprofessional advocate. This will provide some basis for comparison with what happens when an advocate appears for one or both parties.

The hearing room may look like a miniature courtroom, or it can simply be a room with an arrangement of tables. The administrative law judge will ask the parties to come into the room and tell them where to sit. The claimant may or may not bring witnesses; the employer typically has a witness or two in addition to someone serving as spokesperson (the spokesperson will normally testify as the employer). The judge will then call the proceedings to order (in Wisconsin, the judge creates a formal record by tape-recording the proceedings) and elicit from the parties a statement of the formal issue such as

> *Claimant:* I was discharged, but no misconduct was involved.
> *Employer:* The claimant was discharged for misconduct.

It is common for the judge to have to prompt the parties for these statements by asking a few questions based upon the initial determination. (The issues considered in the initial determination also affect the length of time scheduled for the hearing, with the typical misconduct case being allocated between sixty and ninety minutes, and the typical "quit for good cause" case being allocated forty-five to sixty minutes.)

After the judge and parties have framed the issue, the judge will determine which side to hear first. In misconduct cases, the employer generally goes first; in quit-for-good-cause cases, the claimant generally goes first. The reason for this order is that the party going first generally has the burden of establishing his, her, or its position. In a discharge case, the initial presumption is that a discharge is not for misconduct, so the employer must establish that misconduct did occur or benefits will be granted. In a quit-for-good-cause case, the presumption is that the claimant quit for a reason other than good cause; thus the claimant must establish that there was good cause for quitting, or benefits will be denied. One implication of this burden of proof is that if the side which has that burden fails to appear at the hearing, the judge's decision will usually favor the side without the burden of proof. (If neither side shows up, the judge will dismiss the appeal.) It also means that if only the side with the burden of proof shows up, but cannot establish its case, the judge will rule for the no-show side!

With the issue stated and the order of testimony determined, the judge swears all persons who will testify. In a misconduct case, the judge then will determine who from the employer's side should testify first. Questioning will start with the witness's position with the employer, length of employment, and relation to the issues in the case. The judge will ask the employer's witness about the claimant's job, including title, duties, dates of employment, and the manner in which the employer notified the claimant of the dismissal. The judge will explore the nature of the alleged misconduct next; this might encompass attendance problems, tardiness problems, neglect of duties or poor work performance, or violation of work rules. The judge will ask the witness for records documenting absenteeism, tardiness, etc. The judge will want to know how the employee was informed of what was expected by the employer (such as an employee manual containing the expectations or a list of posted work rules) and whether the employer had previously warned the claimant about infractions. The judge will explore the existence and application of a "progressive discipline" system. The judge will complete questioning, then ask the witness to add anything else that seems relevant. The claimant then may cross-examine the witness, although the claimant seldom has many, if any, questions.

Often the first witness for the employer will be a personnel official who oversaw the discipline process, made the final termination decision, and informed the claimant of the termination. Frequently, this witness was not directly involved in the misconduct, and a second witness, such as the claimant's immediate supervisor, testifies regarding the specifics of the misconduct. After the judge completes his or her questions, the employer's spokesperson gets the opportunity to ask additional questions, and the claimant has the opportunity to cross-examine. Depending upon the nature of the events, the employer may have brought additional witnesses; the judge need not call these witnesses if, in his or her judgment, their testimony would be duplicative or would not be relevant to the issues to be decided.

After hearing the employer's side, the judge calls the claimant as a witness. The judge will confirm again the work history with the employer and then ask the claimant to detail the circumstances of his or her dismissal. Often the employee will dispute the employer's statement about prior warnings or explain the circumstances that lay behind the alleged misconduct (i.e., tardiness might be blamed on a malfunctioning car or problems with child care or oversleeping). Sometimes the claimant will assert that the conduct, while a violation of the employer's policies, was, in fact, common behavior, and that the employer had singled out the claimant in some way. The judge normally has available a copy of the claimant's statement to the claims deputy at the time the claimant applied for benefits. Frequently the judge will enter this statement in the record, asking the claimant to read the statement and to verify that it accurately reflects what the claimant told the deputy (it is not uncommon for the claimant to dispute some aspect of the statement, but this is difficult if the claimant has signed the statement). After the judge's questions, the claimant has the opportunity to add additional information, and the employer's spokesperson gets a chance to cross-examine; these questions are usually perfunctory.

The employee will sometimes bring witnesses to support his or her position: a former co-worker to testify that the behavior in question was common, a family member to testify regarding the circumstances leading to tardiness or absenteeism. The judge will hear these witnesses only if, in his or her judgment, they are relevant to the decision to be made. If the witness does testify, the judge will question him or her first, followed by the claimant and the employer's spokesperson.

It is not uncommon for the employee to have failed to bring a witness who would be relevant or to have failed to bring documentation of some type. The judge will not grant a continuance to allow claimant (or the employer if additional witnesses or documentation would help the employer's case) to obtain that additional testimony or documentation. The only time I have seen a continuance granted is if the hearing starts to go over the time allotted and the parties for the next hearing are waiting in the hall. A hearing might be rescheduled if one of the parties notifies the hearing office at the last minute of problems in getting to the hearing (such as an unexpected emergency or a car breakdown en route).

After hearing all of the testimony, the judge will frequently give the parties the opportunity to make a brief closing statement. The judge then closes the hearing, the parties depart, and the next hearing begins. Sometime in the next week or so, the judge will dictate a decision that the appeals office mails to the parties. The judge never renders an oral decision nor, in my observation, gives a clear indication of how he or she will rule (the occasional exception being dismissals when the party with the burden of proof fails to appear).

This description presumes no representation for either the claimant or the employer (other than the inside spokesperson for the latter). Two variations are worth noting. First, if the issue is one of "quit for good cause," the order of presentation reverses, with the claimant (who has the burden of establishing good cause) testifying first. "Good cause" includes major unilateral changes in working conditions (e.g., a reduction in salary of more than 33 percent, a substantial reduction in working hours, transfer to another job location that is an unreasonable commuting distance compared to the former location, etc.), sexual harassment, or pressure by the employer to engage in illegal behavior. It also includes an employee's leaving for a better paying job[27] or becoming physically unable to do the job with the employer unwilling or unable to accommodate the claimant's physical needs.[28] While the burden and issues differ, the hearings in "quit" cases tend to be similar to those in misconduct cases, albeit a bit shorter.

Second, the hearings in cases involving nonseparation issues are much shorter and often quite cut and dried. A claimant who forgot to mail in a claim card, or who did not report to the unemployment office when instructed to do so, may appeal the denial or termination of benefits; however, it is difficult to make a case that the failure to comply with the UC regulations was for "good cause." In separation cases, the claimant-appellant (who appears at the hearing) obtains a reversal of the initial determination in 28.7 percent of the cases when the employer appears to contest the appeal and 58.5 percent of the cases when the employer does not appear. In nonseparation cases, when the claimant appears at the hearing, the judge reverses the denial or loss of benefits in only 30.3 percent of cases. The nonseparation appeals may be allotted as little as fifteen minutes, and seldom are more than thirty minutes scheduled for such hearings. The judge relies on the testimony of the claimant, plus any relevant documentary evidence; sometimes the claimant will bring a witness to testify in support of an explanation (i.e., to corroborate a claim that mail delivery is unreliable or that someone else regularly picks up the mail and forgets to give it to the addressee). Having such corroboration does not necessarily provide sufficient weight to win a reversal, because, even if an explanation is true, it may not constitute "good cause." In some cases, the regulations may not even recognize good cause; for example, in one case a claimant lost benefits for failing to engage in a work search as required by the regulations. She explained that she had not done so because the claim card had explicitly stated that the "work search was waived." The judge denied the appeal, as did LIRC, because, while recognizing that the claimant had acted in good faith based upon the information on the claim card, that claim card information was wrong and the regulations did not recognize any exceptions to the work search requirement, including misinformation from the UC program itself.

One interesting aspect of the appeals process is that the only way to reverse the decision of a claims deputy is to go through the appeals hearing process. There is no way to short-circuit that process, even when the denial was due to some clear administrative error. For example, I observed one hearing in which both the claimant and the employer appeared (the latter by telephone). The stated issue was whether the employee had quit for good cause (i.e., to take another job with a new employer, from which the claimant had since been laid off); this being Wisconsin, both employers were in the business of building milking parlors. The claimant testified that he had quit employer 1 to take a job with employer 2, giving two weeks notice; he testified that he believed continued employment to be more likely with the new employer than with employer 1. After several months, he was laid off by employer 2. Employer 1 testified regarding the claimant's last date of employment, pay rate, and quitting of the position; employer 1 had no knowledge of what transpired with employer 2. Employer 2 was not present, but did appear to be a party to the hearing. After the hearing the judge told me that the only reason employer 1 had appeared was to verify that the employee had not been fired for misconduct. The initial claim had actually been denied due to confusion over the name of the second employer; originally registered as A&B Construction, the employer had changed its name to B&A Construction because there already was a company named A&B Construction. When the claimant filed, he listed A&B Construction, and when contacted, A&B Construction said it had no record of the employee; the claims deputy denied the claim. None of this was mentioned during the hearing; the judge came to the hearing with documentation showing what had happened. Once it was clear that there was no misconduct issue with employer 1, the judge had the information she needed to decide the case.

Advocates in UC Appeals Hearings

Given the active involvement of the administrative law judge in unemployment appeals hearings, one can reasonably ask whether there is a significant role to be played by advocates for the claimant and/or the employer. The judges are experts; they know what the regulations require and what evidence will support a claim of misconduct or a claim of "quit for good cause." Before the hearing, the judge has the opportunity to read the statements on which the claims deputies based the initial determinations. This provides the judge with background on what is at issue in order to focus the hearing on the evidence needed to come to a proper determination.

Nonetheless, there is evidence that an advocate can make a difference. A study of 10,972 UC appeals decided during April 1979, from twenty-four states, found that the overall success rate for claimants was 30.8 percent when the employer appeared at the hearing; when the claimant was represented, this success rate increased by about half to 45.4 percent. While these figures are suggestive, they are far from definitive.[29] The success rate for claimants rose even further, to 49.3 percent, when both parties were represented; moreover, the success rate for employers actually fell when they used an outside advocate (from 69.2 percent overall, to 54.1 percent when the employer brought a representative, and to 50.7 percent when both sides brought a representative).[30]

A more recent, but more limited, analysis was carried out in Ohio for UC appeals decided during 1994. Drawing upon data generated from the management information system used by the Ohio Unemployment Compensation Board of Review, Emsellem and Halas report that Ohio employers were represented five times more often than were claimants (9 percent of appeals versus 45 percent). Overall, claimants were successful in 32.5 percent of appeals, but this rose to 45 percent when the claimant was represented. In contrast, employers won 65 percent of appeals regardless of whether they were represented.[31]

These figures probably reflect a combination of factors. First, representatives may make a difference in the ability of a party to prepare and present its case (which is the argument I will develop later).[32] Second, the declining level of success for employers with representatives may mean that employers are more likely to bring representatives to problematic cases (this seems consistent with the slightly higher level of success for represented claimants when the employer is represented also); on the employer side, it is the employer who effectively controls the presence or absence of a representative. Third, claimant representatives, who tend to be attorneys often paid on a contingency basis of some sort, law students working as volunteers in a clinic setting, or union officials,[33] usually make the decision whether or not to appear on behalf of a claimant. That is, while the claimant may seek out a representative, the representative may decline to appear on behalf of the claimant if the appeal has a very low likelihood of success.[34] The higher level of success for claimants with representatives probably in part reflects this selection process.[35]

In assessing the relationship between the presence of advocates and the outcome of a UC appeal,[36] one needs to consider two factors not included in the 1979 analysis: the nature of the issue (which impacts upon which side has the burden of proof), and the side making the appeal (because the initial determination provides at least some indication of the merits of the case). The 1991 Wisconsin data allow these factors to be considered. Before introducing these variables, let me compare the patterns in these data to the 1971 figures. In the Wisconsin data set, there are 7,947 cases in which both sides appeared and in which the judge made a decision clearly favoring one side or the other. Note that I omit from the remainder of my analysis appeals where one or both parties failed to appear, or that did not involve an issue related to job separation.[37] The former omission reflects the simple fact that, while not essential, who appeared at the hearing dwarfs all other factors in importance in determining the outcome;[38] the latter omission reflects the fundamentally different nature of hearings involving nonseparation issues (i.e., the employer is not really a party to those hearings, and they become essentially nonadversarial in nature).

Table 2 shows the percent of appeals won by the claimant, controlling for representation. The table shows the following overall patterns.

Overall, claimants won 42.5 percent of appeals, 41.5 percent when they were unrepresented and 50.4 percent when they did have representation. Looking at it from the employer's standpoint, they won 57.5 percent (100 percent – 42.5 percent) of the appeals, and it made essentially no difference whether or not they were represented (58.4 percent when they were represented and 57.3 percent when they were not).[39]

When both sides brought a representative, claimants won 44.6 percent of cases and employers 55.4 percent.

When the claimant brought a representative and the employer did not, claimants won 53.4 percent and employers won 46.6 percent.

When the employer brought a representative, and the employee did not, the claimant won 41.6 percent and the employer won 59.4 percent.

This pattern is not entirely consistent with the other studies summarized above. First, claimants appear to win a substantially larger proportion of the appeals: 42.5 percent in Wisconsin in 1991 compared to 30.8 percent nationally in 1979 and 32.5 percent in Ohio in 1994.[40] Second, unlike the 1979 national study, but consistent with the 1994 Ohio study, the employer's likelihood of success does *not* appear to decline when a representative appears (nor does it go up with representation as does the claimant's). The greater success by represented claimants is consistent with the other studies, although the impact of representation does not appear to be as great (only about an 8 percentage point gap here compared to a 15 percentage point gap nationally in 1979 and a 13 percentage point gap in Ohio in 1974).

TABLE 2.   Claimant Success by Representation (in percentages)

	Employer Represented	Employer Represented	Employer All Cases
Claimant	44.6	53.3	50.4
Represented	(296)	(565)	(861)
Claimant	41.0	41.6	41.5
Unrepresented	(1,426)	(5,660)	(7,086)
Claimant	41.6	42.7	42.5
All Cases	(1,722)	(6,225)	(7,947)

Source: Bureau of Legal Affairs, Unemployment Compensation Division, Wisconsin Department of Industry, Labor, and Human Relations (compiled by the author).

Note: Figures in parentheses are number of cases.

Introducing controls for who appealed provides some measure of the merits of the case if one is prepared to assume that the initial determination is an indicator of the merits. On an overall basis, there is little difference in success controlling for which side appeals:[41] claimants win 31.3 percent of the cases they appeal, and employers win 32.8 percent of the cases they appeal.[42] Table 3 shows the relationship with representation depending upon who appealed. What is clear in this table is that the difference in success between claimants and employers is more a function of who appealed than it is a function of representation. Clearly, rather than focusing on claimant success, we need to look at appellant success—in other words, the likelihood that the side initiating the appeal will win.

Table 4 is structured exactly the same as the previous table, but shows appellant success rather than claimant success. In this table we can begin to see a fairly clear pattern. For both claimant and employer appellants, the likelihood of success is around 30 percent without representation; this is true regardless of whether the respondent has representation. The situation changes markedly if the appellant has representation. For claimant appellants, the likelihood of success rises to 36.8 percent if both sides have representatives and to 47.6 percent if only the appellant has a representative; the overall success rate of represented claimant appellants is 44.2 percent. For employer appellants, the success rate is 38.2 percent if only the employer has a representative, and 40.8 percent if both sides have representatives; the overall rate of success for represented employer appellants is 38.6 percent.

In round numbers, these figures suggest that the likelihood of success might go up as much as 30 to 50 percent if a claimant has a representative. Even so, this does not rule out the possibility that what is going on here is

TABLE 3.   Claimant Success by Representation Controlling for Which Side Appealed (in percentages)

	Employer Represented		Employer Unrepresented		Employer All Cases	
	Claimant Appealed	Employer Appealed	Claimant Appealed	Employer Appealed	Claimant Appealed	Employer Appealed
Claimant	36.8	59.2	47.6	70.6	44.2	65.8
Represented	(193)	(103)	(422)	(143)	(615)	(246)
Claimant	28.5	61.8	30.0	69.1	29.7	67.4
Unrepresented	(889)	(537)	(3,976)	(1,684)	(4,865)	(2,221)
Claimant	29.9	61.4	31.7	69.2	31.3	67.2
All Cases	(1,082)	(640)	(4,398)	(1,827)	(5,480)	(2,467)

Source: Bureau of Legal Affairs, Unemployment Compensation Division, Wisconsin Department of Industry, Labor, and Human Relations (compiled by the author).

Note: Figures in parentheses are number of cases.

a selection process rather than a representation effect. Further support for the argument that representation matters would come from adding controls for which side has the burden of proof. As discussed previously, in misconduct cases, the employer must demonstrate that misconduct occurred and it followed proper disciplinary procedures in discharging the claimant; in "quit" cases, the claimant must demonstrate that the quit was for one of the narrowly defined reasons that entitles an employee to receive unemployment benefits. Tables 5 and 6 show appellant success separately for misconduct cases and for quit cases.

Table 5 shows misconduct cases where the employer has the burden of proof. When the initial determination is for the employer, and the claimant appeals, the rate of success for claimants is 56.6 percent if only the claimant is represented, compared to 35 to 40 percent in other situations (the overall rate of success for claimant appellants in misconduct cases is around 40 percent). When the initial determination had been for the claimant, and the employer appeals, the highest success rate for the employer is when both sides have representatives (46.2 percent). When only the employer has a representative, the employer prevails in 37.9 percent of the appeals, but when only the claimant has a representative, the employer-appellant succeeds in only 27.1 percent of claims. The overall rate of success for employer appellants in misconduct cases is 31.9 percent. The gaps here are quite high and probably cannot be attributed to case selection only. When just the claimant has representation in misconduct cases, where the burden of proof lies with the employer (and the employer is unrepresented), the claimant is successful in 72.9 percent (100 percent − 27.1 percent) of the cases where the initial determination had favored the

TABLE 4. Appellant Success by Representation Controlling for Which Side Appealed (in percentages)

	Employer Represented		Employer Unrepresented		Employer All Cases	
	Claimant Appealed	Employer Appealed	Claimant Appealed	Employer Appealed	Claimant Appealed	Employer Appealed
Claimant Represented	36.8 (193)	40.8 (103)	47.6 (422)	29.4 (143)	44.2 (615)	34.2 (246)
Claimant Unrepresented	28.5 (889)	38.2 (537)	30.0 (3,976)	30.9 (1,684)	29.7 (4,865)	32.6 (2,221)
Claimant All Cases	29.9 (1,082)	38.6 (640)	31.7 (4,398)	30.8 (1,827)	31.3 (5,480)	32.8 (2,467)

Source: Bureau of Legal Affairs, Unemployment Compensation Division, Wisconsin Department of Industry, Labor, and Human Relations (compiled by the author).
Note: Figures in parentheses are number of cases.

claimant and 56.6 percent of the cases in which the initial determination had favored the employer.

Turning to "quit" cases (shown in table 6), where the burden is on the claimant, the claimant-initiated appeals succeed less than 20 percent of time when the claimant has no representative, but about 25 percent of the time with representation. For employer appeals, the rate of employer success does not vary in a clear systematic way with representation, although the numbers of cases for some of the combinations of categories is very small.

Thus, absent an independent judgment about the merits of individual cases, we can only find patterns that seem consistent with the view that representation in unemployment appeals hearings enhances the represented parties' chances of success. Unlike the sketchy analysis of the 1979 data, we find no strongly anomalous patterns. The next question to consider is how and why representation can make a difference given the adjudicator-centered model employed in UC hearings.

The Role of Advocates in Unemployment Compensation Appeal Hearings

Even with the best-intentioned and most skillful administrative law judge, advocates can play an important role in UC hearings. For purposes of this discussion, I presume an advocate who is knowledgeable and experienced in handling UC cases in a particular locale.

TABLE 5.   **Appellant Success by Representation Controlling for Which Side Appealed, Misconduct Cases Only (in percentages)**

	Employer Represented		Employer Unrepresented		Employer All Cases	
	Claimant Appealed	Employer Appealed	Claimant Appealed	Employer Appealed	Claimant Appealed	Employer Appealed
Claimant	40.0	46.2	56.6	27.1	50.8	35.1
Represented	(125)	(78)	(233)	(107)	(358)	(185)
Claimant	35.0	37.9	38.6	29.4	37.9	31.5
Unrepresented	(411)	(375)	(1,789)	(1,132)	(2,200)	(1,507)
Claimant	36.2	39.3	40.6	29.2	39.7	31.9
All Cases	(536)	(453)	(2,022)	(1,239)	(2,558)	(1,692)

Source: Bureau of Legal Affairs, Unemployment Compensation Division, Wisconsin Department of Industry, Labor, and Human Relations (compiled by the author).

Note: Figures in parentheses are number of cases.

Preparing the Party for the Hearing Room Situation
A first thing that a knowledgeable advocate can do is to brief the party and the party's witnesses on what to expect in the hearing. For example, the short time period allocated for each hearing places pressure on the judges to conduct succinct, efficient hearings. A party that fully understands this may be less put off by the often hurried feel of many hearings. Furthermore, an advocate who knows the styles of the individual judges can be more specific, given that some judges come across as brusque and impatient while others are able to conduct efficient hearings while avoiding this.

Helping to Frame the Issue
While the administrative law judge must try to deal with the issues in the case in the context of specific regulations, which serves to create a set of standard issues or questions, the advocate can play an important role in framing the issue in a way that best serves the goal of the advocate's client. For example, if the core issue is one of employee misconduct in the form of tardiness, the employer's advocate can frame the issue of misconduct broadly to emphasize that the employee had a record of disciplinary problems that went well beyond tardiness; the tardiness issue can be portrayed as the straw that broke the camel's back. In the same case, the employee's advocate can frame the issue in terms of lack of adherence to a progressive discipline policy, even while acknowledging several incidents of late arrival at work.

The advocate can also help the judge recognize who can most efficiently provide testimony that speaks to the key questions to be decided. Often the judge can determine this from the initial determination

TABLE 6. Appellant Success by Representation Controlling for Which Side Appealed, Quit Cases Only (in percentages)

	Employer Represented		Employer Unrepresented		Employer All Cases	
	Claimant Appealed	Employer Appealed	Claimant Appealed	Employer Appealed	Claimant Appealed	Employer Appealed
Claimant Represented	23.7 (38)	36.4 (11)	27.2 (114)	57.1 (14)	26.3 (152)	48.0 (25)
Claimant Unrepresented	18.6 (345)	55.1 (78)	17.1 (1,484)	49.8 (229)	17.4 (1,829)	51.1 (307)
Claimant All Cases	19.1 (383)	52.8 (89)	17.8 (1,598)	50.2 (243)	18.1 (1,981)	50.9 (332)

Source: Bureau of Legal Affairs, Unemployment Compensation Division, Wisconsin Department of Industry, Labor, and Human Relations (compiled by the author).

Note: Figures in parentheses are number of cases.

materials. When the record is unclear, the judges could, in theory, use the initial statements to get a better understanding of the case, but they do not customarily do this (judges use the initial statements almost exclusively to determine only which side has the burden of proof). The knowledgeable advocate can help the judge at this point by identifying their key witness. Sometimes the judge will ask who should testify first ("who can tell me the most about the circumstances of the discharge?"); at other times, an experienced advocate who knows that the particular judge will not take offense at a suggestion from the advocate will make a recommendation without being asked, or tell the judge that the person the judge initially picked to testify first is not the witness with the best information. To make a recommendation in response to the judge's request requires someone who at least understands the points at issue; to effectively tell the judge that the judge's first inclination as to whom to call is wrong requires an advocate who either is supremely self-confident (if not arrogant) or an advocate who knows the individual style of the particular judge.

Bringing the Evidence to Make the Case
The advocate plays the most important role not so much in what happens at the hearing but in preparation for the hearing. The single most important failing of unrepresented claimants and employers is to appear at the hearing without the witnesses or documentation necessary to make the case if the other side contests the issue. One anecdote told to me by a former administrative law judge dramatically illustrates this; it also illustrates how a knowledgeable advocate can use the hearing system rules to the advantage of the advocate's client.

> In a misconduct case there is no requirement that the claimant testify because the burden of proof falls on the employer in misconduct cases; that is, if the employer cannot make a sufficient case that misconduct had occurred, the employer will lose the case. In fact, it is not unknown for an employer-appellant to lose a misconduct case even if the claimant fails to appear at the hearing.[43] Even though an appeals hearing in a misconduct case often has a quasi-criminal air to it, the claimant is not protected from having to testify by the Fifth Amendment's protections against self-incrimination.
>
> In a hearing involving a claim of misconduct, the employer-appellant planned to call the claimant as an adverse witness. When the claimant's advocate realized that this was the employer's intention, the advocate told the claimant to get lost. When the employer tried to call the employee, the judge asked the employer whether the claimant had been subpoenaed; the answer was "no." When the employer objected that the

claimant had to be there, the judge explained that the claimant did not have to be present, and in any case had appeared in the person of the advocate. Because the employer was not able to sustain its burden of proof without the claimant's testimony, the judge affirmed the initial determination for the claimant.

While this is an extreme example—even an experienced advocate for the employer might not have thought to subpoena the claimant—it does illustrate how an advocate can use knowledge of the rules of the game to influence the outcome of the appeal. More often the failure to bring appropriate documents or witnesses is very mundane.

For example, in one case I observed where part of the alleged misconduct involved frequent tardiness, the judge would not accept testimony from the employer's key witness on the tardiness issue because the witness (the nursing supervisor at a nursing home) did not work on the same shift as the claimant and had not witnessed the late arrivals. The judge also excluded affidavits of persons from the claimant's shift who had direct knowledge of the late arrivals. The business manager, who served as the employer's spokesperson at the hearing, had remembered to bring the time cards (which showed a total of 115 late minutes over the last twenty days of the claimant's employment), but when the claimant testified, she was unwilling to acknowledge the accuracy of the time cards, commenting that "I always initialed or added something to the time card." In this case, the weak evidence on the tardiness issue was damaging but not devastating because the alleged misconduct of the claimant went well beyond this one issue, and the employer had brought witnesses to the other, more serious breaches of on-the-job conduct.

Contrast this example to another one involving a health-care facility (in this case a hospital), where the employer's spokesperson was an experienced UC representative from an outside consulting firm. The issue in this case was tardiness, and the employer's evidence included testimony from the manager of the housekeeping department in which the claimant worked as well as materials from the claimant's personnel file. That file included irrefutable documentation of the claimant's tardiness, including a list of dates tardy derived from the sign-in sheets, dates absent, and records of prior discipline due to tardiness (verbal warnings, written warnings, and a three-day suspension). The personnel records here were crucial, because in a case involving frequent tardiness, if the employer fails to bring acceptable business records showing the tardiness (i.e., time cards or sign-in sheets), and the claimant denies the allegation of frequent tardiness, the judge must decide who to believe.

If the case involves allegations of misconduct and only the personnel manager from the employer shows up, with no one who was witness to the misconduct and no form of acceptable documentation (e.g., discipline notices acknowledged and signed by the employee), all the claimant must do is deny that the misconduct occurred.

The evidentiary requirements in UC hearings are central to the role of the advocate. The hearing notices sent to the employer and the claimant tell them to bring relevant documents and evidence.

> The Administrative Law Judge is required to base the decision in the case solely on sworn testimony and documents presented at the time and place of hearing. Verbal accounts of the facts are permitted only by "eyewitnesses" or other persons having direct knowledge. Statements about what the witness heard from someone else must generally be disregarded as "hearsay." Letters or written statements, even if notarized, cannot substitute for the personal appearance of a witness. Opportunity must be provided to ask the witness questions. If written evidence such as records or reports are to be offered, the original document should be brought to the hearing if possible. The person responsible must be present to testify.[44]

While this statement is straightforward, someone unfamiliar with the hearing process may have substantial difficulty figuring out in advance what evidence speaks to what issue. An experienced advocate will know precisely what documents support the client's case and precisely which witnesses the judge will need to hear.

This knowledge is particularly important given that almost all UC appeal hearings occur in a single session. That is, while the UC appeal hearing relies upon an adjudicator-centered procedure that resembles the adjudication process used in civil-law countries, UC appeals retain what students of comparative law and procedure refer to as "concentration": fact-gathering is concentrated into a single event.[45] The traditional civil-law approach is episodic, what Kaplan described as the "conference method" of adjudication.[46] If the UC appeal hearing were episodic rather than concentrated, the administrative law judge could make clear to the parties what specific witnesses and/or documents needed to be produced at the next session. However, both the timeliness requirements and the resource requirements preclude an episodic approach to UC appeals.

Asking the Questions to Make the Case
While a significant proportion of UC claims and UC appeals involve issues that are clear-cut, the events leading up to a discharge or a quit can involve a lot of history. This background can affect the framing of the

issue and the presentation of evidence. An advocate who knows this history can ask questions of witnesses that would never occur to the judge who has only the initial determination materials and the answers to questions the judge has already asked to help guide his or her questioning of the witnesses. This is particularly true of adverse witnesses who may be selective in their recitation of events; while the type of cross-examination associated with jury trials is inappropriate in UC hearings, the adjudicatory-centered approach used in these hearings is not always adequate to capture all of the information that is relevant for the decision to be made. At the same time, as I will discuss in detail below, an advocate who does not understand the unique aspects of the UC appeal process—even an attorney with a lot of advocacy experience—can ask irrelevant questions and call (or try to call) witnesses who are repetitive or irrelevant.

The Role of the Advocate: Summary
Administrative law judges are trained to run hearings in a manner that strives to provide a fair procedure in the absence of advocates. For many appeals, perhaps even most, this works. In part this is because many appeals are cut and dried; that is, the initial determination was correct, and there is no legal basis for the appeal even if the appellant is unhappy about the initial determination. Most appeals (almost three-quarters) are by claimants, and claimants often have no understanding of the regulations that governed the initial determination; they probably appeal less from a specific sense that the determination was wrong and more from a generalized feeling that they should get unemployment compensation. The second tardiness example described above, the one where the employer had systematically gone through a program of progressive discipline before terminating the claimant, is a good case in point. The claimant acknowledged the pattern of tardiness (he had in fact been late to work over eighty times in less than twelve months) and could do nothing more than give excuses for one or two of the final incidents.

Even in this clear-cut case, however, the employer had to know what evidence was needed to substantiate the tardiness; if one of the parties arrives at the hearing without the witnesses or documents necessary to substantiate its case, the factual correctness of the party's position will not sustain its case. For example, I observed one case involving the dismissal of a teacher's aide for using profanity around the students under her charge and for failing to follow the instructions of her supervising teacher. The school district misdirected the hearing notice, and the district lawyer was unable to arrange to have the needed witnesses at the hearing. The judge denied the attorney's request for a continuance. After the hearing, the judge commented to me that it looked like the claimant "was really abusing these kids," but the judge might have to rule for the claimant because of the poor case put on by the school district. The judge expressed no sympathy at all for the failure of the district to produce the necessary witnesses, because there had been a previous delay (when the district had claimed it had not received notice of the hearing) and the district knew that the case was coming. While this case did not involve lack of knowledge on the part of the employer, it does demonstrate the way a party's preparation for the hearing can limit what the judge can do, regardless of what the judge thinks actually happened.

What Happens When an Advocate Appears at a UC Hearing

When neither side has a representative at a UC appeal hearing, the responsibility for extracting the relevant testimony and documents falls clearly and unambiguously on the administrative law judge. Formally, the judge still has this responsibility when one or more parties is represented by an advocate. In fact, when one party but not both has an advocate, the burden on the judge may be even greater than when neither party has an advocate, at least with regard to insuring that the unrepresented party gets a fair hearing. However, with regard to the presentation of the case for a represented party, the judge has the option of allowing the advocate to present the case for the advocate's client. Judges differ in their inclination to defer to an advocate: some are reluctant to let any advocate take the lead in presenting the case, some will only turn the case over to an advocate they know will succinctly get out the evidence the judge needs, and others are inclined to let most advocates handle the presentation of their clients' cases. Overall, attorney advocates as a group appear to receive more deference from judges, but there are nonattorney advocates whom the judges recognize as extremely competent (in fact, more competent than most attorneys).

Earlier, I contrasted two cases involving discharge of an employee in which tardiness was at least part of the reason. The hearing involving the advocate for the employer provides a good example of how an advocate can succinctly get all of the key elements of his or her client's case in front of the judge. An abbreviated reconstructed transcript of that hearing shows the role played by an effective advocate.[47] There were five persons present at the hearing (the abbreviations shown in parentheses will be used in the transcript).[48]

The administrative law judge (ALJ)
The claimant (CL)

The employer's advocate (ADV)
The witness for the employer (W)

The transcript omits the judge's opening statement, along with other procedural elements (e.g., swearing the witnesses).

ALJ: What is the employer's position on this case?

ADV: The claimant was discharged for misconduct in the form of excessive tardiness.

ALJ [to CL]: What is your position? Were you discharged for tardiness?

CL: I was discharged, but not for tardiness. I was tardy for valid reasons.

ALJ: Because this is a question of misconduct, I will take the testimony of the employer first. Mr. [ADV] you may question your witness.

ADV [to W]: What is your position with the employer?

W: I manage the department that handles housekeeping for the hospital.

ADV: How long have you been in that position?

W: Since July 1990.

ADV: When did the claimant begin work at the hospital?

W: November 22, 1988.

ADV: What was his last day of work?

W: May 21, 1991.

ADV: What was his job?

W: He worked as a housekeeper.

ADV: What was his work schedule?

W: He worked full time, first shift; the days of the week varied from week to week.

ADV: What was his pay rate?

W: $5.75 per hour.

ADV: Who discharged him?

W: I did.

ADV: When was he discharged?

W: At the end of his shift on May 21.

ADV: What precipitated the discharge?

W: The final incident was on May 18, the prior weekend when he reported to work late.

ADV: Tell me about the discharge meeting . . . who was there, and what happened?

W: The meeting took place in the office of the vice president for personnel. The employee was there, as was the vice president, the shift supervisor, and me. I informed [the employee] that his employment was being terminated because of a pattern of frequent tardiness. I told the employee that we had tried to work with him to overcome the problem, and that we had run out of alternatives. This could not continue. The employee asked if the discharge was effective immediately, and I told him that it was.

ADV: Does the hospital have an employee handbook?

W: Yes.

ADV: Does the handbook contain a policy concerning tardiness?

W: Yes.

ADV: Did the employee receive a copy of the handbook?

W: Yes, and I have here the receipt signed by the employee acknowledging that he had been given a copy of it.

ADV [to ALJ]: I would like to offer the handbook and the receipt as exhibits.

ALJ [after marking these as exhibits 1 and 2, ALJ hands them to the employee and asks]: Is that your signature?

CL: Yes, it is.

ALJ [to ADV]: Continue.

ADV: Does the handbook include a discipline procedure?

W: Yes, it does.

ADV: Was that procedure followed?

W: Yes, it was.

ADV: Does the discipline procedure include a list of causes for discharge?

W: Yes, it does.

ADV: Is tardiness included in that list?

W: Yes, it is mentioned in Policy 13.

ADV: Who made the decision to discharge the employee?

W: I did, after consulting with the vice president for personnel and the shift supervisors.

ADV: What occurred on May 18?

W: He was 50 minutes late to work . . . he claimed to have overslept due to a power outage.

ADV: Did he have a history of tardiness?

W: Oh yes . . . we had gone through all the steps of our progressive discipline procedure.

ADV: Is there proof of this?

W: Yes, it's all documented in his personnel file.

ADV: Do you have the relevant materials with you?

W: Yes [*hands a sheaf of papers to the advocate, who then hands the papers to the ALJ to be marked*].

ADV: What is the first page of the item marked as exhibit 3?

W: It is a memo listing the dates tardy, taken from the sign-in sheets . . . the reasons the employee gave for being tardy on various occasions, the dates the employee was absent, and the record of prior discipline.

ADV: Who wrote the memo?

W: I did.

ADV: What did you use to prepare the memo?

W: The other records from the personnel file which are attached to the memo.

ADV: Tell me about the prior disciplinary actions that had been taken.

W: There had been several verbal warnings, two written warnings, and in March, a three-day suspension.

ADV: What problems are created by tardiness?

W: There are morale problems for the employees who do show up on time, and the supervisor may have to do some rescheduling to be sure that all the work gets done if the tardiness is for more than a few minutes.

ADV: How many employees are there in this section?

W: Forty.

ADV: Have any other employees been the subject of discipline for tardiness?

W: Yes, several . . . somewhere between three and five, including at least one other person who was discharged.

ADV: No further questions.

ALJ: How many times was he tardy?

W: Eight-two, going back to July 1990 . . . the list of dates goes on for two pages.

ALJ: Are any other reasons given for being late on May 18?

W: Not in the records I have.

ALJ [*to CL*]: Do you have any questions for the witness?

CL: Was the tardiness on May 12, 1991, excused?

W: It was not excused, but I took no action regarding it.

ALJ [*after a few moments of silence*]: Any other questions?

CL: No.

ALJ [*to ADV*]: Any other questions?

ADV: Under the hospital's progressive discipline policy, could the employee have been discharged if he was tardy any time after the March suspension?

W: Yes.

ADV: No further questions.

[the ALJ calls the claimant as a witness]

ALJ: Are you currently employed?

CL: Yes, I started at —— yesterday.

ALJ: Do you recall anything that differs from the prior testimony about your employment and the end of it at the hospital?

CL: Not really. I did give my supervisor a letter on May 20 that told why I was tardy on the 18th. [*Hands a copy to the ALJ.*]

ALJ [*marks the letter as exhibit 4*]: Was the letter discussed at the discharge meeting?

CL: Not really.

ALJ: Why did you give them the letter?

CL: I wanted them to know that I had been trying real hard. After the suspension in March, I went to the employee assistance program for help, and the problem had improved substantially. I wasn't being irresponsible. I asked them for another chance.

ALJ: What was the response to the letter?

CL: They acknowledged it, but the decision to fire me had been made.

ALJ: Were you late eighty times?

CL: Yes, but before [name of the employer's witness] came to work in July 1990, tardiness was never a big issue. I was tardy a lot during the first two years I worked at the hospital, but I didn't get any reprimands until November 1990.

ALJ: How many times were you tardy after the verbal warning in November?

CL: Sixteen until the suspension in March.

ALJ: Did you get warnings for any of these tardinesses?

CL: Yes.

ALJ: Why were you tardy after these warnings?

CL: At least three times my car wouldn't start and I was thirty to forty minutes late; most of the other times I was only four or five minutes late.

ALJ: Tell me about the times you were tardy in May.

CL: I don't remember what happened on May 1. On May 12, I called in at 6:30 because my ride hadn't shown up. My supervisor sent someone to pick me up, but I didn't get to work until 7:20.

On May 17, I was ten minutes late. A friend of mine called me at 2:30 in the morning to come get him out of jail; he had been busted for driving under the influence. I didn't get back home until 4:30, and I slept through the alarm. On May 18, there was a bad thunderstorm, and the power went out. My alarm didn't go off. I woke up at 7:30 and called in immediately. My witness can testify about these last two.

ALJ [*pulls a piece of paper out of a file folder and hands it to the claimant, and marks it as exhibit 5*]: Is this the statement you gave to the claims deputy when you filed for unemployment compensation?

CL [*after reading what is on the piece of paper*]: It's mostly correct. I didn't say that it wasn't my fault that I was late, but otherwise it looks right.

ALJ: You were in the employee assistance program?

CL: Yes.

ALJ: What for?

CL: I needed help in my attitude toward work. The program helped a lot.

ALJ: Anything else you want to add?

CL: Not at this time.

ALJ [*to ADV*]: Do you have any questions?

ADV [*to CL*]: What prompted you to write the letter . . . did you think you might be terminated after you were late on May 18?

CL: Yes. I hoped the letter would show that I was serious about the job.

ADV: With your record of tardiness, why not make darn sure you would get to work on time? Why not have a windup clock so you didn't have to worry about a power outage?

CL: I don't know.

ADV: Were you warned after the suspension that any more tardinesses could lead to discharge?

CL: Yes.

ADV: No further questions.

ALJ [*to CL*]: Anything else?

CL: No, but what about my witness?

ALJ: His testimony is not needed. [*To employer's ADV*] Anything else from the employer?

ADV: Nothing further.

ALJ: Any objections to any of the exhibits? . . . there are five of them.

CL: No.

ADV: No objections.

ALJ: The hearing is closed . . . both of you will receive a written decision in the mail within two weeks.

The advocate in this case might seem almost superfluous. This appears to be a clear example of an employee who could not get his act together and whom the employer had tolerated well beyond what one might view as minimum expectations. While this is in many ways correct, one must keep in mind that the burden of proof rested with the employer because this was a misconduct case. The employer had to bring the correct witnesses and/or evidence to the hearing, or the claimant would win essentially by default. In this case, the role of the advocate was in part to minimize the cost of the UC hearing procedure to the employer. An employer might have been tempted to bring to the hearing several witnesses (one or two supervisors who could testify to observing the claimant arriving late to work), someone from the personnel office who would testify regarding the progressive discipline that the hospital had imposed on the claimant, and someone from the employee assistance program to testify about what the employer had tried to do to help the employee. The advocate knew that in this case one key witness combined with the appropriate business records would be adequate to make the case for misconduct and to defend the procedure used by the employer.

Moreover, the advocate knew exactly what points had to be covered in testimony to make the case.

> He established the existence of a discipline policy (i.e., the handbook).
> He established that the claimant knew (or should have known) of the policy.
> He established that policy covered the alleged misconduct.
> He established that the employer had followed the policy in discharging the claimant.
> He established that the employee's misconduct was long-standing in nature, and that disciplinary measures, including one suspension, had not ended the misconduct.
> He established that the employer had not singled out the claimant for discipline.
> He established that the discipline policy allowed for termination if any infractions occurred after a suspension.
> By one or two questions of cross-examination of the claimant, he established that the claimant knew that his job was on the line because of his record of tardiness.

While the judge could have obtained this same testimony, this advocate did it more efficiently than the judge would have been able to do. In fact, the judge was familiar with the advocate (who is not an attorney) from prior appearances, and the judge knew that the advocate was aware of what evidence and testimony the employer needed to provide. Almost certainly, the judge let the advocate conduct the questioning of the employer's witness, because the judge knew that doing so would be the most efficient way to run the hearing.

Lawyer and Nonlawyer Advocates: Does Formal Training Matter?

Throughout this chapter I have been developing the argument that a knowledgeable advocate can make a difference. The core question for my analysis, however, is whether systematic differences exist between the representation provided by advocates with legal training and that provided by advocates with no such training. In this section I will begin to develop the argument that specific expertise is the dominant factor affecting the quality of an advocate's performance. This expertise combines general substantive and procedural knowledge with specific knowledge of rules, process, and players.

The Statistical Story

What happens to the statistical patterns discussed in the previous sections when we introduce controls for the type of representative? While the UC appeals office does not code the type of representative, the management information system from which the data come includes the name and address of the various parties and their representatives. For representatives and for employers, the system includes a title. I used the title to code the type of representative into two categories: attorney and agent.[49] The agent category included law students working in a UC appeals clinic, union officials, and persons working for UC-related management and consulting firms. Even starting with almost 8,000 cases, some of the combinations of appellant, case type, and advocate type have too few observations for analysis.

Table 7 shows the likelihood of appellant success for different types of representatives without regard to the type of case; for comparison purposes, I have included in the table figures on appellant success with no advocate. The roman figures show the appellant success rate for cases appealed by the employee (claimant); the italic figures show the appellant success rate for cases appealed by the employer. The last column and last row of the table show the impact of representation for each side without regard to the representative used by the other side. The overall pattern does not show any clear differences between the success of lawyers and agents. The bigger differences are between the represented and unrepresented. For example, employee appellants win 45 percent of appeals with either a lawyer or agent, but only 33 percent with no representative (the roman figures in the last column). Employer appellants win only 31 percent with an inside representative or no representative, versus 43 percent for lawyer representatives and 37 percent for agent representatives (the italic figures in the last row of the table); the difference between lawyers and agents is not significant. Interestingly, here we see that representation of any type only seems to have an effect for appellants, not for respondents: the success rate for appellants is not, in the aggregate, affected by the respondent's decision regarding representation. Employee appellants win 33 to 37 percent of cases across the categories of employer representation (the italic figures in the last column), and employer appellants win 29 to 32 percent across the categories of employee representation (the roman figures in the last row).

The pattern in the body of table 7 provides no indication that, overall, lawyers are more successful than agents. For example, employee appel-

TABLE 7. Appellant Success by Type of Representative, All Cases (in percentages)

Type of Employee Representative	Type of Employer Representative			
	Lawyer	Agent	Inside or None	All
Lawyer	37	45	48	45
	(133)	(22)	(303)	(465)
	40	*44*	*28*	*33*
	(58)	*(18)*	*(104)*	*(182)*
Agent	13	[60]	51	45
	(23)	(5)	(100)	(129)
	50	*[43]*	*33*	*37*
	(10)	*(7)*	*(33)*	*(51)*
None	27	29	30	30
	(530)	(252)	(3,976)	(4,865)
	43	*36*	*31*	*33*
	(310)	*(184)*	*(1,684)*	*(2,221)*
All	29	31	32	31
	(687)	(280)	(4,398)	(5,480)
	43	*37*	*31*	*33*
	(385)	*(209)*	*(1,827)*	*(2,467)*

Source: Bureau of Legal Affairs, Unemployment Compensation Division, Wisconsin Department of Industry, Labor, and Human Relations (compiled by the author).

Note: Figures in roman are for cases appealed by the employee; figures in italics are for cases appealed by the employer; figures in parentheses are number of cases; percentages in brackets are based on very small numbers of cases and should be considered with caution.

lants represented by a lawyer win 37 percent of their appeals with a lawyer when the employer has a lawyer representative and 45 percent when the employer has an agent. However, when the employer is the appellant and the employee has a lawyer representative, the employer wins 44 percent with an agent but only 40 percent with a lawyer. Interestingly, the one fairly clear asymmetry here is when an employer has a lawyer representative but the claimant has an agent; in this situation, employee appellants win only 13 percent of their appeals. As I will suggest below, this probably reflects that fact that many "agents" appearing for claimants are law students who, when pitted against an experienced attorney, do not perform particularly well.

What happens when we introduce controls for which side bears the burden of proof? Tables 8 and 9 break out misconduct and quit cases. Some of the cells in these tables have a very small number of cases. This limits the conclusions that we can draw; nonetheless, some interesting patterns are evident.

In claimant appeals of misconduct cases, the presence of lawyers on

TABLE 8. Appellant Success by Type of Representative, Misconduct Cases (in percentages)

| Type of Employee Representative | Type of Employer Representative | | | |
	Lawyer	Agent	Inside or None	All
Lawyer	40	54	58	52
	(89)	(13)	(167)	(271)
	50	*47*	*24*	*34*
	(42)	*(15)*	*(78)*	*(137)*
Agent	19	[67]	57	50
	(16)	(3)	(60)	(80)
	[57]	*[20]*	*33*	*36*
	(7)	*(5)*	*(24)*	*(36)*
None	33	36	39	38
	(252)	(126)	(1,789)	(2,200)
	43	*33*	*29*	*32*
	(206)	*(137)*	*(1,132)*	*(1,507)*
All	34	368	41	40
	(358)	(142)	(2,022)	(2,558)
	46	*34*	*29*	*32*
	(262)	*(157)*	*(1,239)*	*(1,692)*

Source: Bureau of Legal Affairs, Unemployment Compensation Division, Wisconsin Department of Industry, Labor, and Human Relations (compiled by the author).

Note: Figures in roman are for cases appealed by the employee; figures in italics are for cases appealed by the employer; figures in parentheses are number of cases; percentages in brackets are based on very small numbers of cases and should be considered with caution.

both sides seems to have a canceling effect; claimants win 40 percent of their appeals when both sides have lawyers and 39 percent when neither have lawyers. The same is not true for employer appeals of misconduct cases; the employer wins 29 percent of its appeals when neither it nor the claimant has an advocate, but 50 percent of the appeals when both sides have lawyers as advocates. Continuing with employer appeals, when the claimant has a lawyer and the employer has an agent representative, the outcome pattern is essentially the same as when both sides have lawyers (the employer wins 47 percent). The clearest advantage for lawyers occurs in claimant appeals where one side has a lawyer and the other has an agent. When the claimant is the one with the lawyer, the claimant wins in 54 percent of cases; however, when the employer has the lawyer, the claimant wins only 19 percent (compared to the 39 to 40 percent success rate when both sides have a lawyer or both sides are unrepresented).[50]

Returning to employer appeals of misconduct cases, it is more difficult to compare lawyers and agents, although the pattern is clearly murkier. Agents and lawyers have similar success appearing for employers in appeals where the claimant has a lawyer, although the lawyer does better when the claimant is unrepresented. Interestingly, against an unrepresented employer in an employer appeal, the claimant may do better with an agent than with a lawyer (although the differences here are not statistically significant).

When we turn to quit cases (table 9), the numbers begin to get very small. Recall that the rate of success of claimant appellants in quit cases is low. When neither side has an advocate, claimants win 17 percent of these appeals. If the claimant appears with either a lawyer or an agent, and the employer has no advocate, this reaches 26 to 30 percent, but drops back to 21 percent if the employer appears with a lawyer. An advocate appearing for an employer facing an unrepresented claimant appellant seems to make little difference. For employer appeals of quit cases, the number of cases is too small to allow any face-off comparisons between lawyers and agents. Employers facing unrepresented claimants may improve their chances slightly by bringing a lawyer or agent (57 to 59 percent success rate, versus 50 percent without a representative), but the type of advocate makes no difference. Interestingly, in employer appeals of quit cases, there is no indication that the claimant having a representative makes any difference when the employer is unrepresented. If anything, the claimant is more likely to lose such cases by bringing a lawyer, although there is no effect here that is statistically discernible.

Overall, these patterns show that representation can (and sometimes does) make a difference, but that differences among the categories of representatives are less important than are differences within categories of

representatives. Before considering some illustrative examples, one needs
more detail on the process of representation in UC appeals cases. It is useful to consider separately the claimant and employer sides of the issue.

Claimant Representatives

Excluding friends and family, claimant representatives tend to be one of
three types: union officials, law students, and lawyers. Of these, only the
lawyers generally work on a fee-for-service basis. The union officials who
appear as UC advocates do so as part of their union duties, and the law
students are volunteers. While most of the lawyers appear on a fee-for-service basis, some are friends of the claimants, and some work as salaried
employees of legal service operations.

   While a lawyer may take a UC case when the only thing at stake is the
UC compensation, it is more common for lawyers to appear for claimants
when the UC representation is in some way connected to another proceed-

**TABLE 9.   Appellant Success by Type of Representative, Quit Cases
(in percentages)**

	Type of Employer Representative			
Type of Employee Representative	Lawyer	Agent	Inside or None	All
Lawyer	21	[25]	26	26
	(28)	(4)	(90)	(125)
	[33]	*[33]*	*62*	*50*
	(6)	*(3)*	*(13)*	*(22)*
Agent	[0]	—	30	26
	(3)	(0)	(20)	(23)
	—	—	—	*[33]*
	(1)	*(0)*	*(1)*	*(3)*
None	16	20	17	17
	(198)	(95)	(1,484)	(1,829)
	57	*59*	*50*	*51*
	(44)	*(27)*	*(229)*	*(307)*
All	17	20	18	18
	(229)	(99)	(1,598)	(1,981)
	55	*57*	*50*	*51*
	(51)	*(30)*	*(243)*	*(332)*

Source: Bureau of Legal Affairs, Unemployment Compensation Division, Wisconsin Department of
Industry, Labor, and Human Relations (compiled by the author).

Note: Figures in roman are for cases appealed by the employee; figures in italics are for cases appealed
by the employer; figures in parentheses are number of cases; percentages in brackets are based on very
small numbers of cases and should be considered with caution.

ing. The simple reason for this is the statutory limit on the fee that lawyers may charge claimants in UC cases: ten percent of the benefits at issue. Because of this limitation, representing UC claimants can produce, at best, very modest fees. Most of the claimant lawyers I observed were appearing at the UC hearing because they also were representing the claimant in a discrimination case or an appeal of the termination or a workers' compensation case. In some of these cases, the UC proceeding was serving as a kind of discovery device (i.e., one or both sides were hoping to gain information in the one case that would be useful in another proceeding). Testimony at the UC proceedings is admissible elsewhere, and a party at the UC hearing must be careful not to compromise its position in another proceeding. For example, in one case involving the dismissal of a teacher alleged to have permitted one group of students to attack another student physically, the parents of the victim of the attack were suing the school officials for failing to supervise the teacher adequately. The school officials had fired the teacher, but if the officials defended that discharge for misconduct at the UC hearing, that defense could be introduced by the victim's attorney in the proceeding against the school officials. However, if the school officials failed to defend the dismissal at the UC hearing, they would then be in a bind in the reinstatement proceeding that the teacher's attorney had brought against the school district.

Because of the low fees involved, few attorneys handle UC cases, and most of those who do appear in UC proceedings do so sporadically if not very rarely. The result is that many, perhaps most, of the lawyers are not familiar with the administrative law judges, the procedure used by the judges, or the rules governing eligibility for UC compensation. The result is that while many of these attorneys are good at questioning witnesses, they often ask irrelevant questions or fail to bring the right witnesses to question. The following transcript illustrates this problem. It also shows how an attorney who is not particularly knowledgeable about UC can be outshone by a nonattorney representative who is thoroughly familiar with the hearing process, the evidentiary requirements, and the administrative law judges. The following case involves a discharge for misconduct. The appellant is the claimant. As the transcript shows, the claimant's position is that she did take the item in question, but did so with the understanding that it was okay to do so. In the following excerpt, ATT refers to the claimant's attorney, ADV refers to the employer's nonattorney advocate (Ms. A in the transcript), ALJ to the administrative law judge, CL to the claimant (Ms. B in the transcript), W to the employer's first witness (Ms. C in the transcript; the employer brought two additional witnesses whom the advocate decided not to call to testify).

ALJ: What is the employer's position on the issue?

ADV: The employee was discharged for misconduct—theft of hospital property.

ATT: The employee was discharged but no misconduct occurred.

ALJ: Because the employer has the burden in a misconduct case, I will take their testimony first. Ms. A, who would have the best information about what happened?

ADV: Ms. C.

ALJ [to Ms. C; all witnesses had previously been sworn]: What is your position with the hospital?

W: I am employed as a nurse manager.

ALJ: How long have you been in that position?

W: About a year and a half.

ALJ: How long had Ms. B worked at the hospital?

W: About 14 years.

ALJ: What was her last day of work?

W: She was discharged on October 28.

ALJ: What was her position?

W: She was the unit secretary in the —— unit.

ALJ: What was your relationship to Ms. B.?

W: I was her supervisor.

ALJ: How was Ms. B informed that she was being discharged?

W: In a face-to-face meeting.

ALJ: Were you present at that meeting?

W: Yes.

ALJ: What happened?

W: She was told that she was being discharged for theft of hospital property. The hospital's policy was that any theft of property was grounds for immediate discharge.

ALJ: What did Ms. B say when she was informed of the discharge?

W: She was pretty upset; I don't recall her specific response. The theft had occurred three or four years ago.

ALJ: How was the theft discovered?

W: The hospital received a phone call from the —— Police Department.

ATT: Objection, this is hearsay.

ALJ: Overruled, this is the information upon which the employer acted.

W: The —— Police Department had found a set of wrist restraints marked with —— Hospital. They had picked up a person in an intoxicated state who was wearing the restraints. That person told the police that they had come from Ms. B's home.

ALJ: What happened after the police called the hospital?

W: Personnel contacted me and advised me to confront Ms. B.

ALJ: Did you do this?

W: Yes.

ALJ: Was anyone else present?

W: No, it was just me and Ms. B.

ALJ: What happened at that meeting?

W: Ms. B admitted taking the restraints; she said that they had been just lying around and that she took them as a joke.

ALJ [to ADV]: Do you have any questions of this witness?

ADV [to witness]: You said that the police called the hospital because the restraints were marked. How were they marked?

W: They had stamped on them "Property of —— Hospital."

ADV: How are the restraints used by the hospital?

W: They are used to restrain a patient's hands. It can be because the patient is out of control, but more often it is to prevent a patient from disturbing sutures or an IV or something like that. We don't use them very often on the unit where I work.

ADV: Did Ms. B know about the hospital's policy with regard to theft?

W: Yes, when I confronted her, I asked if she had a copy of the employee handbook. She said that she did. Over the weekend between that meeting and the discharge meeting she read the policy, and she was aware that the policy called for discharge on the first occurrence.

ADV [handing a copy of the employee discipline policy to the ALJ]: I would like to introduce this as an exhibit.

ALJ [after marking the policy as Exhibit 1]: Further questions?

ADV: No, I have no further questions.

ALJ [to ATT]: Questions for this witness?

ATT [to the witness]: Did you see the restraints involved?

W: No.

ATT: Could you describe the restraints and explain how they are used?

ALJ: That was already covered.

ATT: Do you know of any other incidents of misconduct involving Ms. B?

W: I'm not aware of any.

ATT: No further questions.

ALJ: I will take Ms. B's testimony next. What is your name, address?

CL [Provides information requested.]

ALJ: Is there anything about the dates of your employment or your position that you would like to correct?

CL: No, what Ms. C said was correct.

ALJ: What happened at the discharge meeting?

CL: Ms. C called me in and informed me that I was being discharged because I had admitted taking the items, and they needed to be consistent in how they applied the policy regarding theft. I was crying and was very upset.

ALJ: You admit that you took the items?

CL: Yes, but it was eight or nine years ago.

ALJ: Did you file a grievance regarding your discharge?

CL: No, I was in shock. I had worked at the hospital for fourteen years, and I was a good employee.

ALJ [*pulls a piece of paper from the file in front of him, and marks it as Exhibit 2; hands it to CL, who takes a minute or two to read it*]: Is that your signature?

CL: Yes.

ALJ: Is this the statement you gave to the Claims Deputy when you filed for unemployment?

CL: Yes, it is.

ALJ: Did you tell the deputy that you had taken the restraints?

CL: Yes, I did.

ALJ: Did you ask anyone for permission to take them?

CL: No.

ALJ: Why did you take them?

CL: This happened sometime in the early 1980s. We were moving the unit. Lots of old things were being thrown away. The supervisor said that if we wanted any of the things that were being thrown out, we could take them home. There were old lamps, old bedside tables, stuff like that. The restraints were not a complete set. I had never seen them used. I assumed that they would be thrown away, and no one would miss them if I just took them.

ALJ [*to ATT*]: Questions?

ATT: Where were you working?

CL: On the arthritis unit.

ATT: Who was your supervisor?

CL: Jane Smith.

ATT: What did she say about taking things home?

CL: She said that we should use our discretion in taking things home.

ATT: How did it happen that someone was wearing the restraints out on the street?

ALJ: That's not relevant to the issue here.

ATT: I don't have anything further.

ALJ [*to ADV*]: Do you have any questions?

ADV [*handing a document to the ALJ*]: Will you please mark this.

ALJ [*looks at it and then marks it before handing back to ADV*]: I have marked this as exhibit 3.

ADV [*to CL*]: Is this the letter you received confirming your discharge and the reasons for it?

ATT: We will stipulate that the hospital stated that the discharge was for misconduct.

ADV [*to CL*]: Does the letter mention a grievance procedure?

CL: Yes.

ADV: Did you ever contact the person listed as the contact regarding grievances?

CL: I tried, but I was never able to reach her. I couldn't get people to return my calls, and I never reached the correct person.

ADV: Were the things not being used because of remodeling?

CL: No, the unit was moving to a new wing.

ADV: Could the restraints be used in the new area?

ATT: Objection, that would be speculation.

ALJ: Overruled.

CL: I don't see how it could have been used. It wasn't a full set. I had never seen them used on the unit in all the time I had been there.

ADV: Did you get permission from your supervisor to take them?

CL: No, I was embarrassed about asking the supervisor. I had just gotten married.

ADV: No further questions.

ALJ [*to ADV*]: Do you have any further witnesses?

ADV: [after briefly conferring with one of the persons with her] I don't think I need to call either of the other two persons.

ALJ [*to ATT*]: Anything further?

ATT: Nothing else.

[*Neither ATT nor ADV made a closing statement; the ALJ admitted the three exhibits with no objections for ATT or ADV, and closed the hearing.*]

Several important observations may be drawn from this hearing transcript. First, despite the presence of advocates for both sides, the judge took primary responsibility for developing the case.[51] Nonetheless, the role, or potential role, of the advocates was significant. Unless the claimant was prepared to disavow the statement to the claims deputy (which the claimant had signed), there was virtually an open and shut case supporting the discharge for misconduct. The two possible defenses were (1) the employer had failed to follow its stated disciplinary policy, and (2) while the claimant had taken the restraints, that taking did not constitute theft.

The claimant and her lawyer chose to pursue the latter course. There was one piece of potential testimony that was crucial to this strategy: that of either the supervisor who told staff persons they could take unwanted items home, or another employee who was working on the ward at the time who could have testified that "everyone was taking old stuff home." If one presumes that the argument had some factual basis,[52] one must ask why the claimant's lawyer did not try to find a witness to support this argument. Other than the obvious explanation that it was false, the best explanation for failing to bring a supporting witness was that the lawyer presumed that the standard of proof would be "beyond a reasonable doubt" and that a supporting witness was unnecessary. The lawyer clearly did not understand the evidentiary standards that applied in the hearing, as indicated by the two objections he raised during the hearing, both of which were overruled by the judge. Overall, the attorney seemed to have little role in the hearing; his questions were tangential, if not irrelevant (e.g., the disallowed question about how the person picked up by the police happened to be wearing the restraints), and at times unnecessarily repetitive.

In this case, the employer's nonlawyer advocate played a relatively small role. The evidence and testimony supporting the employer's action was sufficient that the advocate probably made at best a marginal difference. The key testimony elicited by the advocate served to confirm that the hospital had correctly followed its disciplinary procedure, and that the claimant had failed to take advantage of the grievance procedure the hospital provided for employees who felt they had been unfairly treated. The advocate's questions to the claimant served to confirm that the claimant had been informed of the grievance procedure and had not pursued it (although the claimant stated that she had tried unsuccessfully to make an inquiry about the grievance procedure). The advocate in this case had appeared before the judge on a number of prior occasions and was familiar with his style. She also knew when the judge had the evidence to affirm the denial of benefits; even though she could have strengthened her case by calling one or both of the additional witnesses, she knew that the judge would prefer to end the hearing without what he would view as repetitive, unnecessary testimony.

One might ask which attorneys are most likely to be effective representatives for claimants. The answer is that the best attorneys for claimants are going to be those who specialize in employment law. It is unlikely that someone not specializing in employment law will have had significant experience in UC hearings, and the potential fee from a UC hearing is too low to permit an attorney to invest significant effort in becoming familiar with the law and procedure relevant for those hearings. While having some expertise as an advocate may help an attorney make a difference compared to appearing unrepresented, the lack of substantive knowledge and the lack of specific experience greatly limits the effectiveness of a nonspecialist attorney.

The best claimant attorneys that I saw were those who do a lot of employment and labor law. In every case that I saw where a claimant attorney seemed particularly effective, it was a case in which the UC claim was only part of what the attorney was handling on behalf of the client. The attorney was not necessarily able to win the case for the client, but the attorney did know what type of evidence was relevant and was able to raise questions about the evidence presented by the employer.

The following fragment from a hearing indicates the kind of questioning one might see from an effective claimant's advocate. This case involved the dismissal of an employee ("Mr. A") from a state agency for allegedly having submitted false travel vouchers. An audit found discrepancies such as phone calls from one location when the employee claimed to be traveling at another location, travel expenses claimed for days when the employee had taken sick leave, claims for meal expenses when he was not eligible (e.g., a claim for breakfast when the employee reported having left home at 7:30 A.M. when the rules allowed for such a claim only if the departure was before 6:00 A.M.), and making personal phone calls using the employer's credit card.

The strategy of the claimant's attorney was twofold in this case: question whether the prescribed progressive disciplinary procedure had been followed and challenge the accuracy of the documentary evidence. The potentially more productive element was the latter because it would be important for the former. (If the employer had engaged in systematic theft, progressive discipline would probably not be relevant, but if what had happened was simply negligence regarding record keeping, that would be a different matter.) The attorney representing the employing agency (LAW) went through a list of infractions and exhibits with the key witness (W); the claimant's attorney (ATT) then cross-examined this witness.

ATT: What procedure was used to audit the phone calls?

W: The auditors reviewed all calls to private numbers.

ATT: Were some of the supposed private numbers actually state numbers?

W: I don't know.

ATT: Does this list contain all of the nonstate numbers that were called?

W: I don't know.

ATT: Did Mr. A explain some or all of the calls as business related?

W: I don't recall.

ATT: Have employees of [agency] had a history of errors on vouchers?

W: Yes.

ATT [*hands a document to the ALJ to be marked, then passes it to W*]: What is this docment?

W: It's a memo dated June 22, 1990.

ATT: What does it deal with?

W: It cautions employees to take more care in filling out travel vouchers.

ATT: What procedure is used in reviewing and approving travel vouchers?

W: We use the standard state procedures.

ATT: Would it be the supervisor's responsibility to verify vouchers against time sheets?

W: Yes.

ATT: Do you know whether the supervisors at [agency] actually did this?

W: No I don't.

ATT: When do employees fill out time sheets?

W: At the end of the pay period . . . sometimes they fill them out at the beginning of the period and then correct them at the end.

ATT: Is it possible that the times and dates recorded on the time sheets may be incorrect.

W: It's possible.

ATT: How about the travel vouchers, are they filled out contemporaneously with incurring the expenses?

W: Not always.

ATT: Have employees put down wrong dates when filling out expense vouchers?

W: Yes. [*Through the last series of questions, the witness has been looking over at the employer's attorney with an expression that says, "Can you get me out of this?"*]

ATT: Did Mr. A offer to make good on errors on the expense vouchers?

W: I don't recall.

ATT: Did Mr. A say that these were mistakes and that he needed training to improve the accuracy of his expense vouchers?

W: Yes.

ATT: Did Mr. A ask for copies of his calendars?

W: I don't recall.

ATT: Were other employees who made personal calls terminated?

W: No.

ATT: What happened to them?

W: I don't know.

ATT: No further questions.

ALJ [to LAW]: Any additional questions for this witness?

LAW: If a supervisor had checked Mr. A's vouchers, would the discrepancies have been apparent?

W: No, they didn't have the phone bills to match to the travel vouchers.

LAW: After the audit, were any other employees terminated?

W: Yes, one other person was discharged.

LAW: No further questions.

ALJ: What is the date of the last travel voucher that you identified as allegedly being fraudulent?

W: April 21.

ALJ: Were the vouchers after this date okay?

W: We couldn't find any discrepancies.

In this hearing the administrative law judge was clearly anticipating an appeal of his decision (regardless of which side the decision favored); he kept asking the witnesses to speak up so the tape recorder (which served as the record of the hearing) got what they were saying. In fact, the claimant's attorney later informed me that the judge ruled in favor of the employer; however, before he could initiate the appeal process, the agency settled with Mr. A (who was also appealing his dismissal to the state personnel commission).

What about nonlawyer advocates for claimants (other than family members or friends)? The records of the UC Bureau of Legal Affairs showed three types of such advocates: law students, union officials, and paralegals (only one person appeared in this latter category). Of these three groups, I only actually observed law students. What I saw was mixed. Generally, the law students, who by definition were not experienced advocates, tried very hard to be strong advocates for their clients.[53] However, I saw two types of recurring problems.

The first problem was that some of the students did not know how to examine a witness. This was not particularly surprising because of the students' lack of experience (many are first-year students, and the UC hearings constitute their very first advocacy experience). The problem showed up in two distinct ways. First, some students simply did not know how to ask questions. Some students tried to ask leading questions of their own witnesses, which either the judge would cut off or the employer's lawyer would object to. At several junctures in one case—a particularly contentious one with a law student representing the claimant and a lawyer representing the employer[54]—the lawyer's objections to the student's questions so frustrated the student that he was virtually begging the judge to assist him in formulating questions in an acceptable form.[55] The student also repeatedly asked tangential, if not irrelevant, questions. There seemed to be little dispute over whether the events deemed to be misconduct had occurred;[56] there was also no dispute over whether the employer had gone through a process of progressive discipline.[57] The claimant's argument for receiving UC benefits rested solely on whether the employer had strictly followed its disciplinary policy, specifically whether the claimant had been referred to an employee assistance program for help in dealing with her personal problems that were creating difficulties at work. The employer presented testimony that information about the assistance program was posted by the time clock in every store.

The second difficulty with the law students' questioning of witnesses was a failure to get across the point of a question or the implication of an answer. One example of this again involved a case pitting a law student advocate for the claimant against a lawyer for the employer; in this case the employer was the appellant. This case presented two issues, one related to the termination of the claimant's employment and the other to whether he was available for work. The issue between the employer and claimant was whether the claimant's work had been substandard (which, in the technical language of UC appeals, constitutes misconduct). The employer, a very small operation (probably less than a dozen employees), manufactured wood trim for windows and doors. The claimant was responsible for setting up equipment, manufacturing, and inspecting the product. The employer maintained that the claimant had produced a particularly large quantity of goods that did not meet the purchaser's specifications. The employer asserted that the claimant was having personal problems that appeared to result in poor work performance, both with regard to materials produced and with regard to the other employees under the claimant's supervision. The employer's testimony made it clear that there was no formal disciplinary policy, and there had been no progressive discipline used with regard to the claimant; the owner said he had warned the claimant about the problems with other employees, but had not explicitly told the claimant that his job was in jeopardy. The testimony of the employer made reference to a variety of incidents, but the precipitating event was that the goods were not acceptable to the customer.[58]

The student representing the claimant asked few questions of the employer's witnesses (the owner's wife and one other employee) or the claimant (the judge did most of the questioning of the claimant). This student advocate had arranged for a witness to testify about the goods that were defective, but he was totally ineffective in asking questions of that witness. The questions sometimes made no sense. When the questions did make sense, the advocate would cut in hurriedly with another question before the witness could finish the previous answer. After five or ten minutes, the judge took over the questioning. Interestingly, there seemed to be no dispute regarding the quaility of the goods, and the advocate's purpose in calling this witness was unclear.

The second general problem with law student advocates was that they often introduced superfluous issues. In one case a car wash employee with a long history of alcoholism was dismissed because he regularly failed to show up for work. The employer (unrepresented) presented a long list of dates of "no call, no show's." The most common reason for these given by the claimant was that he (the claimant) was in detox. The employer provided to the judge a policy document that listed reasons for dismissal, which included absenteeism. The advocate elicited testimony from the employer that the claimant was a good worker, when he was sober and at work; the employer also acknowledged that he knew that the claimant was an alcoholic. In his testimony, the claimant essentially confirmed everything the employer said. When the advocate asked the claimant if he had received a copy of the car wash's work policies, the claimant explained that he had not received them "this time," but acknowledged receiving them during a previous period of employment at the car wash. The advocate then tried to introduce a line of questions about how important the job was to the claimant; it almost seemed as though the advocate were trying to appeal for sympathy from a jury. The judge had previously signaled a lack of sympathy in a question directed to the claimant, "Why should the employer be liable for unemployment compensation here . . . why should they be liable for your drinking problem?" The judge let the advocate ask a series of questions about the claimant's alcoholism, but would not permit the advocate to call a witness who had come to the hearing to testify about the claimant's problems and efforts to deal with those problems. The advocate asked to make a closing statement, but the judge refused to allow this, indicating to the advocate a willingness to receive a written brief citing any case law the advocate felt was relevant.

One observation suggested by these various examples is that the students were working with cases they could not win[59] and were doing the best they could under the circumstances. While this is true in some cases, it is not true in all cases. In one case involving a small company that bound the edges of carpeting to make rugs, the issue presented to the judge was whether the claimant had quit or had been discharged. As the hearing proceeded, it became clear that there had been a rocky relationship between the claimant and the employer; the claimant had been "fired" multiple times but had always come back to work. Exactly what had happened the last time was in dispute. The advocate's questions did not clarify the events at all. At the very end of the hearing, the advocate made a closing statement in which he said, "There is only so much harassment a person can take . . . whenever things did not go right [the claimant] was a kicking post for [the employer]." It can be "good cause" to quit if an employee is "subject to abuse from supervisors or co-workers."[60] However, the advocate brought no witnesses and introduced no substantive testimony that would have built a harassment case.

Overall, the performances of law-student advocates whom I observed were disappointing. By and large, they reflected neither a knowledge of the legal issues involved in many of the cases nor skills in oral advocacy. The more vigorous advocates seemed motivated more by a striving for justice or fairness than by the specific factual or legal issues that underlie determinations of eligibility for UC compensation. Still, while the law students as a group were not particularly effective, the cases presented by them seemed notably better than cases presented by unrepresented claimants (and this is consistent with the statistical patterns). At least part of this probably reflected the students' awareness of basic evidentiary requirements, which led them to insure that key documents and witnesses were present at the hearing. Furthermore, the experience of a variety of other actors in the system indicates that some law students are effective.[61] I have no way of determining whether this reflects the stage of the students' law school training and the experience they already have under their belts, or simply that some students have the knack and others do not.

Employer Representatives

Two primary groups of employer representatives are attorneys and non-lawyer agents employed by or retained by firms that provide services managing an employer's unemployment compensation affairs. Both of these groups divide into two subgroups, but these subgroups differ between lawyers and nonlawyers. Some of the lawyers are employment law specialists, while others have a general practice serving small businesses. Some of the nonlawyers have ongoing, direct relationships with the clients for whom they appear, while others are retained by an intermediary and appear on a purely ad hoc basis. In assessing the quality of representation, one must take into account these distinctions.

In contrast to the limitations that apply to advocates representing claimants, there are no limits on the fees lawyers can charge employers for appearing at UC hearings. As a result specialist lawyers provide very effective representation for employers. These lawyers know the rules governing the payment of UC benefits, including expectations of progressive discipline, employee handbooks with explicit statements about policies, and the like. They know what evidence a judge will need to find that the discharge of a claimant was for misconduct. These attorneys often have general employment law practices that can include extensive experience in dealing with discharge appeals (often in the context of union grievance proceedings). They also know how to examine and cross-examine witnesses to establish a client's case. However, they are not necessarily efficient in their presentation of a case to the UC administrative law judges.

The following partial transcript involves an appeal where the employer's lawyer (ATT) had a fairly strong misconduct case; the claimant (Ms. K, identified as CL in the transcript) also had a lawyer—one with a reputation as a vigorous advocate (LAW). The employer was a private social service agency (which I will call Stop Drug Problems Now—SDPN) focused on drug abuse problems. In this case, the judge chose to turn the development of the case over to the lawyers rather than taking the lead.[62] The employer's attorney is not particularly efficient in how she gets her client's side of the story on the table, although the position seems strong.

ALJ: What is the position of the employer?

ATT: Ms. K was discharged for misconduct.

ALJ [to LAW]: Was Ms. K discharged?

LAW: She was discharged, but our position is that she is nonetheless eligible for compensation.

ALJ [to ATT]: Call your first witness.

ATT: We call Ms. K as an adverse witness.

ATT [to Ms. K]: When did your employment with SDPN begin and end?

CL: I worked there from April 1988, when I founded the agency until May 24, 1991; when my employment ended I was the executive director.

ATT: When did your paid employment start?

CL: About two years after starting SDPN.

ALJ: Could you be more specific . . . when did you get your first paycheck?

CL: Sometime in 1990.

ALJ [pulls out several pages from the file in front of her, marks it, and hands it to CL]: Is this the statement you gave to the UC deputy?

CL [*looks at the sheets*]: Yes, it is.

ALJ: Is there anything there that is incorrect?

CL [*going through page by page*] Page one is okay . . . page two is okay . . . so is page three.

ALJ: Look at the first sentence of the first page . . . what does it say?

CL [*reading*]: "I did not go on the payroll until around April 1990."

ALJ: Is that an accurate statement?

CL: Yes, it is.

ALJ [*to ATT*]: Continue.

ATT [*hands a document to the ALJ, which the ALJ marks as exhibit 2; hands to CL*]: What is this document?

CL: It is a personnel policy document dated April 1990.

ATT: Did you help prepare the document?

CL: Yes I did.

ATT: Did you recommend its adoption to the SDPN board?

CL: Yes.

ATT: When were the policies approved?

CL: I don't believe that the board ever formally approved them.

ATT: Did you use them as guidelines in working with the SDPN employees?

CL: Yes.

ATT: On page 14, is there a classification of employee labeled "executive"?

CL: Yes.

ATT: Which employees fell in this category?

CL: I did.

ATT: Did anyone else?

CL: No, because I was the only one directly accountable to the Board.

ATT: Let me direct you to section 6.0; what does it deal with?

CL: Disciplinary procedures.

ATT: Could you review that section for a moment . . . Does section 6.1 outline a progressive discipline procedure?

CL: Yes.

ATT: Does the section indicate that the supervisor may begin at any step of the procedure depending on the seriousness of the matter?

CL: Yes.

ATT: Let me now direct your attention to the bottom of page 39, the section on terminations for special causes. Does this section provide grounds for termination due to special causes?

CL: Yes.

ATT: When you were executive director, did you believe that you could terminate employees for the causes listed on page 39?

CL: Yes.

ATT: Please look at the next section . . . what does it deal with?

CL: It outlines the appeal process.

ATT: Under what circumstances is the procedure applicable?

CL: It applies to cases where discipline was imposed.

ATT: Does it apply only to cases involving termination or all forms of discipline?

CL: It applies to most situations.

ATT: Does the process allow a terminated employee to appeal the termination?

CL: Most of the time it does.

ALJ [*breaking in, to CL*]: Were you terminated?

CL: Yes.

ALJ: Did you appeal?

CL: I wasn't allowed to.

ALJ: Was there an appeal process available to you?

CL: No.

ALJ [*to ATT*]: Continue.

ATT [*hands a document to the ALJ to be marked, and then passes it to CL*]: Can you identify this document?

CL: It's the termination letter.

ATT: Did you appeal the termination?

CL: No I did not.

ATT: Let's go back to what has been marked as Exhibit 2; did it have a section on outside employment?

CL: What do you mean?

ATT: Did SDPN have a policy forbidding outside employment that conflicted with SDPN?

CL: Not to my knowledge.

ATT: Were you unaware of a policy prohibiting outside employment that conflicted with SDPN?

CL: I was aware of no such policy.

ATT: Did the board ever adopt a set of employment policies?

CL: To my knowledge, the board never adopted any such policies.

ATT: Did anyone ever draft some policies?

CL: Yes, there was a draft.

ATT: Did you use those draft policies as guidelines?

CL: Yes.

ATT: Did you consider yourself subject to those guidelines?

CL: Yes.

[*testimony omitted*]

ATT: What is K&K Associates?
CL: It's a name that was created by me and ——.
ATT: What did it refer to?
CL: We worked together.
ATT: What work did you do together?
CL: We worked together [*CL is trying to avoid answering the question*].
ATT: Isn't it true that K&K Associates made a grant proposal to the city?
CL: Yes.
ATT: Did the proposal have a title?
CL: Yes, it was called Building Together.
ATT: What was Building Together intended to do?
CL: To provide services to youth.
ATT: Was it drug and alcohol related?
CL: You might look at it that way. We envisioned four sessions, only one of which was about alcohol and drug problems.
ATT: Was Building Together done for free?
CL: Partially.
ATT: Does that mean it was partially for pay?
CL: We got some payment from a local women's organization.
ATT: Do you know where they got the money they paid you?
CL: I'm not sure where they got the money.
ATT: Where do you *think* they got the money?
CL: Probably from the county.
ATT: Was any part of the Building Together proposal prepared on SDPN time?
CL: No.
ATT: Did any SDPN staff work on Building Together on SDPN time?
CL: I'm not sure.

The attorney for the employer used his questioning of the claimant to lay a foundation for the employer's contention that Ms. K had engaged in activities that effectively competed with SDPN for funding resources. Throughout Ms. K's testimony, the attorney asked questions about financial irregularities or mismanagement. I have not included those in the transcript above because Ms. K's answers were confusing, perhaps because she was trying to avoid answering these (as well as other) questions posed to her. After about an hour of testimony by Ms. K, the administrative law judge broke in and asked that the employer's attorney call a witness who would testify as to the reasons for discharge. That witness, the president of the board of directors, referred to a suspension letter listing the reasons, which focused less on the conflict of interest than on financial mismanagement; an audit had revealed a number of problems (e.g., a failure to pay payroll withholding taxes, failing to comply with grant contracts, double billing, etc.). While the attorney here may not have been particularly efficient in building a case in support of the discharge for misconduct, she did come to the hearing with the right witnesses, the right documents (with the exception of some bad checks the claimant was alleged to have written), and the right questions.

As suggested previously, not all employer attorneys were knowledgeable about either substance or process. The clearest example of this involved an employee who quit work at a computer store. The employer had lost its contract to sell Apple computers. The issue was whether the claimant had quit for good cause. While the claimant cited a variety of reasons leading to his decision to quit, the primary reason was a change in compensation largely due to the loss of the Apple program: from a salary of $18,000 plus commission (which came to a total of $27,400 in the previous year), the employee was to be paid $6.25 per hour plus commission (with a relatively low prospect for significant commissions).[63] The claims deputy had concluded that the quit was for good cause, and that the claimant was eligible for benefits; the employer had appealed that decision.

The employer's attorney asked questions about a variety of issues. He established that until about a year earlier, the employee compensation plan had been more or less what the new one was to be (i.e., the employee had been paid $6.25 hour, which is about $12,000 per year, plus commission). He also established that the claimant began working full time for a local real estate broker less than a week after quitting the computer store. The attorney thought he had found a fact devastating to the former employee's claimed entitlement to UC benefits: how can you collect UC benefits when you are working for someone else? At the end of the claimant's testimony, the attorney made a motion for what amounted to summary judgment on the grounds that the claimant immediately went to work elsewhere. The administrative law judge curtly rejected the attorney's motion both because the procedure did not allow for such motions and because the motion itself was ungrounded (a claimant is eligible for benefits even if working full time, if there is no income being generated from the new position, which was the situation in this case). The attorney was somewhat confused by all of this and requested a brief recess.[64]

After the recess, the store manager testified, confirming the salary-related points made by the claimant. The attorney's questions of the manager concerned the fact that other employees who had similar changes made to their compensation did not quit—a fact that was irrelevant to the claimant's actions. At the close of the hearing, the judge gave the attorney and the claimant the opportunity to make closing statements. The attorney's primary point was to note that the initial determination, while allowing benefits, found that the new salary the claimant had been offered was not inconsistent with the current labor market; this was yet another irrelevant point to the issues before the administrative law judge. Not surprisingly, the attorney's points did not convince the judge to reverse the initial determination.

An attorney who has extensive involvement with an employer's personnel operation is likely to be most effective in providing representation at a UC hearing. For a large employer, this attorney may be a member of the corporate counsel staff. One example of this situation involved the dismissal of a city employee (Mr. R) for failing to reside within the city as required by local ordinance. The dismissal was part of an ongoing effort by the city to enforce its residence requirement. The judge elicited key portions of the evidence in her questioning of the witness (W), the claimant's former supervisor.

ALJ: When was Mr. R discharged?

W: On November 19.

ALJ: Were you Mr. R's supervisor?

W: No, I had no direct supervision of him.

ALJ: Were you involved in the decision to terminate his employment?

W: Yes, I was informed that he was living outside the city. I contacted the Human Resource Department and the City Attorney, and they investigated the situation.

ALJ: Were you involved in the investigation?

W: Only to the extent of passing on information.

ALJ: When did you first talk to Mr. R about his living situation?

W [looking at notes]: I first talked to him in early November. I told him that his payroll record showed a Madison residence, but we had learned that he was actually living outside of the city.

ALJ: What procedure did you follow?

W: On November 19, in the morning, we held a predetermination hearing at which Mr. R was present. I asked him if he was aware that it was city policy that all employees, as a condition of employment, reside in the city. He said that he believed that as long as he had an address in the city where he could pick up mail that he could live elsewhere.

ALJ: Did Mr. R confirm that he was living outside the city?

W: Yes, he admitted that he had been living in —— for about a year.

ALJ: Under what circumstances can an employee live outside the city?

W: An employee can request permission to live outside the city. Permission is rarely given, and then only for reasons such as health or financial disaster. I cannot waive the residency requirement; only the Mayor can. Under the ordinance, once an employee leaves the city, the position is deemed vacant.

The attorney (ATT) representing the city followed up the judge's questions with a brief series of his own questions that provided the evidentiary basis of the city's decision and showed that the city had followed the applicable disciplinary procedures.

ATT [*after the judge marked a set of papers as exhibit 1*]: Can you identify this document?

W: Yes, it is Mr. R's employment application.

ATT: Does the application say anything about the residence requirement?

W: Yes, on the back; the applicant's signature attests to his residing in the city.

ATT [*after the judge marked another document as exhibit 2*]: What is the document I have just handed you?

W: It is the termination letter with attachments that accompanied it.

ATT: What were those attachments?

W: An affidavit from ————; a change of address form showing the address outside the city; a statement of residency dated September 25, 1990, and another statement of residency dated July 21, 1991.

ATT: What is the purpose of a predetermination hearing?

W: It is intended to give the employee the opportunity to respond to and challenge the evidence.

ATT: Did Mr. R contest the affidavit from ————?

W: No he did not.

ATT: What did Mr. R say about where he was living?

W: He admitted that he had been staying outside the city overnight for about a year, though he claimed he was residing in the city.

The administrative law judge then took Mr. R's testimony. Mr. R essentially confirmed the city's position. He tried to draw a distinction between where he was "staying" ("I didn't think staying at someone else's house was living outside the city") and where he was "residing," identifying the latter with his mailing address. During Mr. R's testimony, the city's attorney whispered to the other person from the city that he "would not waste time on cross-examination," but changed his mind and asked two or three brief questions including, "Is there anything in the employment application that says it's okay to have just a mailing address and phone number in the city?"

This is an example of an in-house lawyer enforcing the well-established policy of an employer. In other situations an in-house lawyer may simply possess or be able to access key information readily. One such case involved the dismissal of an employee of a local utility company for having given out information about the company's internal phone system that allowed a family member to use that system to make unauthorized long-distance phone calls. In this case, which I will not quote, the in-house lawyer representing the employer at the hearing was able to use detailed information about the operation of the internal phone system to show that the claimant had to have specifically given out confidential security codes in order for the access to have occurred. While an outside lawyer could, no doubt, have obtained the information used by the in-house lawyer, it would probably have been a more time-consuming process.

Let us now turn to nonlawyer employer representatives. Recall that the two subgroups consist of representatives who have ongoing relationships with their clients and those who appear on an ad hoc basis. I have already quoted fairly extensively from hearings involving two different individuals from the first category (the case involving the hospital employee who had an extensive record of tardiness, and the case involving the hospital employee who had taken the restraints), so I will not give any additional examples. Two primary elements contribute to the effectiveness of these representatives. First, they appear at hearings on a fairly regular basis. During 1991, one of them appeared at forty-four hearings and the other at seventeen hearings.[65] Based on this experience, they know the procedure and the administrative law judges; for example, in the restraints case, the advocate could tell that the judge had pretty well decided the case after hearing the employer's first witness and the claimant, and the advocate chose not to call any of the other witnesses she had brought. These advocates come to the hearings with the right documents and the right witnesses. The second major factor in the effectiveness of these advocates is their detailed knowledge of their clients' procedures for disciplining and discharging employees. Appearing as advocates at hearings is only one small aspect of what these individuals do; much of their time is spent assisting clients in structuring their personnel systems to minimize liability in cases involving the discharge of employees. When a hearing does come up, they know the procedures that were used, and they know that those procedures, if they were properly used, conform to the requirements of the unemployment regulations. In summary, these advocates, while non-lawyers, are experts in unemployment compensation, both with regard to the laws and regulations and with regard to advocacy.

The second group of nonlawyer employer advocates are individuals whom UC consulting firms retain on an ad hoc basis to represent the firms' clients at UC appeal hearings. These individuals have disparate backgrounds, ranging from accounting to law enforcement. One of the advocates I observed ran an investigation and security firm and did UC hearings as a sideline; another was a retired police officer. These advocates tend to be experienced in the UC setting, but they are not specialists in unemployment compensation (except from their experience in the appeals hearings). They may have experience in an adversary setting (e.g., a retired police officer will have spent many hours in courtrooms and on the witness stand), and they probably feel very comfortable with formal legal proceedings despite a lack of formal legal training.

The problem for these advocates is that they often have not had an opportunity to prepare the case. The UC firms who retain these advocates pay on a per-hearing basis, and the amount the firms pay can be a hundred dollars or less. Frequently, the advocate first sees the client in the hallway outside the hearing room and must rely upon the materials and witnesses someone else told the client to bring to the hearing. Still, on the strength of sheer experience,[66] these advocates can provide real help, even if they may not be as effective as someone with more detailed knowledge of the client's affairs or more time to prepare the case in advance. They can brief the employer's witnesses on what to expect at the hearing; they can find out enough about the case to know when the judge may be missing something important which the advocate can then bring out in his or her questions. They can cross-examine the claimant and the claimant's witnesses to weaken the claimant's case or to strengthen the employer's case; and, given sufficient familiarity with a particular administrative law judge, they know when to keep quiet and let the judge handle things to the client's advantage.

While for purposes of this discussion I have not treated them as advocates, one final group of persons who appear for employers merits discussion: these are in-house nonlawyer spokespersons. For a large employer with a very systematic discipline procedure, nonlawyer personnel specialists can become quite good advocates. Interestingly, their expertise may develop in an interactive fashion: staff may appear for the employer at UC appeal hearings and lose cases due to inadequate procedures, lack of documentation, failure to bring the correct witnesses, and so on. Because of these experiences, the staff may insist that the employer change rules and procedures to conform to the UC regulations; over time, the cases become stronger, and the spokespersons learn what evidence and witnesses to bring to the hearings.

Two different administrative law judges described to me one local manufacturing concern that went through precisely this kind of experience. The relationship between this company and its employees was not particularly good, and the company imposed a severe set of rules (including written policies permitting discharge on a first infraction). When discharged employees sought unemployment compensation, the employer sent staff from its personnel department to the hearings. At first, the employees prevailed at the hearings, because the staff appearing for the employer did not have records or witnesses to support the discharge, and/or the formal policies were unclear or contradictory. Over time, the company clarified its procedures and policies (which were, from the employees' perspective, quite draconian), and the staff became experienced in presenting cases to the judges. After a year or two, the company won most of the appeals, and discharged employees brought fewer appeals.

Conclusion: Representation in UC Appeals

The overall picture that emerges here is complex. First, the differences and effects operate at the margin. Assuming that both the claimant and the employer appear at the hearing, the outcome of many, and perhaps most, cases reflects the merits of the case. Second, some expertise (e.g., in adversarial advocacy) is probably better than none, but it is the combination of general advocacy skills, knowledge of specific hearing practices and players (e.g., how the administrative law judges run hearings), and substantive knowledge of the statutes, regulations, and decisions governing the payment of unemployment compensation that characterizes the most effective advocates. Formal training (in the law) is less crucial than is day-to-day experience in the UC setting.

How can this last statement be reconciled with the statistical observation that when nonlawyer advocates face those who are lawyers (in misconduct cases appealed by the claimant), the latter group has a higher success rate? Recall that if the claimant has a lawyer advocate and the employer has a nonlawyer, the claimant wins 54 percent; in the reverse representational situation, the claimant wins only 19 percent.[67] I believe that the primary reason for this difference is that the largest proportion of nonlawyer advocates for both claimants and employers consists of the two types of representatives who are less likely to be effective—inexperienced law students for claimants and experienced but low-paid advocates who appear for employers on an ad hoc basis (with little time to prepare and little prior knowledge of the employer's practices).

The analysis, both statistical and observational, leaves little doubt that knowledgeable, experienced nonlawyer advocates can be effective in representing parties in UC appeal hearings. It also shows that having legal training does not insure that an advocate will be effective, particularly when there is little familiarity with the specific regulations or procedures governing UC and UC appeals. The overall key appears to be situation-specific experience. Someone walking into his or her first UC hearing, even someone with extensive experience in other adversary settings, will have trouble with the specifics. Similarly, someone intimately familiar with the UC regulations but with no advocacy experience will encounter substantial difficulties presenting a case in an adversarial setting.

CHAPTER 3

The Wisconsin Tax Appeals Commission

What do you do if you are unhappy about what you owe in taxes? In Wisconsin, taxpayers can turn to the Wisconsin Tax Appeals Commission to resolve their disagreements with the Wisconsin Department of Revenue (DOR). The Tax Appeals Commission (TAC), an independent, quasi-judicial state agency, hears and decides appeals from taxpayers concerning a variety of state tax-related matters.[1] In the words of its chairperson, the commission's goal is "to provide taxpayers of the state of Wisconsin with fair and impartial hearings on their tax appeals."[2]

The majority of cases before the commission concern income tax matters. In 1992–93, 60 percent of the filings before the commission were income tax cases, with another 20 percent equally divided between sales tax and manufacturing assessments (a property tax on manufacturing real estate and equipment).[3] The remaining 20 percent of the caseload was scattered over a variety of tax matters.

Tax law is highly technical and often complex. In tax disputes other than relatively straightforward factual matters (e.g., whether a taxpayer reported some of his or her income), expert representation is often crucial to the success of an appeal. Although the taxpayer need not be represented, the Department of Revenue always sends an attorney to appear on its behalf before the commission. The commissioner who presides at a hearing involving an unrepresented petitioner customarily makes a particular effort to insure that the taxpayer has the opportunity to air his or her case fully, within the appropriate procedural limits.

Two types of taxpayer representatives regularly appear: lawyers (usually lawyers who specialize in tax matters) and nonlawyer tax specialists. The latter group includes accountants and nonaccountant tax preparers (such as employees of companies like H&R Block). Some of the nonlawyer/nonaccountant representatives are "enrolled agents," which is a specialist group "admitted to practice before the Internal Revenue Service." In this chapter I consider the comparative effectiveness of lawyer and nonlawyer representatives. As a preliminary matter, I will describe the situation for the unrepresented petitioner. The number of tax hearings I observed is small, in part because of the frequent settlement of tax appeals before the hearing.

While I saw relatively few hearings, both my observations and the quantitative data I collected presented a stark pattern. In contrast to unemployment compensation appeals, where nonlawyer specialists were able to provide very effective representation, the nonlawyer specialists I observed at tax hearings were, with one possible exception, not effective in the hearing context. They may have been very effective in negotiating settlements with DOR, but I can only speculate about this because I observed only public hearings—I saw no negotiation sessions. The nonlawyers whom I saw may have had extensive substantive knowledge; what they lacked was any sense of the procedural elements of the hearing setting. Therefore, the hearings involving nonlawyer advocates more closely resembled hearings where the taxpayer was unrepresented than hearings where a tax lawyer appeared for the taxpayer.

The Tax Appeals Process

Most matters come to the Tax Appeals Commission when a taxpayer objects to a determination by the Wisconsin Department of Revenue. A disgruntled taxpayer must first petition the DOR for a redetermination; the DOR's Appellate Bureau considers the petition and will grant, deny, or partially grant or deny the petition. If the taxpayer objects to the action of the Appellate Bureau, the next step is to file a written appeal with the Tax Appeals Commission.[4] Between 1988 and 1994, the number of appeals filed has ranged between 469 and 634, and the number disposed between 451 and 617.[5] A taxpayer who loses before the commission has the right to appeal to the Circuit Court (as does the Department of Revenue if it loses), but few such appeals occur—seven in 1993–94.[6]

The commission uses procedures that approximate those used by the state's Circuit (trial) Court in civil matters. That is, either side (but usually the Department of Revenue) can employ formal discovery devices (e.g., requiring the production of relevant documents, or compelling responses to written questions in the form of interrogatories). The taxpayer and the DOR can file formal motions, such as to quash interrogatories or to dismiss for failing to meet required deadlines.[7] One exception to the use of the Circuit Court procedures is the relaxation of evidentiary rules; the commission will admit "all testimony having reasonable probative value."[8]

The Tax Appeals Commission actually decides only a small percentage of the matters appealed to it. The vast majority of taxpayers who petition the commission either abandon their appeals or resolve them through negotiation with the Department of Revenue. According to one report, in

1980, only 20 percent of cases had full hearings;[9] by my count, for fiscal year periods 1991–92 through 1993–94, the commission issued decisions on the merits[10] for only 16 percent of the cases disposed.[11]

In some ways these figures are misleading, because the commission uses slightly different procedures for cases that it labels "small-claims." Such cases involve less than $2,500 and present no issue of importance beyond the instant case.[12] The key differences in procedure between small-claims and regular matters are that (1) a single commissioner rather than the commission as a whole may decide a small-claims matter, and (2) the commissioner can render an oral decision at the close of the hearing. For the fiscal year period from July 1992 through June 1994, 34 percent of the disposed cases were small-claims matters, and 40 percent of the cases disposed of by a decision on the merits were small-claims.[13] As these figures suggest, small-claims cases are somewhat more likely to be disposed of by a formal decision than are non-small-claims cases: 20 percent of small-claims versus 15 percent of non-small-claims.[14]

The hearing itself is the setting that places into the record evidentiary matters.[15] Normally, the burden of proof falls on the taxpayer-petitioner; that is, the commission, by law, starts with the presumption that the Department of Revenue's assessment is correct, and the petitioner must show why that assessment is not correct.[16] Before the hearing formally begins, the two sides will usually agree upon a set of standard exhibits, including such things as the relevant tax returns, the request for redetermination and the DOR Appellate Bureau's response, other correspondence between the taxpayer and the Department of Revenue, and "jurisdictional" exhibits (i.e., the petition to the commission). In some cases, the two sides can actually stipulate to all of the factual matters (i.e., there is no factual dispute), in which case there may not be an actual hearing, or the hearing is pro forma; in these cases, the issue before the commission is purely one of interpretation of law or regulations.

The procedure for questioning witnesses depends upon whether the taxpayer is represented. When a taxpayer representative appears, that representative will call witnesses and conduct the questioning to establish the taxpayer's case, as well as cross-examining any witnesses called by the Department of Revenue. The attorney from the Department of Revenue presents the department's case and cross-examines the witnesses for the taxpayer. The presiding commissioner[17] is free to interject questions to clarify issues the commissioner feels are relevant.

When the taxpayer has no representative, which is typically true in small-claims cases, the burden falls on the commissioner to assist the taxpayer in presenting his or her case. The attorney for DOR still cross-examines the taxpayer's witnesses and presents the department's case. The taxpayer may, of course, ask questions of his or her own witnesses and any witnesses called by the Department of Revenue. The result is a hybrid between an adversary proceeding and an inquisitorial proceeding.

One element of the procedure closely resembles what I described regarding UC appeals: the taxpayer must appear at the hearing with the factual evidence necessary to establish his or her case. The commission will not normally grant a continuance for the taxpayer to produce witnesses or records that the taxpayer failed to bring to the hearing. Thus, unrepresented taxpayers who do not fully understand the evidentiary requirements of their cases may have a great deal of difficulty meeting their burden of proof; there is little that even the most sympathetic commissioner can do if the factual evidence is missing.

Winning and Losing before the Tax Appeals Commission

Does representation make a difference in the outcomes in cases before the Tax Appeals Commission? This is not an easy question to answer for a variety of reasons. First, the commission decides relatively few cases each year, so generating enough decisions for statistical analysis can be difficult. Second, unlike with the UC appeals considered in chapter 2, there is no ready indicator of the merits of the case (recall that in UC appeals, I used the initial determination as a crude indicator of the merits). Third, if I can find a statistical difference in outcome patterns across types of representatives, I cannot be sure from the statistical analysis whether those differences reflect variations in the effectiveness of representation or variations in the strength of cases where various types of representatives appear.

This last point is both the most difficult and the easiest. It is the most difficult because I do not have any systematic quantifiable data available to allow me to introduce statistical controls. The one possible exception is that I can control for whether the case was a small-claims matter. On the other hand, this is also the easiest problem to confront because my observational data, detailed later in this chapter, show clearly that attorneys are more effective than nonattorneys, and that data provide a clear indication of why this is the case.

For purposes of analysis, I collected data on decisions for the three-year period (FY91–92 through FY93–94) during which most of my observations took place. I have categorized representatives into three groups: none or immediate family member (as indicated by last name), nonlawyer, and lawyer. I have categorized outcomes into three groups: entirely affirmed (i.e., the commission agreed with DOR's tax assessment), entirely reversed, and mixed; this latter includes decisions "modifying" DOR's assessment and various combinations such as "affirmed and modified," "modified and reversed," and "affirmed and reversed."[18] One tricky question is how to treat sets of cases (i.e., multiple cases grouped together for hearing, argument, and decision). I have done the analysis both ways, treating groups as single cases and as separate cases; because the patterns are the same, I report only the results treating groups as single cases. Note that I have omitted from the analysis a small number of decisions that the commission made after hearings in which the petitioner did not appear; this situation arises when the Department of Revenue can make a prima facie case that the commission should affirm the assessment. I have included cases in which no hearing took place because the petitioner and the Department of Revenue stipulated all factual matters; as I will discuss later, most of those cases involved attorney representatives.[19]

Table 10 shows the tabulation of type of outcome by type of representative. The pattern is clear: attorneys do considerably better than nonattorneys. In fact, nonattorneys do no better (and maybe a little worse) than unrepresented petitioners. Attorneys obtain reversals in 36 percent of their cases, compared to 20 percent for unrepresented petitioners and 15 percent for petitioners with nonattorney representatives. Stated another way, attorneys fail to get any relief for the clients in only 36 percent of the cases compared to 63 to 67 percent for cases without an attorney representative.

It is possible that at least some of the difference between attorney and nonattorney representatives reflects the fact that the former are more likely to be handling small-claims cases than are the latter; only 24 percent of attorneys' cases ($n = 55$) were small-claims compared to 48 percent ($n = 33$) of the nonattorney representatives' cases. However, when I control for whether or not the case was a small-claims matter, the gap between the success of attorney and nonattorney representatives does not change

TABLE 10. **Representation and Outcomes in Wisconsin Tax Appeal Commission Cases (in percentages)**

Outcome (from the taxpayer's perspective)	Representation			
	None	Attorney	Non-attorney	All Cases
Lost	63	36	67	55
Mixed outcome	17	27	18	21
Won	20	36	15	24
(*n*)	(82)	(55)	(33)	(170)

Source: Data collected by the author.
$\chi^2 = 12.33$ $p = .015$

appreciably. Limiting the comparison to cases involving a representative, attorneys obtain at least some relief in 69 percent of small-claims cases (n = 13) and 62 percent of non-small-claims cases (n = 42); the corresponding figures for nonattorney representatives are 38 percent (n = 16) and 29 percent (n = 17).[20]

While this statistical analysis is very limited in its scope, the pattern is very clear: outcomes for cases involving nonattorney representatives more closely resemble those with no representative than those with an attorney representative. In fact, as I will show in the following sections, this is not surprising because the hearings involving nonattorneys generally look more like hearings involving no representative than hearings where an attorney appeared on behalf of the taxpayer.

The Unrepresented Petitioner

In this section I discuss the situation of the unrepresented petitioner. I will describe two archetypical situations involving unrepresented taxpayers. The first involves relatively unsophisticated taxpayers who simply believe that the Department of Revenue has not treated them fairly or has misunderstood their situation. The second involves more sophisticated taxpayers, often those with questionable deductions arising either from tax shelters or from efforts to label an activity as potentially income-producing. The descriptions that follow use specific cases as examples.

The Rented Room

The taxpayer in the first case is a woman of about fifty, whom I will call Ms. A. She speaks in the accented English of a person born outside the United States. She rents an apartment with two bedrooms, and sublets the second bedroom to cover part of her rent. The Department of Revenue had disallowed Ms. A's claim for a homestead credit and had raised questions about the school tax credit to which Ms. A was entitled. Both of these issues revolved around the question of how much of Ms. A's rent should be allocated to the sublet, particularly during times when she had no one sharing the apartment with her.

In this hearing the commissioner asked the attorney from the Department of Revenue (Mr. K) to state the issue so that he (the commissioner) could determine the evidence that he needed to make a decision in the case. Mr. K stated:[21]

> The issue here is the proper determination of the amount of rent paid in 1986 and in 1987. This amount is used in computing the school tax

credit and the homestead credit. The taxpayer claimed that she was holding out fifty percent of the dwelling to be rented out, but she provided us with no records on the amount of rent she received or the period of time she had rented out the space.

Also, she is claiming that she over-reported her taxable income for 1986. This point was not raised in any prior claim to the Department. It first appeared in the taxpayer's petition to the Commission. The Department would move that this aspect of the taxpayer's claim be dismissed because she had not first filed the appropriate amended tax return.

After Mr. K had finished his description of the issue, the commissioner restated the issue to Ms. A, emphasizing the rent issue. Specifically, the commissioner explained that she had claimed all of her rent in computing the credits, but if she was subletting part of the space, she could only claim the difference between what she paid her landlord and what she received from her subletter. When the commissioner asked Ms. A if she understood what the hearing would focus on, she did not reply directly to his question. Instead, she stated that the Department of Revenue auditor who questioned her claims about the rent she received should be reprimanded for failing to find the error she had made in reporting her 1986 taxable income. Later in the hearing, it became clear that the error concerned the reporting of unemployment compensation; while such compensation is fully taxable for federal purposes, a portion of it is not taxed in Wisconsin for persons with total incomes under a specific threshold.[22]

From other comments and body language, it was clear that the petitioner clearly wanted to tell her story—the whole story. At this point, the commissioner formally called and swore in the petitioner as a witness, and she moved from a table opposite the commissioner (and parallel to the attorney for DOR) to the witness stand next to the commissioner (the hearing room resembles a small courtroom). The commissioner proceeded to ask simple questions about the amount of rent Ms. A had paid, the number of subtenants she had had, and the periods of time when she had no subtenant. In the course of her testimony, Ms. A acknowledged that she probably owed additional taxes, but claimed that the amount assessed by the Department was incorrect. That the assessment amount was inaccurate was almost certainly true, but that reflected the Department's standard procedure of assuming the best case from its perspective when the taxpayer failed to provide appropriate documentation; in this case, Ms. A had provided none of the documentation DOR had requested.

At this point Ms. A began to cry and demanded to know how the Department of Revenue found out she had a roommate. The commissioner called a recess to allow Ms. A to regain her composure. When the hearing reconvened fifteen minutes later, Ms. A expressed a strong concern about "being blamed for the errors" on her return. The commissioner assured her that the issue was not one of blame but rather trying to determine the proper amount of tax that she owed.

The commissioner turned the questioning over to Mr. K. His questions sought to determine the exact periods that Ms. A had a subletter during the years in question (she reported her recollections, but had nothing like a list of names and dates), whether Ms. A had any records to verify those dates (she had some deposit records from her bank account, but not with her at the hearing), and whether she had retained any security deposits from roommates in lieu of unpaid rent (perhaps on one occasion she had done this). Mr. K then carefully went through the instructions for tax forms that Ms. A had submitted with her return, asking her what she had reported for specific lines; through this he established that she had not properly followed the forms' instructions.

This concluded the testimony. Ms. A had no witnesses to call, and the department called no witnesses of its own. The commissioner invited Ms. A to make a closing statement, and she simply stated that she was willing to pay the difference between what she had paid and what she owed, but she did not feel she should have to pay any penalty. Mr. K stated the following:

> The department's position is that one-half of the residence was used as a rental property. As a consequence, only one-half of the rent Ms. A paid can be used in computing the school tax and homestead credits. However, if the petitioner can provide physical records showing the dates when roommates were actually occupying the apartment, or records showing the actual rent paid by the roommates, the department is willing to use those records in determining the amount of rent that can be used in computing the credits in question. However, the department's position is that the petitioner's testimony about the period of time when roommates were present is not sufficiently reliable to be used in those computations.

The commissioner gave Ms. A the opportunity for rebuttal. In response, she made two points:

> There were periods of time when I didn't want a roommate and so even though the room was vacant I didn't advertise or seek out a new tenant.

The revenue department should have records of how long my roommates were there. That information should be in tax returns of my roommates. I don't see why they can't use that information to figure out what I actually owe.

Ms. A was quite emotional as she spoke. Either because of the level of emotion shown by the petitioner, or because the evidence was so confusing that he wanted time to sort out what the situation was, the commissioner decided to take the case under advisement and issue a written decision. Since this was a small-claims matter, he had the option of issuing an oral decision at the close of the hearing. In fact, the written decision, issued a couple of weeks after the hearing, modified the department's assessment, giving Ms. A at least part of the relief she was seeking.

The issue in this case was straightforward: what had Ms. A paid in rent after deducting payments from roommates? Ms. A clearly did not know how to substantiate the claims she made about when she had roommates. It may not have been possible to do so four or five years after the fact. However, a knowledgeable advocate could have assisted her in finding relevant records and perhaps reconstructing some dates using newspapers (i.e., classified advertisements) or other sources. The commissioner did as much as he could to assist the petitioner, but without some type of physical records, there was little that he could do. The petitioner's emotional state complicated the situation in some ways, but it also probably led to somewhat more gentle treatment by the attorney for the Department of Revenue than otherwise might have been the case.

Part of what makes this case interesting is that its outcome rode on documentation that the petitioner failed to provide. One of the cases involving a nonlawyer advocate will present a quite similar problem. An interesting question that arises from this case is whether a more sophisticated taxpayer could have done a substantially better job in presenting his or her own case. The next case shows that the problem is not just one of sophistication.

The Tax Shelter

The hearing in this case was a very confused affair, in large part because of the decision of the petitioner (Mr. B) not to bring an attorney. In fact, before the hearing formally started, Mr. B commented to the commissioner that he had not brought an attorney because "I believe that attorney costs in this matter would probably exceed the amount the department claims that I owe." Mr. B was a pilot for a major airline and had sought to shelter his considerable income from tax liability. The specific issue in this case was whether the deductions he had taken in connection with a particular investment—literally a speculative gold mine—were allowable.

After formally opening the hearing, the commissioner explained to Mr. B that

> the Department of Revenue is presumed correct, and it would be his burden to show how the department is wrong;
> Mr. B as the petitioner would go first, followed by the attorney from the Department of Revenue; and
> while the hearing would be conducted in an informal style, the record established by the hearing would be important.

The commissioner then swore in Mr. B and called him to testify. During his testimony he explained that in 1985, the IRS had audited his federal return and disallowed a $25,000 business loss deduction he had taken in connection with the gold mine investment. In 1986, he filed a 1040x for 1983, claiming a loss carryback to 1985. He felt that the state was trying to take away that carryback. The mining operation went bankrupt in 1986, but IRS claimed it was a sham operation, and that he couldn't use it as a tax write-off. But he did lose some money when he sold some of his stock in 1986.

If this seems confusing, that is because it was confusing. The commissioner looked puzzled. The commissioner asked if Mr. B had any checks documenting the payments he had made that he was now claiming constituted losses. This question prompted an off-the-record discussion about what documents would be useful given the issue.

When the hearing went back on the record, the taxpayer noted the the IRS had dropped a penalty that it had first tried to assess. He went on to acknowledge owing tax on part of what is in question, but disputed the DOR's assessment on a loss of $9,450 related to the investment; DOR had partially disallowed the loss (by 30 percent). Mr. B then proceeded to introduce one document after another: photocopies of checks, the IRS assessment, a letter from an attorney attesting to a payment, copies of materials relating to the promissory note that constituted the claimed loss, copies of various materials related to the 1985 IRS audit, the federal 1040x for 1983 with handwritten notes, a partnership tax return for 1985, and others. Where Ms. A in the previous case failed to bring relevant documents, Mr. B seemed to have brought everything remotely related to his tax returns for the years in question. The relevance of most of the documents was unclear, but the attorney from the Department of Revenue said little as they poured forth.

After introducing the documents, Mr. B continued with his confusing testimony. He tried to explain that some property was sold in 1985, and that sale produced a loss that he was carrying back to 1983. His position was that he was entitled to a loss deduction for 1983, given the sale in 1985. At the close of Mr. B's testimony, I had little idea what was going on, and I doubt that the commissioner's understanding was much better. The confusion reflected Mr. B's inability to organize a straightforward presentation of his position, and possibly his failure to grasp the core of the department's position.

After a brief recess, the attorney for the Department of Revenue, Mr. L, offered the department's exhibits. These included jurisdictional materials (i.e., the relevant tax returns, the department's notice of assessment, including the auditor's worksheet showing the adjustments that led to the higher tax liability, and the request for redetermination and the department's notice of action denying it), copies of the IRS's adjustments to the 1983 return disallowing deductions related to losses and interest expenses from the gold mine, a photocopy of a check from Mr. B paying the additional federal tax, and materials related to another IRS audit of a partnership return.

After introducing the exhibits, Mr. L explained that the issue was whether under Wisconsin law Mr. B could claim tax losses exceeding the amount he had actually paid out. Specifically, in 1983, Mr. B invested $15,000 in the gold mine and then claimed losses of $31,000 that same year. Mr. B justified the claimed loss on the grounds that he had in fact signed a note (a "full recourse promissory note") creating an obligation. Mr. L's questions to the taxpayer focused on the note and what Mr. B had actually paid out.

Q: Did you ever pay out the $20,000?

A: No, but I might have to pay it in the future.

Q: Did anyone ever actually receive the $20,000?

A: No, the manager of the mine absconded.

Q: So why do you believe you should be entitled to deduct the $20,000?

A: I did pay interest on the note; under the Internal Revenue Code it was fully deductible. I'm still liable for the note.

Q: Didn't you sign a settlement with IRS acknowledging that you shouldn't have taken the deduction?

A: Yes, I signed a settlement, but that was just for practical purposes.

Q: Is interest still being paid on the note?

A: No.

Q: How many interest payments did you make?
A: Only one.

While Mr. L focused almost exclusively on the 1983 note and the loss that Mr. B claimed related to that, Mr. B kept bringing up an "operating loss for 1986." What this referred to was never clear.

In his closing statement, the Department of Revenue attorney attacked Mr. B as someone "who was seeking to shelter his substantial income from taxes." He went on to talk about the shelter "game," but after a minute or two the commissioner interrupted to ask its relevance to the case. Mr. L asserted that the IRS viewed some shelters as shams, and this was one of them. Mr. B's closing statement was brief: "How can the state demand $9,000 when I only owed the IRS $600?" At this juncture the commissioner explained that some deductions allowable under the Internal Revenue Code were not allowable under Wisconsin law; in particular, Wisconsin did not allow the kinds of carrybacks allowed under federal law, and Wisconsin permitted deductions for losses only when there had been an actual out-of-pocket payment equal to or greater than the claimed loss.

Even though this was not a small-claims case, the commissioner offered to rule orally if the two parties consented, which they did. The commissioner then upheld the department's assessment of the tax due. In response to Mr. B's question about why he should have to pay interest because he had taken the deduction fully believing it was permitted, the commissioner explained that the interest was not triggered by an allegation of wrongdoing, but rather was set by statute and the commission had no power to waive or adjust the interest.

This example shows that the problem of presenting a case is much more than simply lack of sophistication. While Ms. A in the previous case had no idea of what records to keep or to bring to the hearing, Mr. B had records galore! Most of those records, however, had little to do with the issue at hand; and Mr. B had no idea what records, if any, would sustain his claim. It may be that his attorney had advised him that the appeal had too little chance of success to justify the legal fees that would have resulted, but Mr. B had little to lose (other than his own time) by proceeding with the appeal without representation. An alternative interpretation is that Mr. B's presentation of his case was so thoroughly confusing that the commissioner simply decided that Mr. B had failed to sustain his burden to show how the DOR's assessment was incorrect, and upheld that assessment. An experienced representative may have been able to present a case that might have convinced the commissioner that some or all of Mr. B's case had merit.

Tax Attorneys

How does the hearing change when an experienced tax attorney appears for the petitioner? The simple answer is "radically." The hearing is more focused, if there is a hearing at all. In the three-year period for which I have data, about 13 percent of the cases ending in a commission decision had no hearing, because the petitioner and DOR agreed to stipulate the facts; in most of these cases an attorney represented the petitioner.[23] When an attorney appears, the issue is clearly identified, the evidence is organized in a way to aid in following it, and the attorney for the Department of Revenue has to work hard to undercut the position advanced on behalf of the taxpayer.

The Builder

Mr. C built and sold apartment complexes, ranging from as small as four units to as large as 120 units. At the hearing, Mr. M, an attorney, appeared as Mr. C's advocate. Mr C's accountant, Mr. W, was present and testified at the hearing. Because of the relatively small amount of tax involved, the case was a small-claims matter. Both sides, however, wanted to file written arguments, and so the commissioner hearing the case issued his decision some months after the hearing in writing rather than as an oral decision at the close of the hearing.

The case involved the treatment of interest expenses related to a project in a medium-sized city, which I will call Midtown. As Mr. C explained, he would build an apartment complex (taking out construction loans from sources such as banks), rent out the units in the complex, and then sell the complex. The nature of the business required that the complex be more or less fully occupied in order to secure a purchaser. The housing market in Midtown was soft when the construction was completed, and it was a number of years before Mr. C was able to sell the complex.

During the years he was trying to sell the complex, Mr. C continued to pay interest on outstanding loans. In reporting the rental income, Mr. C's accountant had listed on the tax return the net income; that is, rather than specifying the gross income and the interest expense, the accountant had simply reported the difference. The question before the Tax Appeals Commission was whether this was proper procedure. The issue hinged on whether the interest was a business expense (in which case the treatment was proper) or a personal investment expense (in which case Wisconsin's $1,200 limit on such expenses would apply).

Mr. M was an experienced tax attorney who had previously appeared before the commission.[24] At the opening of the hearing, the commissioner

asked each side to state its position, not bothering to discuss procedure or
burdens of proof, because he knew Mr. M did not need to hear this. Both
Mr. M and Mr. S (the attorney for the Department of Revenue) made succinct statements about the issue, with Mr. S citing the specific statutes
upon which DOR was relying.

Mr. M called Mr. C to testify. The first part of the testimony provided
background on how and when Mr. C got into his current line of business,
the nature of the business, and the specifics at issue. In the course of his testimony, Mr. C explained that he "relied upon buying and selling and
building" for his income, adding that he often had to provide financing to
the buyer of one of his complexes.

> *Q:* How does the buyer of one of your complexes usually finance the
>   purchase?
> *A:* I usually have to take paper back when I sell a project. Usually this
>   means that I give the buyer a land contract, which is what hap-
>   pened with the project in Midtown.
> *Commissioner:* When did you sell the Midtown property?
> *A:* In 1982. The sale was delayed from when I built the complex in the
>   1970s, because I had problems getting it filled up.
> *Q:* Was the property ever off the market?
> *A:* No.
> *Q:* Did you have any prospective buyers other than the investor you
>   eventually sold it to?
> *A:* At least one, but he declined because the occupancy was too low.
> [*Mr. M has the commissioner mark two documents as exhibits A and B,
>   and then he hands them to Mr. C.*]
> *Q:* Please identify these.
> *A:* These were prepared by my accountant, Mr. W . . . He's been my
>   accountant for thirty-one years. They show properties that over the
>   years I have developed and sold on land contracts. One is a list of
>   properties that I did alone, and the other is a list of properties that
>   I did with a partner.

I am not going to describe in detail Mr. S's cross-examination, a
meandering trip through Mr. C's tax returns (at one point during this
cross-examination, the commissioner looked as though he were starting to
space out). What was interesting about the cross-examination was the
response of Mr. C's attorney. Mr. M clearly wanted to keep the issue
focused and not divert the commissioner's attention from what he (Mr. M)
believed was the central issue. He did this by frequently breaking in to
state that the petitioner would stipulate to some point or other. He also

objected at several points on the grounds that Mr. C had not prepared the return, and that Mr. W, the accountant who was present, could better answer some of the questions.

One of the central factual questions that Mr. S tried to zero in on during his questioning was whether Mr. C had really been actively trying to sell the property:

> *Q:* Was the property listed with a real estate broker? Was there a listing contract or some type of open listing?
> *A:* No, I didn't list it with other brokers, because I'm a broker myself. I have a broker's license.
> *Q:* Did you advertise the property in any way?
> *A:* I don't recall whether it was advertised.

Mr. M sought to counter this on redirect:

> *Q:* How many apartment units have you built over the last ten years?
> *A:* Many . . . probably a thousand or so.
> *Q:* Could you explain the selling process?
> *A:* The first thing we have to do is fill up the complex. We don't do a lot of advertising, because the other brokers were usually aware of our inventory, and when someone came to them interested in this type of investment, we would be contacted.
> *Q:* Is the multiple listing service used for apartment complexes?
> *A:* No, only for single-family homes.

Mr. M's examination of the accountant, Mr. W, was very brief. He confirmed that he had prepared the exhibits listing Mr. C's various projects (after which Mr. C moved that they be admitted as exhibits). Mr. M asked several questions concerning other aspects of Mr. C's tax return that had been raised by the DOR's attorney. He then concluded with two questions:

> *Q:* Why did you report the mortgage income interest on form B?
> *A:* Because the form requested it.
> *Q:* What was your understanding of the business Mr. C is in?
> *A:* He's in the business of developing, buying, building, and selling real estate.

The cross-examination of the accountant involved a variety of questions, such as whether the accountant was aware of the interest limit, and how the sale of the property in Midtown had been reported.

This case shows how an advocate who understands the hearing process can prepare and present a case. The point Mr. M wanted to get across was very specific. The Tax Appeals Commission could accept or reject that position; unfortunately for Mr. C, the commission rejected his position and affirmed the Department of Revenue's assessment. Mr. M sought to keep attention focused on his client's argument by defusing issues that might shift the commission's attention elsewhere. Mr. C was running a business, and the reporting of the income and related expenses was appropriate, given the nature of that business. Mr. C and his attorney felt sufficiently strongly about this case that they appealed the matter, first to the Circuit Court and then, after losing in the Circuit Court, to the Wisconsin Court of Appeals, where they lost yet again.

The quality of advocacy that I observed in this hearing was typical of cases where an experienced tax attorney appeared for the petitioner. The attorney had tried to boil the case down to the key issues, had organized relevant exhibits, and had prepared the petitioner's witnesses for their testimony. In presenting the case, the attorney tried to keep the testimony focused on the primary issue and avoided introducing superfluous issues or evidence. At times it seemed as though the attorney was working from a well-rehearsed script, and that may have actually been the case.

Nonlawyer Advocates

The Tax Appeals Commission does not place limits on who may appear as an advocate before it, and the appearance of tax specialists other than tax attorneys is a regular occurrence. As advocates, how do they compare to the tax attorney in the previous section? What was very clear from the observations was that almost all of the nonlawyer tax specialists who appeared *with* the petitioners at tax appeal hearings had little or no idea of what an advocacy role required in that setting; this is why I speak of these representatives appearing *with* rather than *for* the taxpayer.

The Beer Distributor

In principle, a nonlawyer could be an effective advocate in a tax appeal hearing, and I did observe one hearing where a nonlawyer did a reasonably good job. Even in this case, the advocate got off to a very rocky start. The case involved the corporate income tax return of a local beer distributor, which I will call Beer, Inc. The owners of Beer, Inc. had established a separate corporation to distribute snack foods; I will call the second corporation Nuts, Inc. The two corporations shared the same facilities and staff, with Nuts, Inc. paying fees to Beer, Inc. for the services it received and the facilities it used. The original fees set had been based on the expected revenue that Nuts, Inc. would generate, with the intention that the proportion of the joint expenses each company paid would be proportional to the revenues generated. The owners believed that the first company could service many of the needs of the new company within existing resources; the result would be to spread overhead expenses across the two companies, effectively reducing the operating costs of the first company. The revenues of Nuts, Inc. did not meet expectations, however, and Nuts had found it necessary to execute a promissory note, held by Beer, Inc., to cover the expenses that Nuts had expected to pay. After a couple of years, the owners realized that they had made an error in their original allocations and, with the advice of their accountant, made a retroactive adjustment to the fees due Beer, Inc. That is, they acknowledged that, given the relative business volume of the two companies, the original payment rates constituted an overcharge to Nuts, Inc.

The tax problem arose because Nuts, Inc. had not actually transferred funds to Beer, Inc. for the amount at issue; rather, there existed only the outstanding promissory note for an amount due Beer, Inc. The adjustment in the payments reduced the amount owed on the note. DOR challenged the transaction claiming that it was an inappropriate write-off of a bad debt. The write-off was deemed inappropriate because the debt was only on paper; Beer, Inc. had never incurred any actual expense. The petitioner's position was that the situation involved not a debt write-off, but rather an adjustment for an overcharge.

The advocate in this case, Mr. A., was a CPA from the accounting firm that handled the affairs of both Beer, Inc. and Nuts, Inc. He was not the member of the firm directly responsible for work on behalf of the two corporations; that accountant, Mr. C, was one of the witnesses. At the beginning of the hearing it was clear that Mr. A was very angry with the Department of Revenue and wanted to show that DOR was being "arbitrary and unreasonable." He asserted that there was no dispute over the facts of the matter, only over DOR's handling of those facts. To prove that DOR was being arbitrary and unreasonable, Mr. A wanted to have an auditor from DOR testify. However, DOR declined to produce the witness, and Mr. A had failed to obtain a subpoena. Mr. A explained this failure as reflecting his understanding that DOR would call the witness in question (DOR had included the auditor in its list of potential witnesses). Only the day before had it become clear that DOR would not call any witnesses of its own.

There followed a lengthy exchange involving the commissioner, DOR's attorney, and Mr. A over the possible relevance of the auditor's testimony and whether the commissioner should grant an adjournment to give the petitioner time to obtain a subpoena for the witness. The commissioner explained to Mr. A that whether or not an auditor at DOR was sympathetic to the petitioner's position was irrelevant. It was the Tax Appeals Commission's responsibility to decide whether DOR's assessment was correct, and the views of the auditor had no probative value. Even if the auditor testified to everything that Mr. A stated he would (e.g., that the auditor had been instructed by his supervisor not to settle the case), the testimony would be irrelevant. The commissioner denied Mr. A's request for the adjournment.

After this rocky start, Mr. A did a reasonably good job presenting a case. He clearly understood his role as advocate and was able to formulate appropriate questions to his two witnesses, the majority owner and president of both corporations, and the CPA who advised the corporation and supervised the preparation of tax returns for the two corporations. The testimony established that the entities were legally distinct, and that the legal requirements to maintain that distinction had been met. The unchallenged testimony established that the original allocation was based on a set of expectations that had not been met, and that the only way that Nuts, Inc. could expect to show a profit in the immediate future was to adjust the allocation. The testimony established that the adjustment appeared on the books of both companies: negatively for Beer, Inc., and positively for Nuts, Inc. This was not a situation of a purely paper debt being created and then written off merely to produce a tax reduction for one company, because, while the adjustment resulted in a reduction in net income for Beer, Inc. (and hence a reduction in tax liability), it created a net increase for Nuts, Inc. and produced a tax liability. (For the year in question, Nuts, Inc. showed a net profit, but this profit was attributable entirely to the adjustment DOR had challenged.) The petitioner's position was simply that, if one looked at the books and tax returns of the two companies together, the total amount of net income and loss shown was exactly the same; it was merely a question of what was being allocated to each corporate entity.

In his cross-examination of the petitioner's witnesses, the DOR attorney raised a number of questions about what had happened. Early in the cross-examination of the corporation president, Mr. A objected to a question as leading; the commissioner overruled the objection, noting that a cross-examiner can ask leading questions. The attorney probed on issues such as the arm's-length nature of the transactions between Beer, Inc. and Nuts, Inc. Perhaps the most important questions had to do with why, given that this was an adjustment to prior charges, it had not been reported on amended returns for the years in which the charges had actually appeared on the books. The accountant, to whom this set of questions was addressed, could not give an explanation.

This last point was important because it related directly to the Tax Commission's rejection of the petitioner's appeal. The petitioner tried to present the image of a transparent transaction—everything removed from the books of one corporation showed up on the books of the other corporation, with the appropriate taxes paid. However, the decision to treat the transaction as a loss in a given tax year almost certainly had had significant net tax consequences across the two corporations. That is, making the adjustment at the time it was made, rather than going back and doing an amended return for prior years, probably reduced substantially the total tax liability (if nothing else, it avoided interest payments and possible penalties). Furthermore, even though the two business entities were legally separate, Wisconsin's tax law gives the Department of Revenue the power to allocate income, deductions, and the like so as to prevent evasion of taxes.[25]

Overall, the advocate did a good job. Whether all the testimony presented was necessary for his case is less clear; an experienced tax attorney may have presented a much more succinct case. Most probably, an experienced attorney would not have wasted time on the issue of whether to subpoena the auditor, and would, if he or she really believed such testimony was crucial, have issued the subpoena to be sure that the witness was present. It might also have been the case that an attorney would have understood the evidentiary issues with regard to proving the existence of a true debtor–creditor relationship or could have shown that the tax consequences of the petitioner's action was in fact neutral with regard to the total amount owed across the two corporations (which was the petitioner's contention). Whether this would have affected the outcome of the appeal is not clear.

These failings notwithstanding, this was the only example where a nonlawyer even came close to providing effective advocacy. Discussions with tax commissioners confirmed that this case was very much the exception, and that the typical nonlawyer was ineffective in his or her advocacy role before the commission. The following cases illustrate the typical problems that nonlawyers encounter.

The Band

The first case involved a taxpayer, Mr. E, who had deducted business expenses associated with being in a band. For each of the three years the band had existed, Mr. E's band-related expenses had exceeded his income from the band. The Department of Revenue had decided that the band constituted more of a personal activity than a business and had disallowed the expense deductions that exceeded income, resulting in an assessment of about $600 in additional taxes. Mr. E appeared at the hearing with his accountant, Mr. N.[26]

Before the formal start of the hearing, the commissioner explained the procedure to Mr. E and Mr. N (i.e., the role of testimony, exhibits, the presumption in favor of the Department of Revenue, and the resulting burden of proof). He asked both the petitioner and the attorney from the DOR (Mr. S) to identify the exhibits each wished to enter into the record. For DOR these included assessment notices, tax returns, petitions for rede-termination, and notices denying those petitions. The taxpayer's exhibits consisted of documentation for the deductions (receipts, travel logs, etc.).

After formally opening the hearing, the commissioner asked the department's attorney to offer DOR's exhibits and to state the issue from the DOR's perspective. Even though tax appeals are initiated by the tax-payer, the commissioner commonly asked DOR's attorney to describe the issue, except when an attorney appeared for the taxpayer; DOR's attorney could describe the issue before the commissioner more succinctly than could an unrepresented taxpayer or most nonattorney representatives. Mr. S described this case as involving

> The issue [of] the deductibility and substantiation of deductions on Schedule C's [the tax form for reporting income and deductions from a business] for the years 1985, 1986, and 1987. The taxpayer claimed that he was in business as a musician, and this led to the deductions. For none of the years in question did the business show a profit. The Department of Revenue questions whether the musician activities constitute a real business activity. The department's position is that there was never any real expectation of profit, and this constituted more of a personal activity than a business activity. As a result, the department denied any deductions that exceeded the proceeds.

After Mr. S had given DOR's position, the commissioner asked Mr. N to explain how the taxpayer disagreed with DOR:

> *Mr. N:* We believe that the goal here was to make a profit, and that there was a real potential that the band could have become a profitable venture. I know that when I was just starting out in my own business, it took several years to really get it going and to begin to show a real profit.

Commissioner: But in what specific ways do you disagree with Mr. S's statement?

Mr. N: We disagree with the department regarding whether there was a profit motive.

Commissioner: Anything else?

Mr. N: The issue is partly the mileage deduction that Mr. E took to travel to practice with the band. This was a real expense. He leased a car primarily for this purpose.

It must have been clear at this point to the commissioner that Mr. N would have difficulty. This became more evident after the commissioner called Mr. E to testify and asked Mr. N to ask questions of his client. Mr. N had no idea what to do. With a little coaching, the commissioner got Mr. N to ask, "Was the band a business venture?" At this point, the commissioner took over the questioning and asked details about the band: its name, where it was based, how often the band members practiced together, where the practices were held in relationship to where Mr. E lived, how the band progressed in terms of getting jobs, whether they hoped to make a recording, etc. Mr. S then questioned the petitioner in more detail about his background as a musician (self-taught), the band's business practices (Did it have an agent? Did they get any professional advice?), marketing efforts, number of performances, and so forth.

Mr. N reemerged in the hearing when the department's attorney asked the petitioner whether he had any receipts to document the cost of the equipment or any of the other expenses. Mr. E stated that he had receipts. What ensued was a confused discussion between Mr. E and Mr. N, with the taxpayer claiming to have given the receipts to the accountant.

DOR's attorney asked Mr. E if he had the receipts with him, and Mr. E replied that he did not. Over the next few minutes, it became clear that DOR had formally requested such documents,[27] but neither the taxpayer nor his accountant had provided them to the department. Mr. S then went through the various claimed expenses, getting Mr. E to acknowledge having made the claims but not having the receipts or records along with him. For example, Mr. E claimed that 77 percent of the use of a car he had leased was in connection with the band, but he had no records or logbooks with him to document this claim. Throughout much of this series of questions, Mr. E's accountant kept trying to break in to make statements about the records and the claimed deductions; Mr. N clearly did not understand the hearing process, nor the nature of giving and taking testimony.

Eventually, the commissioner turned the questioning back to the accountant, Mr. N.

Q: Was the leased car the only vehicle available to you?

A: No, we had another car during this entire period which my wife used, and that we used for pleasure.

Q: How far away did you live from your first job?

A: About a half mile.

Q: How did you estimate the number of miles associated with your work with the band?

A: I tried to make a conservative estimate. The rental vehicle had a 60,000 mile limit on the lease. I knew how far it was to where we practiced, and I knew how often we practiced. I used that to estimate the number of miles I must have covered.

Q [to the commissioner]: Can we still send in the receipts?

Commissioner: No, today was the day.

Q [handing exhibits A, B, and C to Mr. E]: What are these?

A: They are lists of my expenses for 1985, 1986, and 1987.

Q: Who prepared them?

A: You did.

Trying to make the best of a bad situation, Mr. N then proceeded to explain how he had generated the figures on the lists. He emphasized that he tried to be conservative; for example, he said that for 1986 he had cut back the car expenses that were claimed because the "receipts weren't there." When he requested that the commissioner accept exhibits into evidence, the department's attorney objected arguing that summary sheets or lists do not constitute a "record" of an expense. The commissioner accepted the exhibits, noting that "the commission will attach the relevant weight to them in reaching its decision."

Mr. S then asked a few additional questions in cross-examination. During these questions, the accountant tried to break in to explain something, but the commissioner cut him off, saying, "You'll get your chance to testify in a few minutes." After several more questions, Mr. S concluded his cross-examination. The commissioner turned to the accountant, and offered him the opportunity to testify; after a few moments of thought, Mr. N decided not to take the witness chair. That concluded the evidence, and the commissioner asked Mr. N for his closing statement. He made three points.

1. The band was a legitimate business; his client went into it with the goal of making money.
2. This was not simply a hobby; why would he drive forty miles each way several times a week, often in bad winter weather, just for a hobby?

3. He (the accountant) had endeavored to determine the proper deductions based on the facts.

At this point, the petitioner interjected that "we've got the receipts . . . I wish they were here," to which the commissioner responded, "the receipts are relevant only if the band was a real business."

Mr. S's closing statement on behalf of the department made a variety of points. He questioned the expectation of a profit, emphasizing the unbusinesslike way the band operated (no advertising, no manager, no real business records). Even if the band hoped to make money, he questioned the idea that there ever was "a realistic opportunity for profit." He went on to argue that if the commission found that it was a legitimate business activity, the "tax home" for the business was the town where the equipment was stored and where the band practiced; if this were the case, the petitioner's claim of business expenses traveling between his personal home and the business's tax home did not constitute a deductible expense. More generally, he questioned the legitimacy of the claimed expenses, particularly in light of the petitioner's failure to provide the required documentation, despite the department's "repeated requests that the receipts be provided." Mr. S closed his argument by presenting a federal tax case that, as he argued, supported the department's position regarding whether the band constituted a business for tax purposes.

The commissioner offered the accountant the opportunity for rebuttal. Mr. N declined. The commissioner then asked Mr. E if he had anything he wanted to add, and Mr E. asserted, "It was a business. Drumming is hard work. It's not necessarily a lot of fun!"

After a fifteen minute recess, the commissioner returned and ruled that there was not a reasonable expectation of a profit from the band, and consequently the deductions were not allowable. He went on to say that it was not necessary for him to rule on the substantiation issue, but noted that the taxpayer had "failed to meet the necessary burden of proof on this issue." The commissioner closed the hearing by directing the taxpayer's attention to his right of appeal to the Circuit Court.

From the testimony, it sounded as though Mr. E and his accountant had the documentation to substantiate many, if not all, of the deductions claimed on the tax return. However, much like the unrepresented Ms. A in the first case, neither the petitioner nor the accountant realized that the hearing constituted the time and place to produce any and all evidence. Moreover, it appeared that neither understood the prehearing process, as reflected in their failure to respond to the department's request for documents. But this still leaves the question of whether the band constituted a business. Could a knowledgeable representative have produced evidence that would have swayed the commissioner? One could imagine ways that at least a reasonable argument could have been made. Had any posters been put up advertising the band's appearances? If so, examples could have been brought as exhibits. What about publicity photos, or even a copy of the recording the petitioner said the band had produced? A sharp representative could have brought a witness who was a member of a currently profitable band who might have testified about unsuccessful starts or the lean years at the beginning of a band.

Overall, it was very clear that the accountant had no idea what would happen at the hearing. He had no idea what constituted evidence in the hearing context. He had no idea what it meant to put on a case. In fact, the commissioner, not the advocate, developed the petitioner's case, to the extent that there was one to be developed. As I will discuss below, this was typical in cases involving nonlawyer representatives.

The Vacation Cottage

The nonlawyer advocate in the preceding case was the weakest of those I saw. Others had a better understanding of what evidence and documents to bring to the hearing. For example, in a case that posed somewhat similar issues, this one involving the deduction of expenses associated with a vacation cottage that the petitioner claimed was a rental property, the petitioner appeared at the hearing with receipts, travel logs, and phone bills to document his expense deduction, the purpose of the trips to the cottage in question, and the amount of time spent at the cottage. It turned out that the petitioner and his representative had not carefully reviewed the records before the hearing, and this presented problems when, during testimony, they discovered a number of inconsistencies among them.

Hearings in cases with nonlawyer representatives bore more resemblance to hearings with unrepresented petitioners than to hearings with lawyer representatives. This was most evident in who developed the petitioner's case. When a lawyer advocate appeared, it was the lawyer; when a nonlawyer representative appeared (or no representative appeared), it was usually the commissioner. This was evident in the case of the band described above. It also happened in the vacation cottage case.

After about thirty minutes of preliminaries, going over documents and sorting out the issues the parties were to address during the hearing, the commissioner went on the record and called the petitioner to testify. When the commissioner turned to the petitioner's representative and asked him to proceed with his questions for the petitioner, the representative immediately started telling the story himself rather than asking questions of his client. The commissioner broke in and told the representative to let the taxpayer tell the story. The commissioner then proceeded to ask the specific questions needed to develop the case.

> Where is your regular residence?
> What was the purpose of the improvements to the property?
> Have you ever shown a profit?
> How many trips did you make to the property in 1989?
> What was the purpose of those trips?
> How many times did you stay overnight in the cottage?
> Did you go alone or take your family with you?

At some point, the commissioner turned back to the representative for additonal questions. The representative asked several questions about renting out the property. When he asked about rental rates, the petitioner could not recall what had been charged in the earlier years. The DOR's attorney pointed out that the receipts introduced as exhibits showed that information, at which point the petitioner's representative said to the attorney, "Step in any time you want."

After one or two more questions from the representative, the commissioner broke in again to take over questioning. When the commissioner finished his questions and turned again to the representative, the representative had no further questions. After a brief cross-examination by the DOR's attorney, the representative got into the swing of things and asked a long series of questions about dates and documents. Many of the questions, however, served to highlight the inconsistencies in the documents and to raise questions about the petitioner's claims regarding the amount of time he had spent at the cottage. At a number of points, the commissioner interjected questions of his own.[28]

In this case, as in several others I observed, the nonlawyer tax specialist became more of a witness than an advocate. (This had not happened in the band case, simply because Mr. N declined when given the opportunity to testify.) At several points during the testimony of the petitioner who owned the vacation cottage, the representative started answering questions directed at the petitioner, taking the information from some of the records that he and the petitioner had brought to the hearing. The nonlawyer advocate ended up being sworn in as a witness.

The Bad Debt Case

Some of the nonlawyers were able to ask questions, but not always in a way that conformed to the structure of the hearing process. One such case involved the treatment of a bad debt owed to an estate. In this case, the

CPA who appeared for the petitioner was more able to ask relevant questions of the petitioner and the petitioner's son, who appeared as a witness. The commissioner frequently interjected questions, and at times the commissioner and the CPA became involved in long colloquies. At several junctures, the CPA was simultaneously asking questions of both the petitioner and her son. At another point, the representative asked one of the witnesses to read aloud to the commissioner a paragraph in a document admitted as an exhibit. The commissioner, however, cut off the representative, telling him it was unnecessary to read the material because it was already in evidence, to which the CPA remarked that he "hadn't realized it was in evidence."

As the hearing progressed, it became clear that the advocate had more information than did the witnesses. The commissioner had directed several questions to the witnesses, but the advocate provided the answers. A colloquy ensued between the commissioner and DOR's attorney over whether to swear in the representative as a witness. The commissioner called a brief recess to think it over (in fact, he seemed a bit flustered at this point); when he returned, the commissioner and DOR's attorney had a brief, off-the-record discussion about a Tax Appeals Commission decision dealing with the question of whether an advocate can also be a witness. When the commissioner went back on the record, he swore in the representative and had the representative state that his prior statements (about a tax return that was not in evidence) were true. Later in the hearing, the Department of Revenue's attorney was given the opportunity to cross-examine the accountant representative, who testified that he had not become aware of some of the evidence in the case until "9:05 this morning."[29]

The Car Wash

In some cases, the commissioner would suggest that the best way to get the evidence on the record might be for the DOR to present its case first. When this happened, the department's attorney would typically call the petitioner as an adverse witness. The commissioner would try to ask questions to bring out points not raised by the department's attorney that might support the petitioner's position. This happened in a case involving two issues arising from the sale of a car wash. One issue revolved around the date that the petitioner had returned a seller's permit to the Department of Revenue. This permit is part of the sales tax system, and the date in question affected the petitioner's liability for sales tax in connection with the sale of the car wash. The second issue concerned the allocation of the selling price between real property, equipment, and an agreement for the seller not to start a competing business; this had significant implications for depreciation deductions.

The petitioner's representative acknowledged at the opening of the hearing that he did not know how to go about putting a case before the commissioner. The commissioner suggested having DOR go first, and the representative immediately agreed to this. DOR's first witness was a DOR staff person. The testimony of this witness established that the DOR's position on the first issue was indisputable. As it turned out, the postmark on the envelope returning the seller's permit was beyond the allowable date; the law allowed no flexibility. DOR's attorney introduced the envelope in evidence, and the DOR staff person testified as to the receipt and processing of the envelope. After a bit of hesitation, the petitioner's representative asked a series of questions of the witness about the permit, and in doing so demonstrated that he did not know that it was the date of postmark rather than the date of receipt that mattered. In general, the representative's questions did little to help the petitioner's case.

The more interesting issue had to do with the allocation question. The key witness on this point was the petitioner. In the course of the petitioner's testimony, it became clear that there had been a lack of communication between the petitioner and his accountant over issues surrounding the sale of the car wash. More important, however, was what happened when the DOR's attorney completed his questioning of the petitioner and the accountant began asking questions. After a few initial questions that were straightforward, the accountant starting asking questions of an acutely leading nature; the accountant would essentially make a statement about what happened and then ask the petitioner if the statement was correct. After one or two half-hearted objections, the department's attorney just let it go.

A little later, the accountant began to give up the pretense of asking questions at all and started simply explaining what he, as the accountant, had done. When the commissioner pointed out to the accountant that he was making statements rather than asking questions and that the statements did not constitute evidence, the Department of Revenue's attorney suggested swearing in the accountant as a witness. This was done, and the accountant proceeded to affirm that his earlier statements were true. What then occurred was a mixture of testimony from the petitioner and the accountant, with the accountant (and occasionally the commissioner) asking questions of the petitioner, and the commissioner asking questions of the accountant. After the accountant finished his questions of the petitioner, the commissioner and the Department of Revenue's attorney asked additional questions of the accountant.

At the close of testimony, the department's attorney proposed that he and the accountant present closing arguments orally and that the commissioner issue an oral decision. The commissioner agreed to the oral argument but stated that he did not want to decide the case that day. Before proceeding to hear the arguments, the commissioner noted that the only issue in question had to do with allocating the sales price; he stated that "the date issue [regarding the return of the seller's permit] is pretty much settled under the applicable law because of the postmark on the envelope." On the sales price issue, the department's attorney argued that the allocation should be governed by what was stated in the sales agreement. The accountant responded by arguing that the Department of Revenue would not accept any arbitrary allocation: "the allocation of value to the components must be reasonable, and my allocation is reasonable."[30] Despite the stumbling nature of the accountant's presentation, the commissioner must have found the petitioner's evidence and the accountant's argument at least somewhat persuasive because the commission decision modified the Department of Revenue's assessment on the allocation issue.[31]

The Investment Case

One last case deserves brief comment because it shows clearly how it is the combination of substantive expertise on tax matters with the kind of procedural expertise that lawyers seem to have that makes for an effective advocate. I observed one hearing involving an attorney who was not knowledgeable on tax matters. This hearing concerned two separate cases that the commission combined for purposes of hearing evidence and reaching a decision. The investment case dealt with the dissolution of a corporation involving the transfer of the corporation's assets to its stockholders. The question at issue was whether such a transfer of assets, which in this case consisted solely of a six-unit apartment house, was a taxable transaction. The four stockholders were two husband-and-wife couples; technically, there were two separate cases, one for each couple. For one case, no representative was listed, but the husband (Mr. F) in that couple was an attorney; for the second case, Mr. F was listed as the representative.[32] At the hearing, the commissioner treated Mr. F as the advocate, even though it was immediately clear that he had no familiarity with the commission's procedure.

At the beginning of the hearing, the commissioner asked Mr. F to make an opening statement. In that statement Mr. F indicated that the four were stockholders in the corporation, which was dissolved as of January 1, 1988. They kept the same depreciation schedule, but as of January 1, 1988, all income was reported on their individual tax returns. The Department of Revenue wanted a new depreciation schedule based on the value at the time the corporation was dissolved. Also, DOR was claiming that the transfer itself was taxable, although Mr. F didn't know why. Furthermore, if they had adopted the depreciation schedule the Department wanted, the state would actually end up getting less tax from them than under the original depreciation schedule.

The DOR attorney's opening statement simply stated the department's view of the issue: "Do the taxpayers have a nonrecognition of gain when the corporation liquidated its assets? . . . Does the transfer of the corporation's assets to its stockholders represent a taxable transaction?"

After the department's opening statement, the commissioner turned to Mr. F and asked him to present the petitioner's case. Mr. F introduced the depreciation schedule as an exhibit, and he observed that it was the same before and after the corporation's dissolution. The petitioner then stated that was the extent of his case. The commissioner explained to Mr. F that the opening statement does not constitute evidence, to which Mr. F replied, "The petitioner rests."

The DOR attorney called one spouse for the first couple and asked a series of questions about the corporation, its purpose, its assets, and its dissolution. Mr. F asked no questions of the witness. The DOR attorney then called Mr. F (as one of the petitioners), who essentially confirmed what the previous witness had stated. In response to a question from the commissioner, Mr. F clarified the type of corporation in question. After Mr. F's testimony, the department rested its case.

Even though this was a small-claims case, the commissioner told the parties that he would not decide the case at the hearing, because he needed time to study the documents. He then asked whether the parties would prefer to make oral arguments or file written briefs, and they opted for the former. When the commissioner asked Mr. F for his closing argument, Mr. F replied, "The petitioners rest on their opening statement." After the DOR's closing statement, Mr. F did make several points in rebuttal, points that showed his lack of understanding of the case. He restated his argument that the department's position would actually lead to a lower tax liability, and he questioned whether the department's assessment was timely. On this last point, he was under the mistaken impression that the claim was against the dissolved corporation when, in fact, it was against the two couples as individual taxpayers.

What this case shows is that simply having legal training and experience (Mr. F was probably in his late forties or fifties and had probably been practicing law for at least twenty years) does not make one an effective advocate. From his style in the hearing, I doubt that Mr. F had significant courtroom experience. Clearly, he knew nothing at all about how the Tax Appeals Commission operated, and he failed to grasp the issues underlying the department's position. The commission affirmed the department's assessment, and the petitioner's appeal to Circuit Court was unsuccessful.

Conclusions

In my analysis of representation in unemployment compensation hearings, I found that the effectiveness of representatives was less a function of formal background than it was of specialized experience. Nonlawyers who work in the UC setting are able to gain the knowledge and experience necessary to be highly effective advocates in UC settings. Lawyers with no UC experience often fail to deliver effective representation, because they cannot transfer the advocacy experience and expertise from other settings to the UC setting.

The analysis of the tax appeals hearings highlights another dimension of the problem. Here I observed nonlawyer representatives with extensive substantive expertise. The problem is a lack of procedural expertise. The nonlawyers who appear with taxpayers at hearings simply do not know what it means to appear as an advocate in a formal hearing. These representatives may be able to explain how and why they prepared the tax return the way that they did, but they have no sense of what constitutes evidence. They know what constitutes records for tax purposes, but they are at a loss as to how those records should be used for evidentiary purposes in the hearing.

Typically these nonlawyers do not understand the difference between representing and testifying. They simply want to explain how they prepared the tax returns in question and why they did it that way. In fact, it was common for the nonlawyers to serve more as witnesses than as advocates.

What becomes clear as we consider the juxtaposition of the UC setting and the tax setting is the importance of combining substantive and procedural expertise. In the UC setting, the interesting problematic representative was the lawyer who might have been an experienced litigator, but who had little or no familiarity with the specifics of the UC arena. That lawyer might not have understood either the requirements of the UC regulations or the formalities of the procedures used by the administrative law judges. A lawyer in this situation almost certainly knew nothing of the individual styles or preferences of the administrative law judge who was conducting the hearing. While the lawyer's effort to fall back on pure advocacy expertise failed to help the client's interests, the commitment of the judges to insuring a fair hearing probably meant that a nonspecialist lawyer did not particularly harm the client's case.

In the tax setting, it was the advocate with extensive substantive expertise but no procedural expertise who was problematic. While it is doubtful that any tax practitioner, lawyer or nonlawyer, spends a significant proportion of time appearing at hearings, the training in procedure and evidence combined with the formal advocacy experience tax lawyers do have provides a background that better serves the client in the hearing context.

In the next chapter, I turn to Social Security disability appeal hearings, a setting where there are both lawyer and nonlawyer specialists. In this setting, we can ask the question of whether there is a difference in the effectiveness of the experienced nonlawyer specialist and the experienced lawyer specialist.

CHAPTER 4

Social Security Disability Appeals

The Social Security Administration (SSA) oversees a variety of social welfare programs in addition to "standard" Old Age and Survivor Insurance (OASI) programs. The two largest programs provide payments to individuals who have disabilities that preclude gainful employment or would preclude such employment if they were adults.[1] The Social Security Disability Insurance (DI) program functions as a form of insurance where potential recipients obtain coverage by payment of Social Security taxes for a required period of time; payments to recipients of DI come from the Social Security Trust Fund. The Supplemental Security Income Program (SSI) is more of a general welfare program providing benefits to disabled persons not covered by DI and whose income and assets fall below threshold limits.[2]

Because benefits from these two programs depend upon something other than a simple demographic category (i.e., age), disagreements regularly arise over claimants' entitlement to benefits.[3] For example, a person who believes he or she is entitled to Social Security disability benefits files a claim with the Social Security Administration. SSA refers this claim to a state agency to determine whether the claimant meets the definition of disability. If the claimant is deemed to be disabled and meets the eligibility requirements in terms of payment of Social Security taxes, the claimant will receive disability payments. If the disability is not established, the claim is denied. In recent years, SSA has received between 1.0 and 1.3 million Disability Insurance claims (see fig. 1);[4] in 1993, the number of claims rose to 1.4 million. SSA receives about the same number of SSI claims.[5] SSA denies half or more of these applications, with the denial rate running between 50 and 60 percent in recent years.

When SSA denies a claimant's application, the claimant may appeal that denial. The first step is to request a "redetermination," which essentially involves having the same agency that initially reviewed the application take another look at the materials, including any additional supporting documentation. If this is unsuccessful, the claimant can file an appeal to an independent office within SSA called the Office of Hearings and Appeals (OHA).[6] A cadre of administrative law judges decides OHA

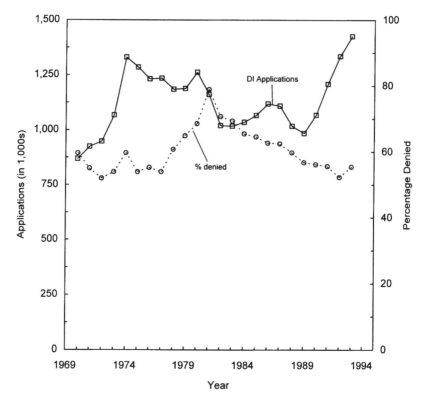

Fig. 1.   Social Security disability claims. (Data from Social Security Bulletin, Annual Statistical Supplement 1994, 266.)

cases.[7] Claims denied by an ALJ may be appealed to the Appeals Council (which may also review cases on its own motion), and after that cases may be taken to the federal district court. My focus is on cases at the Office of Hearings and Appeals.

Over the last twenty years, the number of appeals handled by OHA has fluctuated substantially (see fig. 2). The caseload rose sharply in the early 1980s (when the Reagan administration attempted to cut back eligibility for DI benefits) and then fell again sharply in the mid-1980s. Since about 1986, there has been a fairly steady increase;[8] as figure 2 indicates, the increase most recently seems to be driven more by SSI cases than by DI cases.[9]

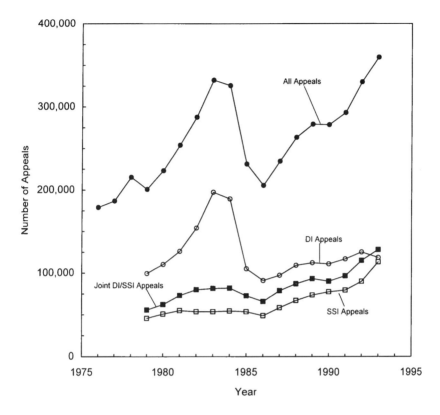

Fig. 2. Social Security appeals, 1976–93. (Data from Social Security Administration's Annual Report to Congress, various years.)

Representation and Success in OHA Proceedings

Claimants who appeal to OHA are entitled to be represented. During fiscal year 1993, representatives appeared on behalf of 65.6 percent of the claimants whose appeals were disposed of by OHA; this figure rises to 83.9 percent for those appeals disposed of after hearings.[10] There is no requirement that representatives be licensed attorneys.[11] Figures 3 and 4 show the pattern of representation, both for all cases and for cases disposed of by hearing.[12] In recent years, attorneys have represented 50 to 55 percent of all claimants and nonattorneys about 15 percent of all claimants.[13] Attorneys have represented 65 to 69 percent of claimants

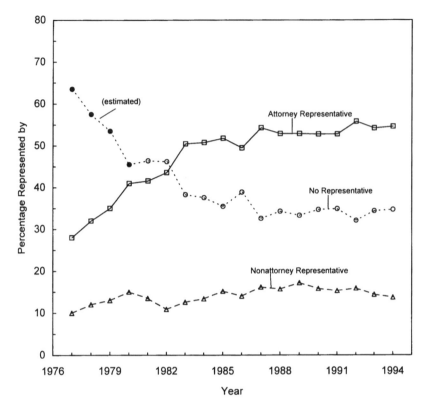

Fig. 3.   Representation in Social Security appeals, all cases. (Data from tables provided by Social Security Administration.)

whose cases went to hearings, with nonattorneys representing 18 to 20 percent. Prior research has indicated that representation in Social Security appeals can make a difference. Popkin looked at a sample of 419 cases decided in 1974 by what was then called the Bureau of Appeals;[14] representatives appeared in only 40 percent of the cases (82 percent of the representatives were attorneys).[15] The success rate for cases with representatives was 71 percent compared to 48 percent for cases with no representative.[16] A second study is part of what is known as the Boyd Report; this was an internal SSA study that looked at 427 cases. Unlike the Popkin study, this one reports success rates separately for lawyer (78.4 percent) and nonlawyer representatives (51.5 percent), as well as for unrepresented appellants (28.3 percent).[17] The success rate for represented

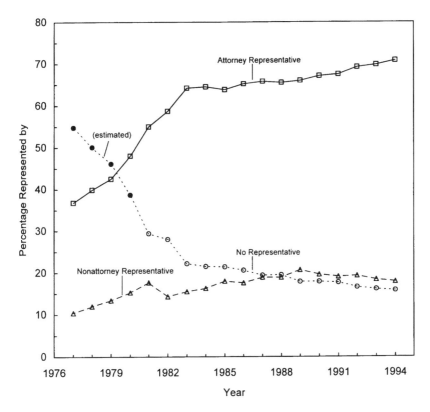

Fig. 4. Representation in Social Security appeals, cases that went to hearing. (Data from tables provided by Social Security Administration.)

appellants is comparable for these two studies, but that for unrepresented appellants differs substantially (for reasons I cannot explain). Despite their inconsistencies, both of these studies from the 1970s indicate that representation makes a difference, and the latter study suggests that lawyers may be more successful than nonlawyers. However, in the twenty years since these studies were conducted, the pattern of representation has changed sharply, with the proportion of cases involving lawyer representatives almost doubling and the proportion involving nonlawyers changing to a similar degree. As figures 3 and 4 show, where the majority of appellants were unrepresented in the mid-1970s, today the majority have attorney representatives. By the early 1990s, the proportion of appellants without any representative at hearings was smaller than the proportion with nonattorney representatives. Given this sharply changed pattern of representation, it is possible that a substantial portion of the gap that existed twenty years ago has now disappeared.

Data from the Office of Hearings and Appeals suggest that the gap in success rates between represented and unrepresented claimants held fairly steady between 1986 and 1992 in the 15 to 20 percent range (see figs. 5 and 6), both for all cases and for cases that went to hearings. Something of a divergence may have started around 1992, with the gap narrowing appreciably for cases decided without hearings but increasing for cases involving hearings. In fact, for fiscal year 1993, the gap dropped to about 11 percentage points (70.6 percent with representation versus 59.7 percent without) for all cases, while increasing to 19.3 percentage points for those cases decided after a hearing (72.0 percent with representation versus 52.7 percent without).[18] This shift may reflect increased efforts by OHA to screen cases in order to decrease the burden of hearings by granting benefits in relatively clear-cut cases through expedited procedures.[19] As figures 5 and 6 also show, attorneys consistently win a higher percentage of cases than do nonattorneys; however, the difference in success rates is very small, typically one or two percentage points, occasionally widening out to as much as six percentage points. The gap between attorneys and nonattorneys tends to be smaller for cases decided after a hearing than is true for all cases. This indicates that in cases decided without a hearing, the difference in win rates for attorneys and nonattorneys must be somewhat greater. In figure 7, which I have scaled very differently than the previous figures in order to make some of the variations easier to see, the solid lines indicate cases handled by nonattorneys and the broken lines those handled by attorneys; those with filled in markers are after hearing, and those with unfilled markers are all cases regardless of whether there was a hearing. The gap between the unfilled markers is generally greater than between the filled markers.

The attorney/nonattorney gap may reflect subtle differences in the style of representation, or it may reflect differences in the cases handled by attorneys and nonattorneys. Most attorneys appearing in OHA appeals work on a fee-for-service basis, usually on a contingent fee basis.[20] This fee structure creates a strong incentive for attorneys to screen out weak cases where the chance of success is lower. In contrast, a large percentage of nonattorney representatives do not work on a fee-for-service basis; many, if not most, work for an agency whose mission it is to provide representation to low-income persons. The agencies providing nonattorney representatives may not be as selective in the cases they accept because, while winning is important, the agency's economic security does not depend upon winning in the direct way that is true for a contingent-fee lawyer.

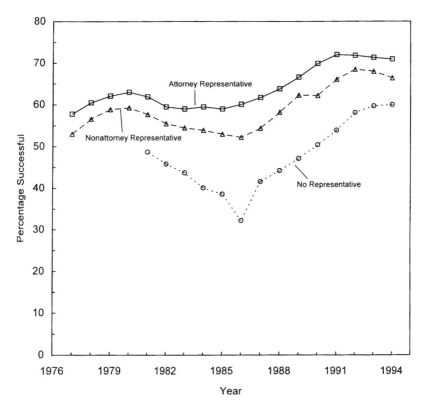

Fig. 5.   Success by representation, all cases. (Data from tables provided by Social Security Administration.)

Another factor has to do with SSA's policies regarding fees for representatives. Two aspects of these policies are important. First, if the representative is an attorney and there is an acceptable fee agreement between the claimant and the attorney, SSA will withhold 25 percent of back benefits due the successful DI claimant for direct payment to the attorney. SSA will not make a direct payment to a nonattorney representative—any fee due a nonattorney representative must be collected by that representative from the client. Second, SSA's policy of withholding from the back benefit and making direct payments to attorneys applies only in DI cases; it does not apply to SSI cases, meaning that the attorney must collect the fee from the client in an SSI case. One result of this policy is that fee-for-service attorneys are more reluctant to take SSI cases than DI cases because of the potential difficulty of getting paid. It should not be surpris-

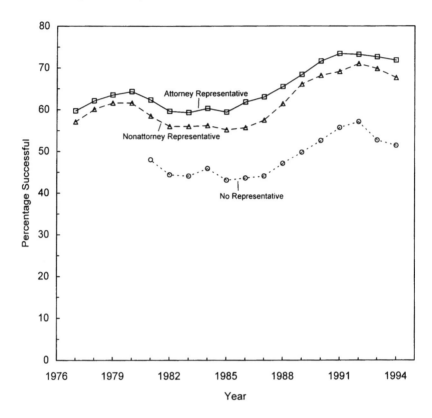

Fig. 6. Success by representation, cases that went to hearing. (Data from tables provided by Social Security Administration.)

ing that the likelihood of an attorney appearing in a DI case is higher than in an SSI case: in FY1993 attorneys appeared for 63 percent of all DI dispositions, but only 46 percent of all SSI dispositions.[21] On the other hand, nonattorneys face the same problems in DI cases and SSI cases if they seek to collect a fee, but in SSI cases they face less competition from attorneys. Moreover, some of the nonattorneys work in programs funded by local government designed specifically to focus on SSI cases, because a person who gets SSI may no longer need benefits from state or locally funded welfare programs. In 1993, nonattorneys appeared for only 8.6 percent of DI claimants, but for 19.2 percent of SSI claimants.[22]

These differences in patterns of representation could conceivably account for the slight gap in success between lawyers and nonlawyers. However, while representational patterns might account for some of the

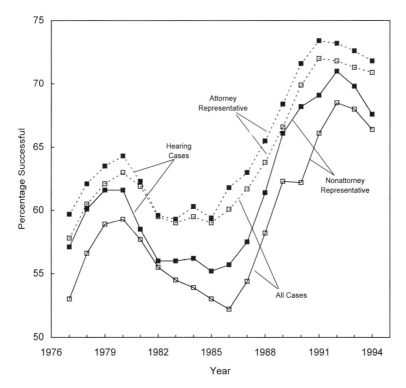

Fig. 7.   Success of attorneys and nonattorneys, all cases and hearing cases. (Data from tables provided by Social Security Administration.)

small success gap between attorneys and nonattorneys, it does not account for all of it. Figure 8 shows attorney and nonattorney success rates separately for all DI and SSI cases;[23] for clarity, I have left out unrepresented claimants and concurrent DI/SSI cases. The figure shows clearly that the success gap between attorneys and nonattorneys remains even with controls for type of case.

What does account for the small, but consistent, difference between attorney and nonattorney success rate? In the discussion that follows, I will argue that it primarily reflects the work of a small group of highly effective attorneys who specialize in Social Security cases and who are extremely good at what they do. I also will suggest that it may be explained in part by economic incentives created by the contingent fee structure used by most attorneys appearing on behalf of Social Security claimants. Before turning

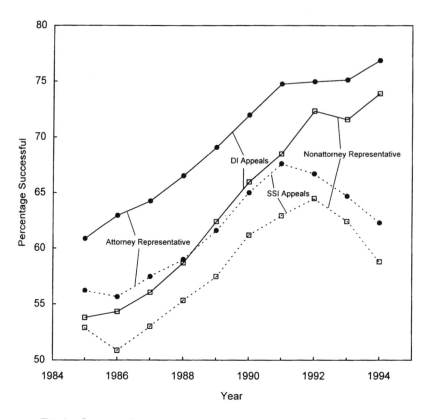

Fig. 8. Success of attorneys and nonattorneys, controlling for type of case. (Data from computer tabulations provided by Social Security Administration.)

to the analysis of my observational materials, I will provide an overview of the Social Security appeal process.

The Disability Appeals Process

The core question in most disability appeals is whether the claimant meets the definition of disability as set out in the relevant statutes and regulations. Jerry Mashaw describes in detail the process of and criteria for determining disability in his study, *Bureaucratic Justice;* only the latter aspect, the criteria, will be of concern here. The Social Security regulations describe the assessment of disability as a five-step process.[24]

1. The claimant is not engaging in "substantial gainful activity"; *and*
2. The claimant has a severe impairment (which is likely to continue for at least one year or end in death); *and either*
3. The claimant's impairment meets or equals one of the impairments appearing in the "Listing of Impairments"; *or*
4. The claimant is unable to do past relevant work; *and*
5. Given the claimant's age, education, work experience, and physical limitations, there are no other jobs available in significant numbers that the claimant could perform.[25]

While regular participants in the disability system refer to the determination process in terms of these five steps (i.e., "we were able to show disability at Step Five"), I find it easier to think in terms of four "stages." The first stage (Stage I) involves meeting a threshold which, if not met, terminates the process with a finding of no disability. If the Stage I threshold is met, there are three different ways to demonstrate disability; these are to be considered sequentially, and hence I refer to them as Stages II, III, and IV.[26]

I. *Substantial gainful activity.*   Is the claimant engaged in "substantial gainful activity" (SGA)? If the claimant has earnings above some threshold amount, an average of $500 per month as of 1990,[27] the claimant is deemed not disabled. For example, a quadriplegic with limited use of his right hand and arm but no use of his left arm or either leg, but who, with the aid of an arm brace to write, works a few hours per day as a bookkeeper and earns just over $6000 per year (after deductions for expenses related to his impairments), would not be disabled for purposes of DI benefits.[28]

II. *Medical listings.*   Given that the claimant is not engaged in substantial gainful activity, does the claimant meet any of the specific medical criteria that are presumptively disabling? These criteria, known as the medical listings (or just "the listings"), contain a mix of very objective criteria (e.g., quadriplegia or severe obesity, defined in terms of a height and weight chart combined with a specified level of hypertension) and criteria involving more judgment by the decision maker (e.g., severe anemia resulting in fatigue).[29] A claimant who meets one or more of the listings and who has no substantial gainful activity is disabled for purposes of receiving disability benefits.

III. *Vocational criteria—The grids.*   If the claimant's medical condition does not meet the criteria of the listings, his or her medical condition may still be such that the claimant is deemed to be disabled. Given that the claimant's medical condition precludes him or her from returning to the general kind of work he or she had previously done, should the claimant

be expected to be able to do other types of work? This "vocational" criterion is obviously highly discretionary, and in an effort to guide this discretion, the Social Security Administration adopted a set of Medical-Vocational Guidelines commonly referred to as the "grids." These guidelines
combine age, education, previous work experience, and the physical exertion a person is capable of (heavy, medium, light, or sedentary) to establish a set of presumptions of disability. Table 11 shows a summary of the
guidelines contained in the grids. For example, a person aged 55 to 59,
without a high school diploma, whose prior work experience consists of
unskilled work,[30] and who is capable of work requiring no more than light
exertion, is deemed to be disabled under these guidelines.

IV. *Nonexertional limitations.* A claimant who does not meet the
criteria set forth in the grids may still be disabled if nonexertional problems (e.g., pain that limits the time a claimant could sit, or vision problems
short of blindness) limit the jobs the claimant could perform to the point
that there are no (or very few) such jobs available.

Both the application and appeals processes turn heavily on documentation. The Stage I determination relies on work and income records that
should be readily available. Issues can arise regarding deductions from
income for impairment-related expenses, and whether some periods of
work should be counted as substantial gainful activity or be treated as
"unsuccessful work attempts."[31] In none of the hearings that I observed
did there appear to be a major issue regarding Stage I.

Stage II determination relies largely on documentation of the
claimant's medical condition. This documentation comes largely from
ostensibly objective materials supplied by the claimant; that is, it does not
rely upon judgments of the claimant's physician that the claimant "can't
work," but rather upon specific, documented diagnoses which the decision
maker assesses and compares to the requirements of the medical listings.
The evidence requested by SSA may be in the form of hospital records and
doctors' notes of treatment and test results; alternatively, or in addition, it
may be in the form of a detailed questionnaire that SSA asks the physician
to complete.[32] SSA need not rely on the claimant's own physician(s); it
may request an evaluation by a "consultative physician," based either on
an assessment of the medical records or a separate examination. Additional evidence regarding disability might come from pharmacists, insurance carriers, former employers, vocational rehabilitation agencies, social
welfare agencies, or law enforcement agencies.[33] In the initial determination, the medical evidence is evaluated by a medical doctor and by a non-
doctor with the title "disability examiner."[34]

At the appeals level, the administrative law judge is the decision
maker. The judge starts with the documentation used at the initial deter-

TABLE 11. Summary of Medical-Vocational Guidelines Used by the Social Security Administration in Disability Determination

Age	Education	Previous Work Experience	Physical Exertion
60–64	6th grade or less	Unskilled	Medium
	7th to 11th grade	Unskilled	Light
	11th grade or less	None	Medium
	11th grade or less	Skilled or semiskilled—skills not transferable	Light
	High school graduate or more—does not provide for direct entry into skilled work	Unskilled or none	Light
	High school graduate or more—does not provide for direct entry into skilled work	Skilled or semiskilled—skills not transferable	Light
55–59	11th grade or less	None	Medium
	11th grade or less	Unskilled	Light
	11th grade or less	Skilled or semiskilled—skills not transferable	Light
	High school graduate or more—does not provide for direct entry into skilled work	Unskilled or none	Light
	High school graduate or more—does not provide for direct entry into skilled work	Skilled or semiskilled—skills not transferable	Light
50–54	Illiterate or unable to communicate in English	Unskilled or none	Light
	11th grade or less—at least literate and able to communicate in English	Unskilled or none	Sedentary
	High school graduate or more—does not provide for direct entry into skilled work	Unskilled or none	Sedentary
	High school graduate or more—does not provide for direct entry into skilled work	Skilled or semiskilled—skills not transferable	Sedentary
45–49	Illiterate or unable to communicate in English	Unskilled or none	Sedentary
	All educational levels—at least literate and able to communicate in English	Unskilled, none, or skilled or semiskilled—skills not transferable	Less than full range of sedentary
18–44	All eduational levels including illiterate or unable to communicate in English	Unskilled, none, or skilled or semiskilled—skills not transferable	Less than full range of sedentary

Source: Adapted from *Social Security Disability Practice* by Thomas E. Bush. Copyright 1997 James Publishing, Inc. Reprinted and adapted with the permission of James Publishing, Inc. For information, call (714) 755-5450.

mination and reconsideration. The claimant can add other relevant material to this documentation for the judge to consider. The claimant or the claimant's representative can ask the judge to make a determination solely on the record without a hearing; however, even if the representative believes the claimant meets the medical listings, a hearing can be useful. This may be particularly true in cases involving psychiatric impairments where simply seeing and hearing the claimant may convince the judge of the claimant's disability.

For cases getting to what I have called Stage III, the claimant's "residual functional capacity" is central. This is assessed based on a standard form completed by a medical consultant. Where the issue is physical capacity, the consultant is asked to assess the claimant's capability and limitations along a variety of dimensions, such as exertional (lifting, standing, walking, sitting), postural (climbing, balancing, kneeling, stooping), manipulative (reaching, handling, fingering), visual, communicative (hearing, speaking), and environmental tolerances (cold, heat, wetness, noise). In cases raising issues of mental capacity, a different set of dimensions is used: understanding and memory, concentration and persistence, social interaction, and adaptation. The state agency evaluators apply criteria set forth in the Program Operations Manual Systems (POMS) to assess the information provided by the consultant and to determine the claimant's ability to perform various types of work in terms of exertion and skill. Also important at this stage is the claimant's employment and work history over the fifteen years preceding the onset of the disability. To be found disabled at Stage III, the claimant must be unable to perform previous work or work similar to that done in the past.

Because Stage III focuses on the exertional ability of the claimant, many cases at Stage III turn on issues of pain, because pain is frequently what limits the claimant's exertional ability.[35] This is a particularly difficult issue for administrative law judges,[36] and this seems particularly true of back pain. Judges typically ask detailed questions to assess both the reality of the claimant's pain and the magnitude of that pain. Sometimes actually seeing the claimant can make a difference in assessing the credibility of a claimant's report of pain. For example, the shortest hearing I observed lasted ten minutes. It involved a fifty-seven-year-old woman who had been severely injured in an auto accident three years previously, suffering a fractured spine, kneecap, collarbone, and shoulder blade, plus visual impairments. At the hearing, she was wearing a neck collar (which her testimony indicated she had worn since the accident), entered the hearing room haltingly, and grimaced in pain when she raised her hand to be sworn in. After only the most basic of questions, the judge turned to the representative, whose sole participation had been to interject at one point that the claimant's associate degree in bookkeeping had been obtained in 1954 or 1955, and said, "Ms. X clearly can't work; I intend to write a fully favorable decision."

At Stage IV, other elements of the residual functional capacity come into play. A claimant may be limited in movement in ways that prevent many kinds of work (e.g., being unable to bend over would preclude working as a light cleaner). Alternately, a claimant's inability to read or do simple arithmetic can preclude many types of work (e.g., working as a cashier). Here the claimant's very specific limitations combined with the jobs available in the local economy may be crucial for the disability determination. Witnesses such as friends, family, and former co-workers may be important in convincing the judge of the claimant's limitations. The judge may have a vocational expert testify, both as to the kinds of jobs the claimant is capable of performing, given his or her medical and mental condition, and as to the number of such jobs available in the relevant geographic area.

Throughout the process, documentation plays a central role. In the appeals process, the representative's role centers on building the documentary case supporting the claimed disability. This may involve insuring that relevant medical reports are in the file, securing additional medical reports to bolster the evidence regarding a particular claim or to counter unfavorable reports already in the file, and possibly withholding some evidence that might not be favorable to the claimant's case. In fact, the ability to obtain the *right* medical documentation may be what separates the very best representatives from those who are simply adequate. A comment that one administrative law judge made to me a week or so after a hearing captures nicely the central role of documentation: "I'm granting benefits in that hearing you saw last week . . . the advocate brought the right documents." In fact, while all claimants are entitled to a hearing in OHA proceedings, when the documentary case is sufficiently clear-cut, experienced representatives will ask for a favorable decision "on the record" and save the time and expense of a hearing. Furthermore, as discussed in the previous section, OHA is making an increasing effort to catch the clear-cut cases early on, and it is encouraging judges to grant benefits in such cases without going through the entire process.

The Administrative Procedures Act (APA) governs the entire appeals process. The provisions of the APA place the formal burden to acquire and consider relevant evidence on the administrative law judge. The result of the APA provisions is that the actual role played by the judge in the hearing itself varies, depending in part on the judge's belief about the representative's ability to present the case. At the hearing, a record of which is made by audiotaping, the judge will explain the nature of the proceedings to the claimant, swear in the claimant and any other witnesses who may be called to testify, and admit the exhibits that are in the file plus any other exhibits the claimant or the claimant's representative cares to offer; the claimant and the representative have the opportunity to object to any exhibits. Sometimes the judge will ask the representative to give some type of brief opening statement; at other times the representative will offer some summary of the case. However, in most of the hearings I observed, the judge simply began taking the claimant's testimony. This testimony focused on (1) educational background and vocational training, (2) prior work experience, and (3) medical condition.

The judge may assume the burden of the questioning (and will do so if the claimant is unrepresented) or permit the representative to do the bulk of the questioning. Usually the questioning starts with background factors such as age, living situation (type of residence, who the claimant lives with, etc.), and driver's license, and then proceeds in the order listed above to cover education and training, work history, and medical condition. After the judge has completed his or her questioning, the claimant's representative may ask questions; the amount of questioning by the representative depends on how extensive the judge's questioning was.

After the claimant's testimony is complete, other witnesses supporting the claimant testify. These witnesses may be friends, family, co-workers, clergy, or the claimant's physician. Only about 30 percent of hearings involve such witnesses.[37] These witnesses are usually questioned primarily by the claimant's representative, although the judge will interject questions as he or she deems appropriate. The judge may also have requested that either a medical expert or a vocational expert (VE) be present to testify. About one-third of hearings have vocational experts present and 10 to 12 percent have medical experts.[38] Almost invariably, the judge questions these experts first. Most prominent is the vocational expert who testifies as to the claimant's vocational abilities and the availability of jobs that a person with applicable limitations would be able to perform in a manner that would be acceptable to an employer. If the VE's testimony seems to indicate that there are jobs the claimant could do, the claimant's representative will typically try to use cross-examination to narrow the job pool by adding appropriate limitations on what the potential employee would be able to do. The VE's testimony often proves crucial. For example, in one case the judge described a hypothetical situation approximating the claimant's condition to the VE he had called, and then he asked, "Is there any work available for someone with these restrictions?" The VE replied that someone with those conditions "would not be employable in any capacity." That statement effectively ended the hearing. The VE's testimony in several other hearings I observed was equally decisive.

At the close of the hearing, the record may be held open for the submission of additional exhibits (e.g., further medical reports). In some cases, the judge may indicate that the decision will be favorable to the claimant, but most of the time the claimant will have to wait several months to receive the written decision before learning the outcome of the appeal. The judge will make the decision, but the decision itself will typically be drafted in whole or in part by a staff attorney.[39] A claimant who receives an unfavorable decision from OHA may appeal the case to the Appeals Council, and from there to federal district court.[40]

A Typical Hearing

Office of Hearings and Appeals proceedings tend to be highly routinized, as suggested by the preceding description. There is usually no formal adversarial element (i.e., there is no advocate defending the original denial), although sometimes the skepticism of the judge or an unfavorable expert witness may give the hearing a bit of an adversary flavor. The following abbreviated transcript gives a feel for what the hearing is like. I have left substantial pieces out of what follows for space reasons, but it should furnish a sufficient idea to provide a basis of exploring the issues of interest here.[41]

> *J:* Good morning, I'm Judge Smith. This is a hearing concerning the Social Security disability benefits for Mary Nelson [*CL*]; she is represented by advocate Sharon Johnson [*A*]. Ms. Nelson, has Ms. Johnson explained to you the way the hearing is conducted?
> *CL:* Yes she has.
> *J:* I will take the testimony this morning and consider it, along with the documents I have concerning your case, and make a decision. You will receive a written copy of that decision in the mail within about ninety days. Ms. Johnson, have you had a chance to review the exhibits, 1–26?
> *A:* Yes I have, and I have no objection to any of them. I would like to ask that the record be held open for one month for some additional reports.
> *J:* I will receive exhibits 1–26; the record will remain open for thirty days. Ms. Nelson, would you please stand so that I can swear you in? [. . .] Let me first ask you some background questions. What is your age?
> *CL:* Thirty-four.
> *J:* Where were you born?
> *CL:* In Milwaukee.

J: What is your current weight?

CL: One hundred eighty.

J: Your usual weight?

CL: About that.

J: Are you right- or left-handed?

CL: Right-handed.

J: What is your housing situation?

CL: I live with my eighteen-month-old child in an apartment.

J: Do you have to go up and down steps, either to get into your apartment or inside of it?

CL: No, it's a first-floor apartment.

J: How did you get to the hearing this morning?

CL: A friend drove me.

J: Do you have a driver's license?

CL: Yes.

J: Do you actually drive?

CL: Sometimes.

J: Do you own a car?

CL: No, I borrow a friend's Ford Mustang.

J: Does it have a standard transmission?

CL: No, it's an automatic.

J: What was the highest grade you completed in school?

CL: Eighth.

J: Have you gone to any kind of technical school?

CL: I started a beauty course, but I didn't finish it.

J: Have you gotten a GED?

CL: No, I haven't, but DVR [Department of Vocational Rehabilitation] told me I would have to get my GED before they could work with me.

J: When did you last work?

CL: June or July of 1991 [about one year before the hearing].

J: What was that job?

CL: I was a waitress at the ——— Cafe for about four months.

J: What was that job like?

CL: I was on my feet all the time, but it was only part-time . . . twenty to thirty hours a week.

J: What was the heaviest lifting you had to do?

CL: Twelve to fifteen pounds.

J [*reading from a document*]: Your job before that was as a sales clerk in a clothing store, from February 1989 to August 1989?

CL: That's right.

J: What was that like?

CL: I was on my feet all the time.

J: Lifting?

CL: None to speak of.

J [*Reading again*]: And before that you worked for three months at —
—— Church as a cleaner?

CL: Yes, it was light cleaning, twenty to thirty hours a week?

J [*Reading again*]: And before that, from July 1987 to March 1988,
you had another waitressing job?

CL: Yes.

[*The judge continues working back through prior jobs, which included
stints as a waitress and several jobs as a cashier in convenience stores,
some of which involved tasks such as stocking shelves.*]

J: Okay, let's talk about your health problems. What seems to be the
main problem?

CL: I have lots of pain.

J: Do you take anything for it?

CL: Oh yes, I'm always on painkillers by eleven in the morning.

J: Where is the pain?

CL: It's in my neck, in my back, in my lower shoulders; it's the worst
in my lower back.

J: When do you have the pain in your lower back?

CL: About two weeks out of every month.

J: How about in your upper back?

CL: That's just constant.

J: When did the pain start?

CL: It started when I was at the beauty college. I thought it might be
due to my pregnancy, but it didn't go away after the baby was
born. I think the lower back pain might be related to my menstrual
cycle.

J: Who are the doctors that you've seen?

CL: [*Gives the names of several doctors.*]

J: What have they told you the problem was?

CL: Some have said muscle spasms; they also have said it might be
due to scoliosis [curvature of the spine].

J: Have you tried physical therapy?

CL: Oh yes, I started it a while back. Three times a week.

J: What is the nature of that therapy?

CL: Ultrasound treatments.

J: Has it helped?

CL: Not yet, but I am still hopeful.

J [*Looking at a document*]: According to this, you are currently taking [J lists medications, and CL confirms each one]. Is there anything else?

CL: No . . . I try not to take the muscle relaxer unless I really need it because it makes me drowsy.

J: Have you done anything else for the pain?

CL: I went to a chiropractor for a while, but I quit going because the treatments only helped for a little while.

J: Anything else?

CL: I had diagnostic surgery several days ago, but I haven't heard about the results yet.

J: Anything else?

CL: No, that's all.

J: Do you have trouble walking?

CL: I don't do a lot of walking. The pain gets worse whenever I do anything physical like walking, or cleaning, or dressing myself or my child.

J: What about things like grocery shopping?

CL: When I grocery shop, I want to fall on the floor it hurts so much. It takes me about an hour at the store just to get a few things, 'cause I have to stop so much.

J: What about sitting?

CL: I can sit for maybe fifteen to twenty minutes, and then my back starts hurting. The longer I sit, the worse it gets.

J: How do you occupy your day?

CL: Just doing the basics. Caring for my child, studying for the GED.

J: What about meal preparation?

CL: I try to do real simple things that don't require me to be on my feet for very long.

J: Laundry?

CL: I need help to do it.

J: What about your social life?

CL: I don't have much of a social life.

J: Your appetite?

CL: My appetite is good.

J: What about sleeping?

CL: I can only get five or six hours a night. I keep waking up due to the discomfort. I will try to nap during the day if my son is napping.

J [*To the advocate*]: You may ask any questions you have.

A [*To judge*]: Thank you. [*To claimant*] What brought on the back pain?

CL: I was in an auto accident about five years ago. The car I was in rear-ended a semi. The driver of the car was killed. I was in the hospital for a week.

A: What was it like after the accident?

CL: I hurt all over at first, but it seemed to get better. The pain in my back intensified when I started at the beauty school, and I had to leave the beauty course because of the pain.

A: Could you tell me about the pain?

CL: My neck and shoulders start hurting first, and then it travels down my back.

A: Could you describe the pain . . . in your neck and shoulders?

CL: It's a bunched up pain . . . it feels like a lot of pressure.

A: In your middle back?

CL: It's a hot pain.

A: In your lower back?

CL: It's a dull throbbing. Like someone is squeezing inside.

A: Which is the worst?

CL: The pain in my upper body is the worst because it is constant. The only medication that helps that pain is the muscle relaxer that I can't take during the day because it makes me so drowsy.

A: What's the next worst?

CL: My lower back.

A: On a scale of one to ten, how would you describe the pain in your upper back?

CL: Seven to eight.

A: Your lower back?

CL: Twelve!

A: Middle back?

CL: Three.

A: Does the weather affect the pain?

CL: I never have related the two.

A: Now in his report, Doctor —— says that your condition does not affect your ability to walk or to stand . . .

CL: The doctor never asked me about walking or standing.

A: What else do you do for pain?

CL: Things like deep heat rubs, hot baths, cold packs.

A: Do they help?

CL: The deep heat rubs help for maybe thirty to forty-five minutes. It's the muscle relaxers that really take the pain away.

A: Can you bathe without assistance?

CL: Yes.

A: How much can you lift?

CL: Five to ten pounds.

A: Can you lift your child?

CL: No.

A: Who helps with the child?

CL: His father; he tries to come over and help whenever he can.

A: Can you reach over your head?

CL: Not without substantial pain. It's hard to even fix my hair.

A: Are there any other problems in your life?

CL: Just my health.

A: Are you depressed?

CL: Lately I have been, because I am sick and in pain.

A: Did you ever have problems with depression before the pain?

CL: No.

A: What do you do to take your mind off the pain?

CL: It's hard to take my mind off of the pain. I read the Bible. I'm hoping to get into the pain clinic.

A: Do you spend a lot of time on the phone?

CL: No.

A: Are there any other side effects of the medications you're on?

CL: The Anaprox might be causing bladder infections.

A: Does anyone help with the cleaning?

CL: No.

A: Can you clean your bathtub?

CL: No, it just stays dirty.

A: What about bathing your son?

CL: That is very difficult to do. His father helps sometimes. Other times I do it in the kitchen sink so I don't have to bend over.

A: I have no further questions. I would like the record to be held open for thirty days to get the results of the diagnostic surgery.

This hearing lasted about forty-five minutes.

I describe this hearing as "typical" because it shows the kind of role that the judge tends to take, and one of the roles the advocate can take. Here, the judge brought out the basic background and the core issue (pain), and the advocate's questions focused on developing the severity of the pain and the efforts the claimant had made to deal with the pain. (In fact, hearings frequently focused on the pain issue, particularly back pain, for the simple reason that pain is very difficult to assess, as well as the perceived possibility that pain is being exaggerated to qualify for benefits.) Overall, the balance between the judge and the advocate was fairly even, and I would describe this as the "average" situation.

Advocates in Social Security Hearings

The rules governing the disability programs administered by the Social Security Administration are complex, and the difference between experienced and inexperienced advocates is readily apparent when one observes someone who is new to these cases. As stated by one of the judges: "It's not being a lawyer that makes a difference, but rather knowing what is a disability. Advocates who know what they are doing do a better job than an attorney who doesn't know disability."

The Inexperienced Advocate

The problem of the advocate not experienced in disability law was evident in the hearings I observed involving such advocates. Take the following brief exchange between a judge and an attorney who was making his first OHA appearance.

> *J:* How is Mr. Brown disabled?
> *A:* He has chronic pulmonary disorder as indicated by a pulmonary function test. I would refer you to [*cites a table in the regulations*]. Mr. Brown has been hospitalized three times in the last six months and actually came here directly from the hospital. I would like to keep the record open to add the reports from this latest hospitalization.
> *J:* I will decide at the end of the hearing whether we need these additional reports. Is there anything else?
> *A:* The medications he has been on have had side effects that have created a condition like arthritis. [*Elaborates on this in some detail.*]
> *J:* I have looked at the record, and it does not meet the regulations . . . the listings are not going to do it for him.
> *A:* I tried to get a report on an MVV [maximal ventilatory volume], but the physicians said they don't do MVV on obstructive lung disease.
> *J:* Maybe these doctors don't, but others do.
> *A:* I don't know why Social Security would want unnecessary tests . . .

Clearly, the lawyer did not realize that SSA listings still relied on the MVV as a core element for assessing disability related to the respiratory system.[42] Despite the absence of this medical documentation, the claimant's testimony at the hearing made it clear that he was not capable of working. After the advocate's questioning of the claimant had dragged on for a

while, the judge broke in with "Let me ask a couple of questions . . . maybe
we can end this," and then after a couple of perfunctory questions turned
to the advocate and said, "I will find a way to find him disabled." The
advocate did not realize that this was the time to thank the judge and get
out of the hearing:

> *A:* I have a series of cases that will help you.
> *J:* I doubt it, but you can put them in a brief.
> *A:* I could write you a letter.
> *J:* Do you want to make him wait another month?

The inexperienced advocates seem not to understand the evidentiary
conventions of the hearings. For example, one advocate I spoke with—a
person who had done a small number of Social Security hearings previously—told me before the hearing that he would call only the claimant and
one witness (the claimant's mother—this being an SSI case where the
claimant was a child), and that all medical evidence would be by affidavit.
Apparently, the advocate did not realize that this was the norm, and that
it was uncommon to call the claimant's treating physician(s) to testify.

I observed an even more extreme example of this failure to understand evidentiary conventions in another child disability case. The advocate in that case was a senior attorney from a large corporate law firm providing her services on a pro bono basis. This attorney actually brought to
the hearing her own psychological and vocational experts, presumably
being paid by the attorney's firm as part of its pro bono services; this was
the only case I saw where the claimant had his or her own medical expert,
and one of only two with a vocational expert not called by the judge. The
judge asked the lawyer to call her witnesses, and she started with the psychologist (in every other case I observed, the claimant was the first witness
to testify). The lawyer questioned the psychologist in a very formal style,
but after about ten minutes, the judge became dissatisfied and took over
the questioning to extract the information he needed to arrive at and justify a decision. Eventually, the judge said to the witness, "Just give me your
opinion." The next witness called by the lawyer was the vocational expert
(VE) she had retained. Before the VE started his testimony, the judge commented that the regulations governing OHA proceedings direct the judges
not to call vocational experts on their own initiative in child cases, but this
does not preclude the claimant's representative from calling such witnesses. After the VE's testimony, the lawyer called the claimant and the
claimant's mother; the questioning of all of the witnesses was, for an OHA
hearing, unnecessarily detailed and frequently redundant. The hearing
lasted ninety minutes, which was one of the longest hearings I observed.

An experienced advocate would have done without either of the two experts and would have taken the testimony of the claimant and her mother in thirty to forty-five minutes.

These inexperienced advocates were actually highly experienced attorneys. Other types of problems can arise with someone who is not an attorney and who is inexperienced in these proceedings. For example, I observed one case in which a nonlawyer advocate was appearing for only the second time in a Social Security hearing; she worked for an agency that relied mostly on nonlawyer advocates, but was supervised by an attorney. The advocate came to the hearing with some citations to relevant regulations (which she noted to the judge at the end of the hearing). The problem this advocate demonstrated centered on the asking of questions. After the judge had completed his questions, he turned it over to the advocate, who started asking a series of questions to provide more detail on the claimant's medical condition. Some of the questions were in the form of leading questions, such as, "Did you have heart surgery in 1981?" After two or three such questions, the judge chastised the advocate for asking leading questions and instructed her to ask questions in a nonleading fashion. Because of her lack of experience, the advocate had some difficulty making this adjustment; a lawyer with any trial experience to speak of would have had no trouble adjusting the questioning. One might ask whether the advocate was inadequately prepared for the hearing (i.e., had not been instructed in the proper question form), but there was no reason to anticipate this problem; I frequently saw experienced attorneys and nonattorneys ask leading questions, even in a hearing with this same judge about a year later.[43]

The data reported earlier in this chapter do not allow for a statistical comparison between experienced and inexperienced representatives. In the cases I saw with inexperienced representatives, the documentation was usually reasonably good, and the judge typically intervened to deal with problems at the hearings. To the degree that inexperienced representatives are less successful than experienced representatives, the factors underlying this difference are probably more subtle than the lack of artfulness often evident at the hearing.

The Experienced Advocate

Experienced advocates not only know the rules governing disability and the kinds of evidence needed to establish a case that disability exists, they also know the other players in the system, particularly the administrative law judges. While my research focused on the advocates, the variation in style among the judges was almost as great as among the experienced advocates. Not only did style vary, the judges also differed in their reputed willingness to grant benefits. This difference in reputation was expressed most bluntly in a conversation I overheard while waiting for a hearing to begin. One OHA staffer talking to another staffer referred to a particular administrative law judge as "Mr. Never-Pay-Anybody-Anything." At one time, the Appeals Council in Washington compiled data on the decision patterns of individual judges on a quarterly basis. Some of the experienced advocates would obtain these compilations for the judges in their area under the provisions of the Freedom of Information Act (FOIA).[44]

Experienced advocates clearly play to the reputational expectations of individual judges. I asked one of the experienced lawyers how he approached cases with a judge who has a low probability of granting benefits; the lawyer replied, "I hope he makes a mistake that I can use as the basis of an appeal." Another lawyer echoed the same sentiment and went on to explain, "If I see Judge X [a sympathetic judge] going off on the wrong direction, I try to bring him back; if it's Judge Y [an unsympathetic judge], I just let him go." A third lawyer, when asked the same question (after a hearing with a judge who seemed very unsympathetic, but whom the representative did not know because the judge was visiting from another city), responded that "normally when I have an unsympathetic ALJ [administrative law judge], I try to make the case so airtight that even if the ALJ wants to deny benefits, the ALJ realizes that I will appeal the case and the Appeals Council will remand it back; the judge doesn't want to deal with the case twice. However, a visiting judge may be more willing to deny a case, even if he thinks it will be appealed because if the case comes back on remand, it will be assigned to a new judge."

Experienced advocates also know when a particular judge has heard enough. Sometimes this becomes visibly evident. In one case, the judge started looking very bored. Paying no apparent attention to the testimony the representative was obtaining, he looked at a file and made notes from it. The lawyer, who had appeared before the judge previously, even though the judge was visiting from another office, quickly realized what was happening and ended his questioning of the claimant. Another experienced representative appearing before this same visiting judge, but for the first time, did not know how to interpret the visible hint. After playing with his fingernails for a while, the judge finally said to the representative, "How many more questions?" Finally realizing the judge's impatience, the representative replied, "One or two," and finished up very quickly. Those advocates with the most experience did not need such obvious prompting. After one hearing, an experienced representative told me, "I often make a closing statement citing appropriate regulations, but I didn't do that with this judge, because he knows his stuff, and I didn't want to risk insulting him by telling him things he knew." After another hearing, an experienced representative remarked to her client, "I cut off the questions because I could see that the judge was going our way, and I didn't want to make him impatient."

An experienced advocate will know that it is not necessarily correct to end the hearing in direct response to a signal from the judge that the decision will be favorable. One important aspect of the Social Security appeals process is that the Appeals Council, the body that reviews decisions of the administrative law judges, may review even favorable decisions on its own initiative. In one case involving a visiting judge, the judge asked the representative to "tell me the theory of the case." The representative explained that the claimant had undergone a series of surgeries in the wake of an injury and that the claimant's condition met the listings. (Throughout this discussion, the claimant, who was wearing a neck collar and clutching a cane, was alternately sitting and standing.) The judge asked the representative to clarify where in the exhibits he would find the documentation that the claimant met the listings. The dialogue between representative and judge continued for a few minutes, and then the judge stated, "I'm convinced that your client is disabled, and I will find favorably." At this point, rather than thanking the judge and departing, the representative asked to go ahead and put in basic testimony, just in case the Appeals Council should decide to review the case.

As in the unemployment compensation appeal hearings, knowledge of the judges is an important element of the background that experienced representatives bring to the hearing process.[45] Knowledge of the other regular players, vocational and medical experts, can be equally important. Occasionally, this knowledge is derived not from participation in prior hearings but from other contact with the expert. I observed several hearings in smaller communities around Wisconsin. In one of those hearings, a very experienced representative encountered a vocational expert who was entirely new to Social Security hearings. The case involved a 34-year-old man who claimed to have serious neck and back problems: "If I move my head, it makes my neck hurt, and if I use my right hand, it aggravates my neck." The representative's questioning of the claimant brought out more detail including bad headaches, numbness, tingling and weakness in the right arm (the claimant was right-handed), muscle spasms in the neck, and nausea. These problems were aggravated by the claimant's blindness in his right eye (from an accident at the age of three) which necessitated substantial head movement to see. The original injury was a broken neck suffered in a diving accident fifteen years earlier; it was aggravated in 1989 when a calcium deposit that developed from the *untreated* broken neck chipped off. It was only after the aggravating injury that the claimant realized he

had suffered a broken neck in the diving accident; this realization came
when the doctor he went to in 1989 said to him, "Who did you see after
you broke your neck?"

The judge in the case was not convinced that the claimant's level of
pain was "totally disabling."[46] The testimony of the vocational expert
(VE) appeared to be crucial to the claimant's case. Interestingly, while the
VE had not appeared before in Social Security hearings, the representative
knew him from other contexts and actually introduced the expert to the
administrative law judge before the hearing formally started. As is normal
practice in such hearings, the judge posed a hypothetical case approximating the claimant's condition and asked the VE if there were jobs available
that were sedentary, with no excessive repetitive activity and no lifting over
the head. The VE responded with a number of very specific jobs: buckler
and lacer in the shoe industry, plastic design applicator in the shoe industry, electric heat sealing machine operator, and hand grinder in the button
industry. The representative later told me that he had been initially surprised at the kinds of jobs named by the VE (not the kinds of jobs typically
listed by VEs at Social Security hearings); however, the representative
explained that he quickly realized the list reflected the VE's primary experience working as a vocational counselor in sheltered workshops for the
mentally handicapped. The representative sought to undercut the VE's
testimony by asking detailed questions about the requirements of each of
the jobs identified, in order to show that they would require substantial
head movement, repetitive motion, and concentration. He closed his questioning by getting the VE to acknowledge, after a little hemming and haw-
ing, that a commercial employer would probably not carry a worker who
had to go home early two times a week due to headaches or other types of
pain.[47]

One last way in which an experienced advocate can make a difference
is in avoiding getting things into the record that would be harmful to the
client's case, or by countering such things when they do occur. This might
involve holding back an unsympathetic medical report or trying to counter
such a report by pointing out its inconsistencies with the rest of the record,
or possibly even questioning the competence of a doctor. Alternately, it
might involve getting clarifying questions or comments in when a claimant
says something potentially damaging. For example, a claimant who had a
combination of respiratory and cardiac problems (he had undergone two
bypass operations and still experienced angina) made several comments, in
response to a question that suggested he may have felt able to go back to
work after the last surgery. The representative quickly asked several questions to make it clear that such a return to work could only have been with
the prior employer, who had been carrying the claimant despite all his

health problems; no other employer would have seriously considered hiring the claimant.

As this discussion shows, an experienced representative can make a difference. However, there is nothing in what I have described that distinguishes between an experienced representative who is a lawyer and one who is not. Both lawyers and nonlawyers can get to know the judges, can have detailed knowledge of the regulations, and can ask appropriate questions. What, if any, differences are there between lawyer and nonlawyer advocates?

Lawyers and Nonlawyers

A variety of differences potentially separate lawyers from nonlawyers: the rigor with which they screen and select cases, the thoroughness of their preparation, their credibility with the administrative law judges, and how strongly they feel about winning.

Selecting Cases

One dimension of the case selectivity issue that I explored before was the difference between Disability Income (DI) and Supplemental Security Income (SSI) cases. The proportion of SSI cases in the work of nonlawyer advocates was measurably greater than the proportion in the work of lawyers. Combining this with the overall lower success rate for SSI cases accounts for part of the difference in success between lawyers and nonlawyers. As discussed previously, the most likely reason lawyers accept fewer SSI cases is the potential difficulty in collecting fees in such cases (since SSA does not make payments to lawyers out of back SSI benefits).

Concerns about payment could explain differences in success for lawyers and nonlawyers within the SSI and regular disability categories. That is, lawyers working on a fee-for-service basis might be more careful in screening cases than nonlawyers working on a salaried basis for advocacy organizations of various types. In fact, some of the lawyers I spoke with reported that they were very selective. One lawyer, who devoted about half of his time to Social Security work, reported that he "screened out 80 percent of the potential clients who called him about a Social Security disability case," particularly anyone who said, "I'm trying to get on Social Security." Other lawyers indicated acceptance rates of 50 to 60 percent, or 65 to 70 percent. However, other experienced attorneys report accepting all, or nearly all, of the potential clients who contact them.[48] Furthermore, the concern about fees is not limited to lawyers; one nonlawyer representative who collects fees from his clients does a lot of screening by telephone: "I ask potential clients two key screening questions. Are you *now* working? Does your doctor say you are disabled?" Without much more systematic data on screening practices, information that does not now exist, there is no way to assess rigorously how much, if any, of the differential success rates of attorneys and nonattorneys may be due to such practices.

Preparing Cases

Attorneys may be better at preparing cases than are nonattorneys. This factor is difficult to assess, because preparation is fundamentally qualitative; however, one indicator suggests the lack of a clear difference in preparation. Considering the centrality of documentation in establishing disability, if lawyers prepared their cases more fully than did nonlawyers, one might expect that the former would tend to provide more exhibits than did the latter. For about two-thirds of the hearings I observed, I noted the number of exhibits received by the judge. In cases with lawyer representatives, the average number of exhibits was 30.9; in cases with nonlawyers the average number was 33.2. If anything, this would suggest that nonlawyers sought more documentation than did lawyers, although the difference here is too small to be meaningful (and therefore it is statistically nonsignificant).[49]

Credibility with Administrative Law Judges

This does not mean that the hearings involving lawyers were just the same as those involving nonlawyers. In cases involving lawyer representatives, the judges may more or less turn the hearing over to the representative to develop the case, while assuming more of the burden themselves when the representative is not a lawyer. There is a very clear tendency in this direction. In about a third of the hearings where lawyers appeared, the judges made a few introductory comments, admitted the exhibits, and turned the hearing over to the lawyer to develop the testimony, even with lawyers who were not experienced in Social Security hearings. I did not see this happen a single time when the representative was a nonlawyer (and most of the nonlawyers I saw had a lot of Social Security experience). I observed representatives from two agencies that employed both lawyers and nonlawyers, and the lawyers from both had questioning turned over to them from the start of the hearing. In most (about two-thirds) of the hearings involving nonlawyer representatives, the questioning was divided fairly evenly between the judges and the representatives, while this happened in very few hearings where a lawyer representative appeared. Overall, lawyers were the dominant questioners in three-quarters of their hearings;

where nonlawyers appeared, the representative was the dominant questioner in less than one-sixth of the hearings.

Clearly, judges tend to run hearings with lawyer representatives differently from the way they run hearings with nonlawyer representatives. Recall that under the Administrative Procedures Act it is the judge's responsibility to insure that a complete and appropriate record is made upon which to base his or her decision. When a nonlawyer appears as a representative, the judge approaches this responsibility differently than when a lawyer appears. However, does this account for the difference in outcomes between lawyers and nonlawyers? The fact that, in deciding how to run the hearings, the judges did not appear to distinguish between experienced Social Security lawyers and lawyers without such experience suggests to me that it is not likely that the differential handling of the hearings accounts for the difference in outcomes. Moreover, if lawyers are, in fact, better representatives than are nonlawyers, the greater role assumed by the judge should actually close that gap rather than account for the gap.

None of the explanations discussed here appears to readily account for the small gap between lawyers and nonlawyers. There is no crude difference in the documentary cases built by lawyers and nonlawyers, although I have no way to assess the quality of the documentation (and I doubt if there would be any systematic way to make such an assessment, even if the files were available for inspection). While the rules governing disability are complex, they are regularly administered by nonlawyer disability examiners, and an intelligent nonlawyer representative should be able to learn the regulations as well as a lawyer could.

This leaves differential performance in the hearings as a possible explanatory factor. Lawyers might be better as oral advocates because of some combination of formal training in advocacy and experience as a trial lawyer. They might be better at questioning witnesses, responding to adverse testimony by experts, and/or making arguments to the judge by citing appropriate regulations or case law. However, the greater role played by the judges in cases with nonlawyers would serve to offset any such additional advocacy skill. Thus, the factors mentioned here, particularly the role played by the judge, may be better at explaining why there is relatively little difference in the success of lawyers and nonlawyers. These explanations do little to account for what differences do exist.

Desire to Win

One other explanation for the difference between lawyers and nonlawyers might simply be that lawyers try harder, because they are more concerned about winning cases. The desire to win could come from two sources, one of which—the need to win in order to get paid—I will deal with in some detail later. The other source of differences in wanting to win might reflect more general background factors. Many of the nonlawyer advocates who do Social Security cases come from the helping professions: social work, rehabilitation counseling, the ministry, and so on. Their motivation centers on helping the claimants. By contrast, both those who are attracted to law school and the law school experience itself place more emphasis on competition and winning. The American justice system is adversarial in its orientation, and one cannot go through law school without being socialized into the values of the system. Of course, there are lawyers who are very concerned about helping people and social workers who care a lot about winning; nonetheless, differences in background might affect aggregate patterns.[50]

Administrative Law Judges' Attitudes toward Nonlawyers

Before closing this argument, I should note that the judges' views of the quality of advocacy by lawyers and nonlawyers overall varies. Judges readily acknowledge that nonlawyers can do a very good job as advocates, and some judges made comments suggesting that, on average, nonlawyers may be as good as lawyers. However, in the hearings I observed, I did detect a pattern indicating that some judges differentiated between lawyers and nonlawyers in how they conducted the hearings, while others did not; for example, some judges would essentially turn the hearing over to a lawyer but would not do so when the advocate was a nonlawyer. Moreover, at least some of the judges held the nonlawyer advocates who appeared before them in lower regard than the lawyer advocates. This was most clearly indicated in some comments made not by a judge but by a VE after a hearing was over and the nonlawyer advocate and his client had left the room. The VE expressed extreme displeasure at the idea that "taxpayers are paying these advocates when there are [fee-for-service] lawyers available to provide representation. . . . I resent the use of my tax dollars for such things . . . why should my tax dollars be used to pay for *inferior representation* [emphasis added]." Throughout this brief discussion the judge made comments indicating that he agreed with the VE's view, particularly regarding the quality of representation provided by the nonlawyer advocates.[51] However, while the ALJs attitudes toward nonlawyer advocates varied, I have no data that show that it was the judges views toward the advocates that account for the patterns I have described above.

The Very Best Advocates

There is another explanation for the small difference in the success achieved by lawyer representatives compared to nonlawyers. It focuses on the relatively small group of lawyers who specialize in Social Security practice, devoting at least a quarter, and usually more, of their time to such cases. A few lawyers devote all of their time to Social Security practice. In my observations, these lawyers clearly stood out in how they handled the hearings. Furthermore, their performance did not reflect case screening practices whereby they skimmed off relatively easy, straightforward cases. Interestingly, they seemed to like the challenge of difficult cases—cases either lost or declined by other representatives.

For example, a hearing I observed handled by one of the lawyers whose practice was devoted entirely to Social Security cases involved a claimant previously represented unsuccessfully by a nonlawyer. After losing at the hearing level, the nonlawyer had dropped out of the picture, and the claimant had sought new representation. The lawyer appealed the case to the Appeals Council, which remanded the case for further consideration back to the Office of Hearings and Appeals. This was one of those hearings in which the judge turned the hearing over to the lawyer after swearing the witnesses and admitting the exhibits. The lawyer went through the claimant's work history (in which all the jobs were unskilled or semiskilled, such as food preparation in a hospital dietary department). The judge frequently interjected questions directed to the lawyer (e.g., what was the claimant's longest period of employment). After completing the work history, the lawyer went on to have the claimant detail her medical problems. Those focused first on pain: migraines, shooting pain in the head, neck, and shoulders, dull pain down through the arms, hands, and wrist. In response to the lawyer's questions, the claimant characterized the pain as "sharp, shooting," "dull," and "burning," depending upon the location. The lawyer continued with questions about the pain (its sources, the limitations it imposed, its impact on her recreational activities) as well as questions about other types of problems (depression, alcohol use, drug use, etc.). After the lawyer completed his questioning of the claimant, the judge called a vocational expert who testified that there were no jobs available that the claimant would be able to perform. When the judge invited the lawyer to question the VE, he simply asked the VE to list the key limitations in the claimant's "residual function" upon which the VE based his judgment. Throughout the hearing, the questioning was extremely smooth and thorough. After the hearing, the judge commented to me that this lawyer "is always well-prepared [in contrast to] some attorneys who are less prepared."

Even more interesting was another case handled by one of the specialists. One of the nonlawyer advocates whom I observed on several occasions had previously declined this case; the nonlawyer had told me that he had "problems with some doctors who won't give you good reports . . . I tell clients to go to another doctor. I'm reluctant to take clients who don't have medical documentation." This was a case that presented evidentiary problems. The nonlawyer had run into problems getting the medical records and other evidence he felt he would need. Without the records, the nonlawyer felt the case would be difficult to prove and declined representation.

The specialist lawyer took on the challenge of the case. The core issue was extreme obesity combined with a back injury, which the lawyer asserted made this "a listings case." One of the issues was the date of onset, and the problem here was establishing the claimant's weight on specific dates. Getting information on weight was a problem because of the limits on the scales in most doctors' offices. Furthermore, there was one medical report showing the claimant's weight at 315 pounds, which was well under the listings' requirement. The kinds of difficulties the nonlawyer representative encountered with the case are clear.

The lawyer elicited the following points through his client's testimony.

1. The claimant had injured his back in 1985 when he had been pinned against a tree by a car. When he attempted to resume normal activity nine months later, his back gave out when he tried lifting something in his garage.
2. The claimant made an attempt to resume work in 1988 by trying to start a "cottage industry." He had previously been a musical instrument maker with a local manufacturer of brass instruments. He could not work in the factory because the physical setup was incompatible with his condition. He tried to set up a shop at home where he could assemble horns, but he found that he could only work for an hour or so a day, and his output was so minimal that he was producing very few finished horns.
3. Until 1987, the claimant's weight had been around 290 [which would not qualify under the obesity listings, given his height]. After some additional surgery in April of 1987, he stopped smoking and started gaining weight. After the surgery, he started "topping out" on the scale at his doctor's office, which went only to 350 pounds.
4. The lawyer asked the claimant about one of the medical records among the exhibits, a report from a visit to a chiropractor in 1989,

which showed the claimant's weight as 315. The claimant explained that that must have been an error in transcription; he was topping out on the chiropractor's scale, and the typist must have misunderstood "350" as "315." During this period, the only way medical personnel could get an actual weight for him was to send him to the shipping department at the hospital and have him weighed on the shipping scale.

Testimony also covered in great detail the nature of the claimant's back pain, the efforts he had made to deal with it, and his ability to function on a daily basis. To further establish that the claimant's weight in 1989 was as he testified, the lawyer brought along some photographs to enter into evidence. The photo showed both the claimant and his daughter, and the lawyer used the apparent age of the daughter in the photo as a way of establishing when the photo had been taken.

This lawyer's style of presentation of the case reflected a great deal of confidence. He worked without a list of questions (which a number of the best lawyers regularly employ), relying on only minimal notes. Furthermore, unlike most of the experienced representatives, he was willing to decline a judge's suggestion. After the presentation of the evidence, the judge indicated that he "could go along with the listings," but asked whether the claimant would be willing to amend the onset date to December 1989. The lawyer did not immediately reply, sitting there thinking about the request; the judge interjected, "you don't have to." The lawyer explained that he was reluctant to go along with the later onset date because of how the benefits would be calculated. The hearing closed without the lawyer agreeing to the judge's suggestion. However, after checking the impact of the later onset date on the benefits calculation and explaining the situation to his client, the lawyer communicated to the judge that the later onset date was acceptable.[52]

As I stated above, one impressive aspect of the style of this group of specialist lawyers was the thoroughness with which they prepared and presented cases. The following example shows an interesting approach to insuring a very thorough presentation of medical conditions. In this hearing, after making his introductory remarks and receiving the exhibits, the judge turned the questioning over to the lawyer. The lawyer briefly covered some background areas (age, marital status, education, and the like) and then turned to the claimant's physical problems, stating, "I like to start at the feet and work up." He then asked the claimant, "Do you have any problems with your feet?" He continued with questions about the claimant's calves, knees, lower back or hips, upper back or shoulders, hands and arms, neck, and head, one after another, very systematically.

For each region of the body, the lawyer asked additional questions to bring out things the client failed to mention (e.g., carpal tunnel syndrome). After going from toe to head, the lawyer turned to heart problems, diabetes and its effects (including dizziness, vision problems, itching), memory problems, anxiety, and prior alcohol use. The thoroughness of the lawyer's questioning concerning the claimant's medical conditions was impressive.

My informal, post-hearing conversations with these lawyers often turned to the particular judge before whom they had just appeared. The lawyers knew the individual judges thoroughly, what they liked and disliked, and their decisional propensities.[53] Moreover, when they had a hearing involving a visiting judge, these lawyers would frequently call a lawyer from the judge's home area to get a briefing on what to expect. Similarly, when one of the judges from the Milwaukee office was temporarily assigned outside that area, these lawyers fielded calls from lawyers who would be appearing before the Milwaukee judge.[54]

This group of specialist lawyers clearly stood out in my observations, in terms of their confidence, their thoroughness, and their detailed knowledge of the system (both in the legal sense and the people sense). Some of this reflects experience, but that was not all of what was going on; the "toe-to-head" lawyer had actually been in practice for only about a year (he was an associate of one of the other Social Security specialists). The fact that it was only lawyers among those whom I observed who fell into this top group suggests that it might be something about either legal training or who goes to law school. That is, it may simply be that lawyers are more aggressive, more concerned about winning, because of training or self-selection, and this shows up in a particularly strong way in some lawyers who become the top practitioners in their field.

One remaining question is why do the top lawyers tend to be in private practice? I observed two lawyers who did a significant amount of Social Security work as staff members of legal service agencies. While they were both very good, neither was at the level of the top private practitioners. One possible explanation is that caseload pressures or some other factor limited the amount of time and preparation they could devote to Social Security cases. An alternative explanation is that the private-practice lawyers, all of whom handled the cases on a contingency basis, had a clear incentive to win in order to be paid. There are two ways of increasing the likelihood of winning: be very rigorous in screening cases, choosing only easy wins, or take only winnable cases (as opposed to easy wins) and prepare them sufficiently to win. The top practitioners fell into this latter group. This group was very likely to appeal cases that they lost before judges, first to the Appeals Council and then, if necessary, to federal district court.

If this latter explanation, focusing on the no win-no fee incentive structure, is correct, Social Security provides an example of a relatively nice fit between the lawyer's and client's interests. Most of the discussion of contingent fees focuses on the conflicts of interest between lawyers and clients created by the contingent fee in the typical litigation context (e.g., personal injury cases).[55] Much of that conflict is created by the pressures on the lawyer to obtain a quick resolution even if the amount recovered is significantly less than a case is potentially worth. In this context, from the client's viewpoint the stakes are relatively constant (because the stakes are primarily in the form of prospective benefits determined by statute rather than damages that involve highly subjective elements such as pain and suffering or lost future earnings).

The one potential conflict of interest concerns delay. It is in the claimant's interest to obtain a favorable decision as quickly as possible so that he or she can begin receiving benefits as quickly as possible. Given the SSA's policies regarding attorneys' fees—that it will withhold and pay directly to the attorney up to 25 percent of the back Disability Insurance benefits due—the attorney may want the case to sit for a while so that the back benefits build up and the fee will be larger. Interestingly, I have found no manifestations of this potential conflict. None of the judges I talked to informally raised this problem, and I have seen no time-to-disposition breakdowns comparing the time OHA took to dispose of appeals with and without lawyers. This probably indicates that the bulk of the time comes not at the OHA level but at the initial determination and reconsideration levels.[56] Furthermore, the incremental-fee associated with a two- or three-month delay is probably not sufficient to create a real incentive for such a delay; and the attorneys' needs to maintain cash flow probably discourage the types of delays that would have any significant impact on fees.

There is one last, rather subtle, reason that the group of specialist lawyers is more successful than are other representatives, either nonspecialist lawyers or specialist nonlawyer representatives. As I noted previously, a characteristic of these lawyers was their detailed knowledge of the administrative law judges before whom they regularly appeared. This knowledge is mutual: the judges know the lawyers who appear regularly, including which ones come in with strong, thoroughly prepared cases and which ones do not. After one hearing involving one of the lawyer-specialists, the judge remarked to me (with the lawyer still in the room) that the lawyer "always comes in well prepared; some attorneys are less so." One of the lawyers mentioned to me that hearing assistants had reported to him comments made by judges indicating their expectation that he would bring in a thoroughly prepared case, covering any gaps in the exhibits through testimony or by introducing additional exhibits.

The result of the judges' knowledge and expectations of the specialist lawyers may function as a kind of signaling. The judges know that these lawyers would not take the case unless they believed they could prove the disability claim.[57] Furthermore, the judges know that these lawyers will not hesitate to appeal, to federal court if necessary,[58] an unfavorable decision when they have a strong case, and that they will make a strong case on appeal. This does not mean that the judges will automatically grant benefits in cases where these lawyers appear. It does mean that they may give these cases a more thorough look when they are inclined to deny benefits than would be true for nonlawyers or nonspecialist lawyers.

Conclusions: Representation in Social Security Disability Appeals

As with the unemployment compensation setting considered in chapter 2, the big difference in Social Security appeals appears between the represented and unrepresented claimant. In another pattern similar to that of the UC setting, a clear difference occurs among representatives with regard to the specialized expertise they bring to Social Security advocacy. A clearly defined group of nonattorneys demonstrate substantial expertise in the Social Security appeal process. Unlike the situation of the UC setting where few, if any, attorneys are specialists in UC law and the hearing process, the Social Security setting has produced a small but identifiable group of specialists within the legal profession. While in the UC cases the pattern of relative success of lawyer and nonlawyer advocates was inconsistent, Social Security cases show a small but consistent difference between attorney and nonattorney representatives in the aggregate. Based on my observations, I have argued that this gap reflects several factors.

> Differences in the types of cases handled by lawyers and nonlawyers (the DI/SSI distinction)
>
> Greater credibility afforded lawyers by administrative law judges (greater willingness by the judges to allow the attorney to develop the case in the hearing)
>
> The presence of the core group of specialists who (a) are very effective in presenting their cases, and (b) who serve as a cue to judges that a case is very strong
>
> The incentives of the contingent fee structure, which give the typical attorney representative a larger stake in the outcome of his or her

Social Security cases than is true for the nonattorney representatives (many of whom are salaried staff in social service–oriented agencies)

While there is a measurable difference between the success of attorneys and nonattorneys, it is striking how small that difference actually is. The fact that the difference is small may partly reflect the documentary nature of the appeal process: for many, if not most, cases, the key is having the right exhibits. This is a very specific type of technical expertise that has relatively little to do with many of the skills that are taught in law school. Thus, given a knowledge of the rules that govern the system, advocacy skill is going to make a difference largely at the margins. Of course, if you are one of those marginal cases, that difference is very important, although in the Social Security system, if a claimant loses on one application, the claimant can simply start the process over again. The loss may be largely in terms of back benefits rather than future benefits.

CHAPTER 5

Labor Grievance Arbitration

The message of the preceding three chapters is mixed: representation usually makes a clear difference, but the impact of the type of representation presents a much murkier picture. In one setting (tax appeals), the type of representation makes a large difference. In a second (social security disability appeals), it makes at best a very small difference, and in the third (unemployment compensation appeals), it makes no difference at all. In this chapter I turn to a fourth and final venue: grievance arbitration under labor contracts.

What makes this setting interesting is that it *regularly* pits experienced nonlawyer advocates against experienced lawyer advocates. At the same time, there are important differences among lawyer advocates: some are specialists in labor law who do a large volume of grievance arbitration work, while others are generalists (usually members of in-house legal staffs) who spend a relatively small portion of their time on labor issues and an even smaller portion on grievance arbitration. The grievance arbitration, which is usually the last step of a multistep grievance procedure,[1] takes place within the context of a long-term continuing relationship between the union and management.

Like the unemployment compensation cases, grievance arbitration involves an adversarial process.[2] Of the settings I observed, the arbitration hearing most closely resembles the traditional courtroom situation (minus the jury). The arbitrator assumes the role of an umpire rather than taking an inquisitorial approach (as was often the case in the three previous settings). Furthermore, it is not uncommon, at least in some settings, for the parties to employ a court reporter to make a record of the hearing,[3] and the advocates regularly prepare written briefs after the hearing for submission to the arbitrator.[4] However, because of the continuing nature of the relationship between the parties, the adversarial quality of the hearing itself tends to be somewhat muted, as is often evident in the style of cross-examination (e.g., a reluctance to make strong personal accusations, or to bring out negative aspects of past relationships). The formality of the hearing varies, depending upon the preferences of the parties and their advocates. In the words of one arbitrator, "the parties can tailor the procedure to their needs, and many adopt unique systems of their own."

Grievance arbitration arises in the context of contractually based labor–management relationships. Labor contracts normally include a clause outlining specific procedural steps that unions and their members must follow if they encounter grievances arising out of the contract. Some of these grievances are quite broad, involving the interpretation of contract language as it applies to the entire group of covered employees (e.g., the tasks covered by the contract or the circumstances in which specific pay provisions apply). Other grievances concern a single employee (e.g., discharge for misconduct, denial of a request for leave), although how the contract is interpreted in the one employee's case may have implications for other employees.

The grievance procedure normally starts with relatively informal interaction and progresses through a series of increasingly formal steps, at the top of which stands formal arbitration. Courts have generally treated the decision of arbitrators as final, except when there is some claim of impropriety on the part of the arbitrator or a claim that the arbitrator considered issues outside the contract in reaching a decision. Grievances reach the arbitration stage either because efforts to negotiate a resolution have failed or because the dispute is over something one side or the other views as nonnegotiable. A large proportion of cases filed for grievance arbitration do not result in a decision by an arbitrator. Most of these cases settle, although some may be abandoned by the grievant.

The role of the arbitrator in the settlement process varies. Some arbitrators are experienced and trained in mediation;[5] many have no such background. In situations where the parties are paying the arbitrator for his or her services (typically on an hourly basis), the parties do not want the arbitrator to engage in mediating or other time-consuming activities. In some situations, particularly when the parties are not paying the arbitrator by the hour, the person assigned to arbitrate a case might offer his or her services as a mediator before the formal arbitration hearing begins, and in some cases the arbitrator's efforts will lead to a settlement. Similarly, on the day of a scheduled hearing the arbitrator might twiddle his or her thumbs while the parties negotiate a settlement (the grievance arbitration equivalent of a settlement at the courthouse door).

Often there are major unstated issues that have led to the arbitration. There may be ongoing conflict between a worker and his or her supervisor. The grievant may be someone that the union feels some special obligation to defend. The employer may feel it must stand behind a supervisor, even when the supervisor's decision was questionable. These issues may not be formally presented to the arbitrator, but the arbitrator knows that often more is going on than either side reveals.[6] The arbitrator's role is to decide the dispute as it is presented, not as it actually is.

The "law" governing the arbitrator's decision is a combination of the contract itself and past practices. Standards for interpretation come from reported arbitrators' decisions and relevant court cases. If an issue is not explicitly covered by the contract, then the arbitrator will look to past practice to see if there was a clear pattern, and if there is such a pattern, will decide the case consistently with that practice. In some cases there may be relevant contract language, but actual practice does not conform to that language. In those cases, the arbitrator will look to past practice unless there is recent contract language specifically disavowing past practice and evidence that the recent contract language has, in fact, been put into practice (or at least that the disavowal of past practice has itself been held to). Sometimes the question is the interpretation of contract language, with the union and the employer differing as to what the parties intended specific language to mean. This can be particularly troublesome with regard to what was and was not to be covered by a contract clause (that is, even if the language itself is clear, the coverage of the language may be ambiguous). In those cases, the content of bargaining discussions becomes relevant, and the notes maintained by the bargaining participants become important pieces of evidence.

Cases involving discipline, either discharge for cause or some lesser disciplinary action, may turn on different kinds of issues. Usually the contract provisions concerning discipline are not themselves in dispute. In discipline cases, the points of contention are likely to be whether the employee actually committed the act or acts for which the employer imposed discipline, whether the employer followed proper disciplinary procedures (i.e., whether the employer met accepted standards of due process), or whether the discipline imposed was appropriate given the nature of the acts and mitigating circumstances. Thus, factual questions about what did and did not happen can be extremely important, and the values of the arbitrator concerning appropriateness of discipline can come into play. Clearly, the issues dealt with in grievance arbitration can be complex, both regarding the relevant facts and the relevant "law." The nature of the testimony required to establish (1) what happened, (2) what didn't happen that perhaps should have happened, (3) what the contract language was intended to mean, (4) what was meant to be covered by the contract language, and (5) the nature of actual past practice, can be extensive and complicated. The decision in one case can have major implications for future cases, for future contract negotiations, and for future relationships among the parties.

Given this complexity, it should not be surprising that some form of representation is the norm in grievance arbitration. A problem here is defining what is and is not representation. Clearly, the hiring of a lawyer from a private law firm constitutes representation. Similarly, an individual grievant appearing without a lawyer or an officer of the union as his or her advocate is unrepresented. In between these two extremes, a great deal of ambiguity exists. For example, on the employer side, the advocate could be a company employee relations manager who regularly handles grievance arbitrations, or possibly a member of the in-house legal staff, part of whose job is to represent the employer in grievance arbitrations. On the union side, the advocate could be the business manager of the local who periodically does grievance arbitration hearings, or a staff person from a regional service office of the union who regularly does arbitrations for a number of local affiliates of the union (and who might have a master's degree in industrial relations).

The process of selecting the arbitrator who hears a given case is usually spelled out by a clause in the contract. Sometimes this clause will specify that the arbitrator will be provided by an agency such as the American Arbitration Association. Alternately, the selection of the arbitrator can be by mutual agreement of the parties, typically using a list maintained by an organization such as the Federal Mediation and Conciliation Service. Arbitrators are usually experienced individuals, with a background either in labor law or in industrial relations; arbitrators need not be lawyers.[7]

The hearing process itself is formal but flexible. Most standard rules of evidence apply, but because the decision maker is a specialist (rather than a lay jury, as in the typical civil trial), there can be some relaxation regarding issues such as hearsay. In the hearing, the order of presentation depends upon the issue. In discharge or discipline cases, the employer normally presents its case first; in other types of cases (e.g., those dealing with issues such as work assignments, benefits, or pay rates) the union will often present the grievant's case first. Opening statements by the advocates are common. While the proceedings are adversarial rather than inquisitorial, the arbitrator does, on occasion, interject questions to witnesses, either for clarification or to try to get a straight answer from a witness who is being evasive. At the close of testimony, the advocates may make closing statements or choose to file written briefs on a schedule decided upon by the parties and the arbitrator.[8]

The grievance arbitration process is an extremely important part of contemporary labor relations, and, as one might expect, scholars have examined a variety of factors that might influence outcomes.

Experience of the arbitrator[9]
Gender of the arbitrator[10]

Occupation and/or training of the arbitrator[11]
Professional affiliations and activities of the arbitrator[12]
Nature of the grievance[13]
Reason for discharge[14]
Gender of the grievant[15]
Clarity of contract language or employer policies[16]
Occupation of the grievant—e.g., blue collar, white collar, professional[17]
Prior disciplinary record of grievant[18]
Seniority of grievant[19]
Industrial setting—e.g., manufacturing, nonmanufacturing, public—federal or state[20]
Region of the country[21]
Mitigating factors[22]
Volume of grievances involving the parties[23]
Nature of representation of the parties[24]

This is not the place for an extensive review of that research. Of relevance here is the impact of the last of the factors listed above: the nature of the representation of the parties.

Three published studies report the impact of representation.[25] All three operationalize representation simply as lawyer versus nonlawyer. The results of the studies are inconsistent. Two of these studies looked at a mix of types of cases. One was based on a random sample drawn from Arbitrator Case Report forms filed with the American Arbitration Association's national headquarters,[26] and the other used cases published in *Labor Arbitration Reports* and in *Labor Arbitration Awards.*[27] Both studies cross-tabulated the representation variable with outcome and found no statistically significant variations related to the representational combinations (i.e., both sides with an attorney, employer only with an attorney, union only with an attorney, neither side with an attorney). One problem with both of these analyses, at least as reported, is that they do not control for the nature of the grievance.[28] It is possible that attorneys are more important in some types of grievances than in others.

The third study, by Block and Stieber, limited its focus to discharge cases.[29] One could argue that these cases might be the most relevant for attorney representatives, because they often have a quasi-criminal feel to them (I do not by this mean that the discharge was for criminal behavior, but rather that the focus is on the actions of an individual, much as is true in criminal cases). This study, which included controls for factors such as occupational level, gender, and alleged offense of the grievant, found evidence of attorney effects.[30] Another pair of authors who drew upon the

Block and Stieber study described the nature of the effects as akin to a prisoner's dilemma: the two sides may be better off without lawyers, but if either side has a lawyer and the other side does not, the side with a lawyer is advantaged.[31] Those authors summarized Block and Stieber's results as probabilities of grievant success: if neither side had a lawyer, the grievant won 57 percent of the cases and if both sides had a lawyer, the grievant won 65 percent. On the other hand, if only the union had a lawyer, the grievant won 75 percent, and if only the employer had a lawyer, the grievant won only 46 percent. While at first glance, it might appear that the grievant was advantaged even if both sides had a lawyer, Block and Stieber's multivariate analysis found no difference between "no attorneys" and "both sides having attorneys."[32] Presuming a significant cost for attorney representatives, given a choice between just these two options, both sides would have been better off if neither had an attorney.

Assessing the impact of type of representation in the grievance arbitration is more complex than these extant studies take into account. This is not simply a problem of controlling for relevant other factors; rather the more difficult problem is taking into account (1) differences among attorneys (labor specialists versus generalists), (2) nonattorneys who have advanced training in industrial relations and extensive experience handling arbitration, and (3) the reasons arbitration participants have for using a particular type of representative.

The first point I alluded to previously. The extant studies simply distinguish between hearings where an attorney appears for a particular side and where the advocate for that side is not an attorney. In many cases, particularly in public sector grievance arbitrations, the attorney for the employer may be a member of the inside legal staff who performs a variety of legal tasks; some very large employers may have inside attorneys who are labor law specialists, although I suspect this is relatively rare. On the other hand, an inside attorney working for a union, or an outside attorney for either the employer or the union, is almost certainly going to be a labor law specialist with extensive and varied arbitration experience. An inside nonspecialist might do two arbitration hearings a year while a specialist might be doing two or more arbitration hearings a month.[33] The latter group will have a better knowledge of the arbitrators and of similar cases that might suggest effective ways of presenting the instant case to the arbitrator.

On the nonlawyer side there are important distinctions as well. Specifically, in comparing lawyers and nonlawyers, the presumption is that one is comparing professional advocates with lay advocates. If the union's advocate is the local union's business agent who has come up through the union ranks, this may well be true (particularly in blue-collar unions). On the other hand, many unions have highly professionalized staffs, particularly at the regional council level. Individuals on this staff may have master's degrees in industrial relations and extensive experience handling grievance arbitrations. Like the labor attorney, a staffer from a union council might handle two or more grievance arbitrations a month and have a good working knowledge of the preferences and predilections of individual arbitrators. Furthermore, these regional representatives or service agents may well have been directly involved in negotiating the contract under which the grievance arose and can build on that knowledge to make a case for the union's interpretation when there are differences over how contract language should be interpreted.

In thinking about these different types of representatives, we should consider one other point from the prior chapter. Recall that in Social Security disability appeals, lawyers appeared to have a small but consistent edge over nonlawyers. I argued that this was probably attributable to lawyers who specialized in Social Security work. More specifically, I argued that specialist lawyers could be expected to have an edge over specialist nonlawyers for two reasons: they had a stake in the outcome because they were to be paid on a contingency-fee basis; and lawyers might be expected to be more competitive and win-oriented than the nonlawyers who tended to come out of a social service background. Neither of those differences exists in this setting. Labor lawyers handling grievance arbitration do not work on a contingency-fee basis; moreover, the nonlawyers handling grievance arbitration come out of an industrial relations background and could be expected to be just as competitive and win-oriented as are the lawyers handling grievance arbitration.

One of the problems in comparing lawyer and nonlawyer advocates is the selection problem: lawyers may be used in cases that differ from the cases handled by nonlawyers. No doubt, some parties involved in grievances make strategic decisions regarding representation, at least in some cases. On the other hand, the types of advocates handling grievances may have less to do with strategic considerations than with standard operating procedures. In the discussion below I will present some evidence on this question.

The Setting: Wisconsin Employment Relations Commission

My data and observation come from grievance arbitration cases decided by staff arbitrators working for the Wisconsin Employment Relations Commission (WERC). The WERC is a state agency that provides neutral arbitrators and mediators to deal with public sector labor disputes.[34] In addition, any private employer in the state of Wisconsin may use the services of WERC staff for a nominal fee ($25 in grievance arbitration cases). Besides grievance arbitrations, WERC handles the full range of mediation in the labor-management setting and contract arbitrations.[35]

WERC employs twenty persons who regularly work as arbitrators.[36] Most, but not all, of the staff arbitrators are attorneys.[37] As is true generally in the labor setting, regular participants in arbitration make efforts to keep track of preferences and propensities of individual arbitrators. The relatively small number of WERC arbitrators facilitates this process. The reputation of the individual WERC arbitrators varies somewhat among the regular participants, but the parties can jointly request that a specific arbitrator be assigned to the case, and some contracting parties identify a list of specific WERC arbitrators from which they will draw in a rotating pattern to hear any cases that arise. In the course of a year, WERC staff will decide ("issue awards") in about two hundred grievance arbitration cases, most (75 to 80 percent) of them involving public sector employers.[38]

One cautionary note about my use of the WERC as the source of cases is that having a small number of arbitrators decide cases on a repeated basis for a set of parties differs from other grievance arbitration settings. The WERC arbitrators, in effect, constitute what is referred to as a "closed panel system." In an "open panel system," where the arbitrators are either provided or selected from a large list, the players may not know the propensities of the arbitrators as well as may be the case with WERC arbitrators.[39] Advocates who do a high volume of arbitrations may be advantaged more in this system. Thus, one needs to be careful generalizing my findings to all venues handling labor grievance arbitration.

The Data

I have four different types of data from the WERC setting. First is observation of hearings. These hearings tend to be considerably longer than those in the other settings in this study, and sometimes extend across several days, usually in a discontinuous fashion. Furthermore, these hearings are not public events, although the calendar of WERC hearings is public, making it easy to identify dates when hearings were to be held. I observed hearings in whole or part for ten cases (a total of about thirty hours of hearing time).[40] These hearings involved a mix of types of representatives: outside and inside lawyers for employers, as well as nonlawyer employer representatives, and both lawyer and nonlawyer union advocates.

Second, I have data compiled from grievance arbitration awards issued by WERC arbitrators. Working from the awards themselves, I coded 576 cases in the three-year period from January 2, 1992, through

October 9, 1994.[41] This covered almost all of the awards issued during this period. I omitted consent awards, supplemental awards, and a few cases where I was unable to code the award due to insufficient information. In addition to the decision, I coded the type of issue, the type of union involved, and the type of representatives each side employed. For cases involving discipline, I also coded the nature of the allegation, the type of employee, the gender of the employee, and the length of employment. In the data set, I also recorded the names of the parties, representatives, and arbitrator.

A small sample mail survey of advocates in WERC cases constitutes the third set of data. Using the files from one year (which included the names and addresses of advocates)[42] I took a sample of cases from these files and listed the advocates. Many advocates appeared multiple times; for those advocates, I chose one case at random. A four-page mail questionnaire was sent to a total of 32 employer representatives and 34 union representatives.[43] I received an excellent response rate: 28 employer responses (87 percent) and 26 union responses (76 percent). The survey included questions about the nature of the explicit issue, the presence of any unstated issues, the amount of money (if any) at stake, whether anything at the hearing came as a surprise to the representative, size of the bargaining unit, why the case did not settle, the amount of time the representative devoted to preparing for the hearing and writing the post-hearing brief, and the arbitrators' training and experience.

The final set of data takes advantage of the practice of preparing written, post-hearing briefs. I identified six briefs written by each of four types of representatives (a total of 24 briefs): nonlawyer employer representatives, lawyers representing employers, nonlawyer union representatives, and lawyers representing unions. I then sent a randomly selected subset of four briefs to samples of arbitrators, labor law teachers, labor lawyers, law students, and undergraduates, asking the respondents to identity the type of author of each of the four briefs. This experiment provides information on one of the most "lawyerly" of activities: preparing formal written arguments concerning fact and law. It seeks to answer the question of how well nonlawyers carry out this activity.

The Arbitration Hearing

Because of the relatively small number of hearings I observed, I would not expect to be able to identify subtle differences among types of advocates, and particularly differences in how various types of advocates interact. Nonetheless, the hearings made clear why, at least in some types of cases, formal legal training may not be central to effectiveness.

The Role of History in Grievance Arbitration

The Hospital

One of the crucial questions in many arbitrations focuses on the intersection of past practices with contract negotiations. That is, there is little dispute over what is currently being done; rather, the dispute concerns whether current practice is consistent either with express contract language or with past practice. The latter is important when there is not express language covering a particular issue or when a consistent pattern of past practice runs counter to contract language (i.e., contract language has, in fact, been ignored).

Take, for example, a case involving a large hospital and its nurses' union. The issue concerned shift-differential pay for nurses who worked certain shifts that included one-half hour during the time in which the differential was normally paid. More specifically, were certain employees entitled to receive the differential from 11:00 to 11:30 P.M. and/or from 7:00 to 7:30 A.M.? The hospital was represented by a labor law attorney from one of the largest law firms in Wisconsin; the union was represented by a nonlawyer who provided services, including representation, for nurses' unions in eastern Wisconsin.

The first witness for the union was the chief steward, who had served on the bargaining team that negotiated the current contract. This witness testified about the negotiations that had resulted in the current contract (with the advocate asking her to consult her notes from the negotiation, which were introduced as exhibits). She also testified about past practices (from her own experience working shifts involving the differential) and the history of particular contract language. The witness was clearly well prepared for her testimony, and the union's nonlawyer representative was intimately familiar with the issues, the contract, and the history in a way that allowed her to elicit the testimony efficiently.

The core issue, for at least part of the grievance, was the question of retroactivity: the hospital had begun to pay the differential for the 7:00 to 7:30 time period after the grievance had been raised, but was not willing to make retroactive adjustments back to the beginning of the contract. The union representative knew that this would be a difficult issue and was well prepared to deal with it, providing exhibits demonstrating how retroactivity had been dealt with in the past and showing that the employees' check stubs did not make it clear what rate was being paid.

In this hearing it was clear that the representative's long-standing and extensive involvement in the local's activities facilitated her advocacy. She knew how past grievances had been handled, the history of contract language and negotiations, and the nature of past practices. She was able to combine these to make a strong case very efficiently (the union called only one other witness and presented all of its evidence in less than one hour). The efforts of the hospital's attorney to undercut the union witnesses on cross-examination were unsuccessful.

In contrast to the union's representative, the hospital's attorney was clearly an outsider. He sought to undercut some of the union's testimony with witnesses from the hospital administration, but he did not seem to be directly acquainted with either past practices or the negotiations. He worked from a checklist of questions, which tended to elicit broad statements rather than specific events or experiences. He asked one witness, the director of payroll accounting, whether the union's first witness had worked shifts that would have involved the differential (as the witness testified she had). The director testified that "the payroll records for Ms. X showed no evidence that Ms. X had worked those shifts in 1989 or before"; however, while Ms. X testified from direct experience, the payroll director testified based on records which could have, but were not, introduced as exhibits. (If the records were complete, and they did show that Ms. X had not worked the claimed shifts, why did the hospital's attorney decide not to introduce the records as an exhibit?)[44]

In summary, here was a case that relied heavily on history. The non-lawyer, regional representative's intimate knowledge of bargaining history and past practice directly facilitated her development and presentation of the case. In my sample of WERC cases, this union's representative handled ten cases over the three-year period, winning six (including the case described here); this compares to an overall union success rate in my sample of 37 percent.[45]

The Groundskeeper
A second case further illustrates the role of history, and of the knowledge of history, in the resolution of grievance arbitration cases. In this case, outside attorneys represented both the union and the employer (a school district). The district was responsible for both school programs (including school athletics) and recreational programs, including maintenance of relevant facilities. Full-time staff handled the former, while seasonal staff handled most of the latter. The grievance concerned the district's use of seasonal recreational staff to perform baseball field maintenance duties on Saturdays, rather than bringing in full-time staff on overtime.

Much of the testimony in this case revolved around the nature of past practice, particularly distinguishing between immediate preparation of playing fields for scheduled games and long-term maintenance. The union's lawyer sought to build a case based on past practices and past grievances. She showed that the district had apparently acknowledged the entitlement of bargaining unit members to overtime, and that on several occasions the district compensated persons who were not called in when they perhaps should have been. The district's lawyer effectively countered this testimony by getting the union's witness to acknowledge that all of the past incidents had concerned maintenance on days when games were scheduled. In addition, he demonstrated that the prior grievance settlements stipulated that those settlements applied during the then-current labor contract, and that it specifically said that the settlements were non-precedental (although on redirect, the witness stated that the practice outlined in the settlements actually continued after the labor agreement had expired).

Testimony of additional union witnesses also focused on past practice. The unchallenged testimony established that (1) bargaining unit members had frequently worked with seasonal recreational staff, both on regular time and overtime, (2) bargaining unit members had on a number of occasions declined overtime when it was offered, (3) bargaining unit members had worked Saturday overtime in the past, (4) the union did not know whether Saturday work in the past had sometimes been performed by seasonal recreation staff, and (5) there was no "jurisdiction clause" in the current contract guaranteeing the maintenance work on the ball field (or any other tasks) to bargaining unit members.[46]

In presenting the school district's case, the district's lawyer sought to establish the procedures for assigning overtime, and the significance of the settlement of a prior grievance concerning overtime with the local (which represents various maintenance and custodial workers). From the district's viewpoint, the latter was extremely important. The district had made a one-time payment to the union in return for an agreement that the assignment of overtime was at the discretion of the district. The (former) superintendent recounted the details of that earlier grievance (which concerned after-hours building checks) and the settlement that the district reached with the local; the district's position was that the settlement covered all overtime involving the local. Interestingly, the district's position regarding the general overtime issue went largely unchallenged; the union's lawyer did try to shake the witness's position that the agreement applied to this grievance, but did not produce any witnesses to testify to the background of that earlier settlement or the union's understanding of that settlement.

In the previous case (the hospital case), the union representative had a witness testify in detail about prior agreements, including reference to and introduction of union members' notes of those negotiating sessions. There are two interpretations of the union's lack of response to the district's position on this issue: either the central role it played in the district's case surprised the union's lawyer, or the union did not have an effective counter to it. My sense is that the lawyer was not fully briefed on this issue, and that it did come as something of a surprise. I suspect that the lawyer had not played a role in negotiating the earlier agreement (which was probably handled by a nonlawyer regional representative) and had relied upon members of the bargaining unit to identify the central issues for development in the hearing. If the union had been represented by someone with more intimate, direct knowledge of the background, that representative might have been better prepared for this issue.[47] However, even anticipating the general overtime agreement, the union would probably have lost. The arbitrator's decision relied on the past practice which dealt only with overtime for day-of-game maintenance, not long-term maintenance.[48]

Regardless of the outcome, both representatives in this case were extremely professional and comfortable with the arbitration hearing process. The lawyer representing the union here was more "lawyer-like" in her conduct of the case and questioning of witnesses than was the nonlawyer representing the nurses' union. However, the case turned not on skill in questioning witnesses but in the details of history that the nonlawyer had a better grasp of due to the nature of her involvement in the union than did the lawyer.

The Problem of Detail

Some of the cases decided by labor arbitrators concern very specific, and at times confusing, details. Effective advocacy in those cases requires both a grasp of the particular details and skill in presenting them. One such case concerned a total of 15½ vacation days for five employees of a school district. In this case, the district was represented by an outside lawyer from a major management-oriented labor law firm, and the union was represented by a nonlawyer regional representative.

The grievance arose when the district changed the way it calculated employees' entitlement to vacation. The change was complicated by the fact that, as acknowledged by both sides, past practice and contract language were inconsistent. The contract stated that employees accrued vacation on their anniversary date of employment; that is, an employee entitled to ten days of vacation per year who was first employed on October 15 did not earn those vacation days until October 15 of each year. Until 1984, the practice had been to treat vacation as accruing throughout the year, allowing employees to take days off prior to their first anniversary date. (One reason for doing this was that things were slow during the summer, and the district preferred that an employee who began work on October 15 take some vacation days that first summer, rather than using lots of vacation time during the school year.)

The contract was then changed so that vacation accrued on January 1 each year (rather than on the employee's anniversary date); new employees had to get through two January 1's before they became entitled to any vacation. The grievance was over how much vacation employees who had started their employment prior to 1984 should be credited with in the transition from anniversary date to January 1. In particular, how should days taken in advance of the anniversary date be treated? The employer sought to deduct all vacation days taken prior to the first anniversary date from what was now being credited to the employees; the union argued that those dates should not be subtracted. As I understood what transpired at the hearing, the key question sounded like it revolved around when the vacation days in question had actually been taken. If those days had been taken before the first anniversary date, one side's position seemed more equitable, while if they had been taken between the first anniversary date and the January 1 after the anniversary date the other side's position was more equitable. It did not seem that the contract language was specific as to how this should be handled.

Interestingly, neither representative presented testimony that spoke to this point, although exhibits introduced at the hearing did, according to one witness, contain that information. When the union's representative started asking questions of the witness about the accuracy of those documents, the district's lawyer started objecting to one question after another. The arbitrator overruled those objections, and it may have been that the lawyer was trying to intimidate the union's representative. Things got so argumentative at one point that the court reporter who was trying to take down the testimony became angry and told those present she could not make an accurate record if they continued in that style.[49]

While I have presented the issue as one of equitably handling vacation days taken in the past in calculating entitlements after the transition to the January 1 accrual date, there is another way of looking at what was going on. The union may have been trying to gain extra vacation days for the five employees by using this transition as a way of getting the early vacation days involved "forgiven." The union's statement of the issue suggests that this might be the case: "Did the parties waive prior claims of vacation given or not given, and wipe the slate clean when the shift was made to the January 1 accrual date?" The district's lawyer suggested as much when he argued that the union was "allocating more vacation than called for under the contract." If the vacation days in question had been taken before the first anniversary date (rather than between the first anniversary date and January 1), the district's position that the union was trying to get something extra would be correct.

This question becomes irrelevant if the negotiations dealt explicitly with the transition issue. As previously noted, neither of the representatives seemed to pursue the question of what transpired in the negotiations about the January 1 accrual date. The *arbitrator* asked one of the district's witnesses what had been communicated during the negotiation about repudiation of past practice and got a nonresponsive, roundabout answer. When the union decided to call no witnesses, the arbitrator asked if anyone present from the union could provide information on this point and ended up swearing in the union's representative at the hearing, who referred to his notes on the negotiation to give the union's position on this question.

Most of the testimony concerned past practices (about which there seemed to be no disagreement). The arbitrator at one point specifically asked how the district arrived at its calculation of what had been used and should be deducted from the employees' accrued vacation. The answer was not particularly helpful. The arbitrator's award was in favor of the district, finding (1) the negotiations leading to the shift to January 1 did not "forgive" any vacation days previously advanced and (2) all of the days at issue had been taken before the anniversary dates of the various employees. The arbitrator observed that no one actually lost anything as a result of her decision.

The Role of Experience

One of the striking aspects about the representatives in grievance arbitration is that most have significant experience. For example, in my survey of representatives, I asked the representatives how long they had been handling grievance arbitration cases. The mean for union representatives was 14.3 years and the mean for employer representatives was 16.4 years. Only three of fifty-four (about 5 percent) representatives had less than five years of experience, and only ten (less than 20 percent) had less than ten years of experience.

One hearing I observed in which the union's representative lacked experience made clear its importance. This was a difficult case, and even a very experienced advocate would have been unlikely to prevail. The case involved the discharge of a longtime employee whose classic case of midlife crisis had resulted in severe problems in his family relationships, which, in turn, led to drug abuse. The discharged employee operated heavy equipment for a parks and recreation department of a small city. The event that immediately precipitated the discharge was involvement in two accidents, one of which he did not report to his supervisor. One point that never came out in the hearing, but that I learned later, was that substantial hostility existed between the supervisor and bargaining unit members, prompting many to believe that the supervisor had been looking for an excuse to fire someone as a means of getting even.

The city's representative was an experienced outside attorney; the union's representative was a regional representative who had been on the job for only one or two years. Because this was a discharge case, the initial burden was on the employer to show that the discharge was for just cause. The employer asked that the witnesses be sequestered (excluded from the hearing room so that a witness could not hear the testimony of those before him or her). The opening statements by the advocates were brief. The employer's lawyer simply stated that the grievant had been involved in two accidents, one of which he did not report. Furthermore, the grievant had been suspended a year earlier as a result of prior driving infractions and an accident. The union's representative did not dispute the events that led to the discharge, but noted: (1) that the grievant had a virtually untainted work record until two years ago, (2) that mitigating circumstances in the grievant's personal life accounted for the problems that had occurred, and (3) that the employer had made no efforts to assist the grievant in dealing with those problems.

The employer called only two witnesses. The first was the victim in the unreported accident. The victim, whose car had been parked at the time it was struck by the heavy truck the grievant was driving, knew the grievant. When the witness discovered that his car had been damaged, he called the police. Before the police got back to him, the grievant called and explained what had happened (the grievant recognized the car after he struck it), and he offered to pay for the damages. There was no cross-examination of this witness.

The employer's second witness was the grievant's supervisor. In response to questions by the employer's lawyer, the supervisor

> recounted the grievant's disciplinary record, introducing at appropriate times notes of his meetings with the grievant (which were then offered as exhibits);
> detailed the cost of the damages to the first witness's vehicle;
> described the disciplinary steps taken; and
> reviewed the work rules requiring employees to report any accidents immediately to the police department.

When specifically asked, "Why did you decide to dismiss [the grievant]?" the supervisor replied, "His driving record created a hazard on the highway, which, in turn, created liability for the city."

The union representative's cross-examination of the supervisor was long and detailed. Much of that examination focused on whether the supervisor was aware of anything that might account for the grievant's change in performance. Many of the responses to these questions were "I don't recall," or "I'm not sure." Many of the one-word responses ("yes," "no," "correct") were inconsistent, for example,

> *Q:* Were you aware that he was arrested and convicted of DWI?
> *A:* Yes.
> *Q:* Would this suggest a problem with alcohol or drugs?
> *A:* No.

As I watched this exchange, I recorded in my notes that the "witness really seems to be stonewalling." Nevertheless, the representative was not able to shake the witness from his position. The situation I observed was an obvious one for strong, leading questions. The representative showed no evidence of being able to use leading questions with an intransigent witness. For example, at one point the representative asked, "Do you remember making a comment on April 27 that there was a change in [the grievant's] attitude?" The representative could have asked something like the following: "Isn't it true that in April you said to John Jones that [the grievant's] whole attitude toward his job had changed?"

The union's case consisted of testimony from the grievant and several supporting witnesses. The primary points of the union's case were (1) that the employer must have known of the grievant's serious personal problems, (2) that available disciplinary alternatives short of dismissal (such as moving the grievant to a position where he would not operate heavy equipment) were not considered, and (3) that, given the grievant's problems, the employer should have made an effort to refer him to the employee assistance program that was intended to help employees with severe personal difficulties that interfered with their job performance.

The grievant's own testimony primarily emphasized the personal turmoil he had been going through. No effort was made to deny the incidents that led to the discharge, although the grievant stated a belief that one of the accidents was not entirely his fault. The union's representative also asked the grievant to explain what steps he had taken to get his life back in order. The cross-examination of the grievant by the employer's lawyer, which was relatively brief, emphasized that the grievant knew he violated work rules by not reporting the accident, and that the grievant had not sought to explain his personal problems to his supervisor.

This was a tough case for the union, and perhaps not winnable by any advocate. The arbitrator's decision took account of the grievant's personal problems and the grievant's efforts to deal with those problems, particularly the substance abuse. However, the arbitrator noted that the grievant had received ample warning that he was in trouble and had waited until after the last incident to try to do something about the core substance problem. Furthermore, the city had fully complied with its progressive discipline policy, and the grievant had been explicitly warned prior to the last pair of accidents that any further incidents could result in disciplinary action "up to and including discharge." Still, one must ask whether a more experienced representative, more skilled at cross-examination, could have obtained admissions from the employer's witnesses that they were specifically aware of the grievant's problems and had decided to leave the grievant to his own devices. If such an admission had been obtained, along with some explicit indication that supervisory personnel had discussed, but not acted on, the option of telling the grievant to get help from the employee assistance plan, the arbitrator might have concluded that while the employer had fulfilled the requirements of its progressive disciplinary policy, it had failed to act in good faith.

Going Through the Motions

In some cases, it appears that at least one side is simply going through the motions of presenting its case. Usually this involves situations where one side is pursuing the grievance for reasons other than the grievance itself. For example, in one case the director of a county nursing home had unilaterally decided that employees would not be permitted to take personal days under certain circumstances. From the director's viewpoint, the change in policy was reasonable, but it unilaterally modified long-standing practices. The county sent a lawyer from its corporation counsel's office to represent the nursing home (the union's advocate was a nonlawyer regional representative), and this representative mounted a minimal defense. The case was so clear that the arbitrator offered to make an on-the-spot ruling, but the county's representative declined, probably because he wanted to save the supervisor the immediate embarrassment. One might ask why the county did not simply resolve the grievance at an earlier stage and avoid arbitration. Probably the nursing home director's superiors felt it necessary to back the director, even though she had made a mistake in changing the leave policy without consulting the union and/or her superiors. Perhaps they felt that the director would learn something about how to handle such issues in the future by going all the way through the grievance process and losing.

In a second case, which actually consisted of at least two cases involving the same grievant, it was the union that may have been going through the motions. The union's representative was a nonlawyer regional representative, and the employer, a small city, brought in an outside lawyer.[50] I observed most of the hearing concerning one grievance and a fragment concerning the other. The one I saw the most of involved a letter sent by the city to the employee concerning her job performance. The employee "grieved" the city, claiming that the letter constituted disciplinary action and was not justified by her actual performance. The city's position was that the letter did not constitute disciplinary action, but was simply a performance evaluation warranted under the circumstances. If the letter did not constitute discipline, then it was not subject to a grievance. Interestingly, in one sense, the union lost the arbitration because the arbitrator found that the letter was justified, but in another sense the union won because the arbitrator found that the letter did constitute discipline and hence was properly the subject of a grievance over whether there was just cause for disciplinary action.

More problematic was the second grievance (of which I saw only a small part of the hearing but did read the full decision). This grievance concerned whether the city could properly forbid employees who were members of the volunteer ambulance crew from going on ambulance runs during work hours. The union claimed that past practice made such activities a form of benefit to the employees, and that by unilaterally forbidding the employees from engaging in this activity, the union had withdrawn a benefit. The employees involved in the case were active union members, and I suspect that the union viewed the city's action as a way of harassing the union.

In fact, at the hearing, it became clear that there was substantial hostility between union and management. I had no way of assessing the basis of that hostility or of determining whether the city was out to get the employees in these cases (one of whom was the spouse of the local president) or whether it was merely dealing with a nonproductive employee, seeking to end employee activities (going on ambulance runs) that disrupted work routines. What was clear from various indications was that each side questioned the truthfulness of the other side's witnesses.

Why did the union pursue these grievances? Clearly, the grievant in the first case was having significant conflicts with her supervisors. Because I saw relatively little of the hearing in the second case, it was not clear how disruptive the absences for ambulance runs were to work flow, or whether permitting such activities constituted a past practice. The union obviously wanted to make the point to the city that it would fight various actions the city took, particularly when those actions seemed to be targeted at union leadership. While the union did not formally prevail in these two cases, it did force the city to incur substantial expense, in the form of outside legal fees. Moreover, in another case involving the discharge of the same grievant as in the first case, the union lost at arbitration but successfully appealed the arbitrator's decision to Circuit Court on the grounds that the arbitrator's decision went beyond permissible criteria.[51]

Assessment and Summary

No clear picture emerges from the observations. The nonlawyer representatives I observed appeared to have a combination of experience and intimate knowledge of past practices, negotiations, and ongoing relationships that allowed them to do a reasonable job of representation; furthermore, at least on the union side, many of the nonlawyers had attended training courses on handling grievance arbitration.[52] Experienced outside labor lawyers had technical skills (e.g., methods of intimidating opposing advocates, very good cross-examination and questioning skills, brief-writing experience, etc.) that could potentially give them an advantage. However, these advantages may have been undercut by lack of detailed, ongoing familiarity.

Winning and Losing in Grievance Arbitration

My sample of cases from the WERC decisions permits an analysis of the overall outcome patterns in the grievance cases decided by WERC arbitrators. Because only the arbitrators' decisions were readily available, I limited my analysis to variables that I could readily code from the text of the decision. One could imagine other variables—such as prior grievances, amount of time and effort put into preparing for the hearing,[53] some measure of case merits, and so on—that might predict outcome, but which I did not have available. As one considers the results of my analysis, the limitations of the information I used should be kept in mind.

One minor problem in analyzing these data arises in coding the outcomes. In most cases, the arbitrators either "sustain" the grievance, meaning that the union wins, or "deny" the grievance, meaning that the employer wins. Some grievances involve multiple issues and produce a split outcome, and in some grievances, particularly disciplinary grievances, the arbitrator determines that there was "just cause" for discipline but that the discipline imposed was excessive. To measure outcome, I created an indicator that I coded 1 for sustained and 0 for denied; this covered 92 percent of the 575 cases that were codable. For the remaining 8 percent of cases with mixed outcomes, I coded the outcome as .5 when it appeared to be a fairly even split decision, .75 when it seemed weighted toward the union, and .25 when it seemed weighted toward the employer.

In coding outcomes, I was not able to deal with more subtle aspects of winning and losing. Recall, for example, the case I described above in which the employer had sent the grievant a letter critical of the employee's work performance. The grievant claimed that this letter (1) constituted discipline, and (2) did not have just cause (i.e., was unwarranted). The employer claimed that (1) the letter did not constitute discipline (and hence was not properly the subject of a grievance), and (2) in any case, was warranted by the grievant's job performance. The arbitrator denied the grievance, and I coded the case as a win for the employer. However, in denying the grievance, the arbitrator found that the letter did constitute discipline (and hence was properly the subject of a grievance) but that there was just cause for issuing the letter. While the union was disappointed that the letter stayed in the employee's personnel file, it could view the decision as a partial victory because of the finding that the employer's action was disciplinary. My coding does not take account of these subtleties, because to do so would have required going well beyond the decisions themselves, which were the basis of my coding.

In my analyses, I handled the outcome variable in one of two ways. In those analyses that did not require me to reduce the variable to a dichotomy, I computed the mean of the outcome variable. For purposes of discussion, however, I treat this mean as if it were the proportion of cases won by the union, which I will usually report as a percentage. In some multivariate analyses, I either dropped from the analysis those cases that I had not coded as clear wins and losses for the union, or I collapsed the partial wins and losses with the full wins and losses (omitting the "ties").

Table 12 shows the outcomes, indicated by the percentage of grievances won by the union, for all cases, for discipline cases, and for discharge cases. The table controls for the general type (lawyer versus nonlawyer) of representative used by both sides. Strikingly, there is no evidence of differential outcomes for lawyers and nonlawyers in this table. While, for example, the percentage of cases won by lawyer representatives appearing on behalf of unions is somewhat higher than the percentage for nonlawyers, the differences are not statistically significant (meaning that the observed difference could easily arise by chance). Furthermore, in contrast to the Block and Stieber study, which did report a difference between lawyers and nonlawyers in discharge cases, the patterns for all discipline cases and for cases involving discharge are the same as for all cases taken together.

Table 13 shows the differences in union success for all cases when I open up the categories of representatives in the analysis. This table shows three types of union representatives: lawyers, regional nonlawyer representatives, and local nonlawyer representatives. For employers, it shows four types of representatives: outside lawyers, inside lawyers, outside nonlawyers, and inside nonlawyers. There are relatively few in the outside nonlawyer category. Considering only the marginals, this table does, on first examination, suggest some patterns. First, for unions overall, lawyers seem to do the best (42 percent win rate), followed by regional representatives (37 percent win rate), and then by local representatives (31 percent win rate). However, if one applies standard statistical tests (in this case, a chi-square for a 3 by 2 table), the result indicates that this pattern could reflect nothing more than random sampling effects ($\chi^2 = 2.453$, $p < .05$). Similarly, overall for employers, it appears that inside lawyers achieve less success (losing in 45 percent of cases) in grievance arbitration than do the other types of employer representatives (losing in 35 to 38 percent of cases). However, standard statistical tests again indicate that this pattern could easily be attributed to random variations.

Looking at the body of the table rather than the marginals suggests

TABLE 12. Union Success by Legal Background of Representatives (in percentages)

Type of Union Representative	Type of Employer Representative		
	Lawyer	Non-lawyer	All
Lawyer	**44**	**23**	**42**
	(127)	**(14)**	**(141)**
	41	*[38]*	*41*
	(47)	*(4)*	*(51)*
	36	[33]	35
	(28)	(3)	(31)
Non-lawyer	**36**	**38**	**36**
	(316)	**(112)**	**(428)**
	34	*31*	*33*
	(67)	*(33)*	*(100)*
	34	31	32
	(32)	(18)	(50)
All	**38**	**36**	**38**
	(444)	**(126)**	**(569)**
	37	*32*	*36*
	(114)	*(37)*	*(151)*
	35	31	34
	(60)	(21)	(81)

Source: Wisconsin Employment Relations Commission decisions, coded by the author.

Note: Figures in bold are for all cases; figures in italic are for discharge and other discipline cases; figures in roman are for discharge cases only. Partial "wins" may account for some percentages that appear to be inconsistent with the number of cases; figures in parentheses are number of cases.

For all cases, $\chi^2 = 5.06$, $p > .10$.

For discharge and other discipline cases, $\chi^2 = 1.29$, $p > .10$.

For discharge cases only, $\chi^2 = 0.03$, $p > .10$.

some possible patterns that would not be evident in table 12. First, some combinations are relatively unusual. For example, when the union employs a lawyer as a representative, the employer is very unlikely to use a nonlawyer: overall employers use nonlawyers in 22 percent of the cases, but in only 10 percent of the cases when the union is represented by a lawyer. The employer uses an outside lawyer in 53 percent of the cases overall; interestingly, this is more often the case when the union has a regional nonlawyer representative (74 percent of those cases) than when the union has an outside lawyer (56 percent of those cases). While one might think the two sides make strategic choices in the type of representative employed, this pattern is not consistent with that kind of strategic behavior. Otherwise, one might expect that employers would be most likely to turn to outside lawyers when the union used a lawyer as its representative.

Of more importance is the possibility that differences in outcome may depend upon the pairing of types of representatives, but not simply as lawyers and nonlawyers. This can readily be seen by focusing on the two by two subtable formed by the first two rows and first two columns of table 13 (lawyers and regional representatives for unions, versus outside and inside lawyers for employers; see boxed area). The difference that appears here is that when a regional union representative faces an outside lawyer, the regional representative wins only about 31 percent of the cases; for the other pair-offs, the union win rate is fairly constant in the 42 to 46 percent range. That is, the nonlawyer regional union representative does just as well against the inside, nonspecialist lawyer as does a union lawyer does against either the outside lawyer or the inside lawyer.

TABLE 13. Union Success by Type of Representatives (in percentages)

Type of Union Representative	Type of Employer Representative				
	Outside Lawyer	Inside Lawyer	Outside Nonlawyer	Inside Nonlawyer	All
Lawyer	46	42	—	17	42
	(79)	(48)	(1)	(13)	(141)
Regional Nonlawyer	31	45	34	43	37
	(201)	(93)	(16)	(63)	(373)
Local Nonlawyer	28	[65]	—	27	31
	(17)	(5)	(0)	(32)	(54)
All	35	45	38	35	38
	(297)	(146)	(17)	(108)	(568)

Source: Wisconsin Employment Relations Commission decisions, coded by the author.

Note: Partial "wins" may account for some percentages that appear to be inconsistent with the number of cases. Figures in parentheses are number of cases.

Other figures in table 13 reinforce the point that the distinctive player here may be the outside lawyer representing an employer: the inside lawyer facing a regional nonlawyer union representative does no better (losing 45 percent) than does the inside nonlawyer (losing 43 percent). I suspect many of the apparent anomalies in table 13 reflect the small number of cases in the anomalous cells (e.g., the low win rate for union lawyers against inside nonlawyers, or the high win rate for local nonlawyer union representatives against inside lawyers).

The technical statistical term for the type of pattern in the body of table 13 is *interaction:* the impact of the type of advocate representing the union depends on the type representing the employer (and vice versa). Testing whether these differences could be attributable to chance requires dropping the third column, because of the small number of cases. Applying to this reduced table a method for analyzing interactions in contingency tables, which resembles analysis of variance,[54] produces a statistic that barely misses achieving the standard criterion for statistical significance ($\chi^2 = 9.17$, $df = 4$, $p = .057$).[55]

This result suggests that type of representative might well make a difference in grievance arbitration, but that the traditional categories of lawyer versus nonlawyer hide possibly important patterns. Table 14 collapses table 13 into a two by two table in a different way that is more consistent with the internal patterns in table 13. As with table 12, there are two categories for each type of representation: for the union side it is the original lawyer/nonlawyer category, but for the employer side the dichotomy is outside lawyer versus other type of representative (including both inside lawyers and nonlawyers).

The statistical analysis of this table suggests clearly that the type of representative might make a difference, but that the interaction of the two representatives is what matters. One particular combination stands out: an outside lawyer representing an employer does better against a nonlawyer union representative. The other combinations do not differ from one another. The simplest way to see this effect is from an analysis (labeled "Special Model" in table 14) that simply allows the nonlawyer union representative versus the outside employer lawyer combination to differ from the weighted average of the other three representative combinations. This weighted average is a union success rate of 41.9 percent compared to a success rate of 30.6 percent for the union nonlawyer versus the outside employer lawyer. This difference is strongly significant statistically ($\chi^2 = 7.20$, $p = .007$).[56]

Table 15 introduces controls for type of case using the new categorization of type of representative. I have used three categories of case type: dismissal/discharge, discipline short of dismissal, and other type of case.

Clearly the basic pattern of union nonlawyer versus employer outside lawyer deviating from the other representational situations holds up.[57] Analysis of this table shows that the only statistically significant effect in the table is this specific interaction between the type of representative used by the union and by the employer ($\chi^2 = 4.25$, $p = .039$).[58] There are no significant variations by type of issue (at least using the very simple classification used here). Fitting a simple model with just a constant term and a special interaction term shows that unions win, on average, 32.3 percent in situations where a union nonlawyer faces an employer outside lawyer. In the other representational situations, the unions have an average win rate of 41.4 percent.[59]

There are several ways in which it would be desirable to refine this analysis. Variables such as type of union, a more detailed categorization of the type of issue, and something more about the quality of the representatives (beyond formal qualifications) could be included. To do this, one must move beyond tabular analysis. For a dichotomous dependent variable such as winning and losing in arbitration, the appropriate technique is logistic regression. The "dependent" variable in logistic regression is the natural logarithm of the odds of the union winning (in this application),

TABLE 14.   Union Success by Type of Representatives (Collapsed) (in percentages)

Type of Union Representative	Type of Employer Representative		
	Outside Lawyer	Other Representative	All
Lawyer	46	38	42
	(79)	(62)	(141)
Nonlawyer	31	42	37
	(218)	(209)	(373)
All	35	35	38
	(297)	(108)	(568)

Logit Analysis

Full Model				Special Model			
Term	Estimate	χ^2	p	Term	Estimate	χ^2	p
Constant	−.494	—		Constant	−.328	—	
Union	.126	1.57	.210	Special Effect	−.490	7.20	.007
Employer	−.036	0.13	.716				
Interaction	.201	4.02	.045				

Source: Wisconsin Employment Relations Commission decisions, coded by the author.

Note: Partial "wins" may account for some percentages that appear to be inconsistent with the number of cases. Figures in parentheses are number of cases.

what I will refer to as the log odds. One constructs an equation to predict this dependent variable; the equation consists of the weighted values of a set of predictor variables (type of representative, type of issue, etc.), with the weights determined by a standard statistical criterion.

One complication in this analysis is the problem of "partial" wins or losses. Standard logistic regression requires that the dependent variable contain only two categories. To deal with this problem, I actually did the analysis that follows three different ways. In one, I included only those cases that I had coded as unambiguous wins or losses; in the second, I collapsed the partial wins and losses into clear wins and losses, omitting only those that I had coded as a draw. In the third, I applied an alternative statistical technique, ordered probit analysis,[60] that permits the dependent variable to be an ordered set of categories (in my case there were five categories: clear loss, partial loss, tie, partial win, clear win). Given that 92 percent of the cases were clear wins or losses, it was not surprising that the

TABLE 15.   Union Success by Representation Controlling for Type of Cases (in percentages)

	Type of Case					
	Discharge Cases		Other Discipline Cases		Nondiscipline Cases	
	Employer Representative		Employer Representative		Employer Representative	
Union Representative	Outside Lawyer	Other	Outside Lawyer	Other	Outside Lawyer	Other
Lawyer	40	27	45	53	48	38
	(20)	(11)	(11)	(9)	(48)	(42)
Nonlawyer	19	42	26	38	32	42
	(19)	(29)	(20)	(30)	(177)	(150)

| | Logit Analysis | | | |
Effect	Estimate	df	χ^2	p
Constant	−.521	1	—	
Case type	−.168	2	1.26	.534
	.041			
Union representative	.141	1	1.91	.167
Employer representative	−.036	1	0.12	.724
Interaction	.209	1	4.25	.039

$\chi^2_{GOF} = 2.38$ df = 6 $p = .882$

Source: Wisconsin Employment Relations Commission decisions, coded by the author.

Note: Partial "wins" may account for some percentages that appear to be inconsistent with the number of cases. Figures in parentheses are number of cases.

results applying the various approaches were consistent; consequently, I report only the results from the second approach (collapsing partial wins and losses with clear wins and losses).

In this analysis, I expanded one predictor variable and included two additional variables. The expanded predictor was type of case, which here included seven categories: dismissal, other discipline, compensation (wages, benefits, job classification), hours and overtime, job posting and related seniority issues, work assignments and duties, and other. The first added predictor was type of local, which had five categories: nonpublic employee locals, police and fire department locals (representing sworn officers), health care locals, teachers' locals, and other.

Both of these variables are entered into the analysis as a dummy variable; for each variable, one category is treated as a base category, and a weight is computed for each of the other categories to show how much that category differs from the base category after controlling for the other variables in the equation. The choice of the base category is arbitrary. In my initial analyses I used the "other" category as the base, but then shifted the base category to highlight the pattern of differences. For example, in one of the the initial analyses (using the "other" category as the base), the coefficient for work assignments and duties category of the issue variable is –.92; this means that, controlling for the other variables in the logistic regression equation the log odds of the union winning in a work assignment and duties case is .92 lower (the minus sign) than cases falling into the "other" category. Any pair of categories can be readily compared by taking the difference of the coefficients for those categories. For example, in this same analysis, the coefficient for the compensation category was .18; subtracting the coefficient for the work assignment and duties category (–.92) from this (.18) tells us that, controlling for the other variables in the equation, the log odds of the union winning a compensation case was 1.10 higher than winning a work assignment and duties case. In this example, because the work assignment and duty category produced the largest negative coefficient, it is useful to use this category as the base category, so that all coefficients are positive and represent shifts from this category with the lowest win rate for unions. Changing the base category has no effect on the relative values of coefficients. Using the work assignment and duties category as the base, the coefficient for "other" cases would be +.92 and the coefficient for compensation cases would be +1.10, exactly the same absolute values we previously obtained by comparing coefficients.

The coefficient for a given category can be easily converted to a value that tells us the impact on the odds of the union winning (as distinct from the log of the odds). This conversion involves reversing the logarithm process (what is called exponentiation).[61] Exponentiating the 1.1 yields approximately 3.0, which means that, controlling for the other variables in the equation, the odds of the union winning a compensation case is three times higher than that of winning a work assignment and duties case. On the log odds scale, the coefficient is added in (because the log odds equation is additive); on the odds scale, the coefficient is multiplied in (because the odds equation is multiplicative).

The second added variable was a crude measure of how much arbitration work the two representatives did relative to one another. This variable was constructed by counting the number of times each representative appeared in the data set. For each case, I took the ratio of the number of appearances by the union's representative to the number of appearances by the employer's representative (I call this the appearance ratio). Finally, I took the natural logarithm of this ratio. The resulting variable, the log appearance ratio, is equal to zero when the two representatives appeared an equal number of times; it is positive when the union's representative appeared more frequently than the employer's representative and negative when the employer's representative appears more frequently than the union's representative. This is a crude indicator, because it is likely that the regular representatives, particularly private attorneys, appear before arbitrators other than those employed by WERC.[62]

Nonetheless, as the analysis will show, the log appearance ratio is a useful indicator that works exactly as one would predict (the union's success increases as this variable increases). The logistic regression produces a coefficient for log appearance ratio; in one of the analyses below, this coefficient is .32. This means that if the log appearance ratio goes up by one, the log odds of the union winning goes up by .32. Translating this to the more interpretable odds of winning is a bit tricky; for this variable, the coefficient becomes the power of the appearance ratio. Note that because .32 is very close to $1/3$, the following equation suggests that we might view it as equal to that value, which can be interpreted as the cube root.[63] This equation says that if the appearance ratio doubles, the odds of the union winning is multiplied by $2^{1/3}$ or 1.26. If the appearance ratio quadruples, the odds of the union winning is multiplied by $4^{1/3}$ or 1.59. If the appearance ratio is halved, the odds of the union winning is multiplied by .5 or 0.79. Note that all of these calculations assume that the coefficient for the log appearance ratio is .32, which I have rounded to $1/3$ for purposes of discussion; the specific value of the power depends on the coefficient.

$$\frac{win}{lose} = (appearance\ ratio)^{.32} \approx (appearance\ ratio)^{\frac{1}{3}}$$

How, then, should one handle the key variable, type of representative? In the tabular analysis, I used four different approaches.

1. Two dichotomies (one for each side), coded simply as lawyer and nonlawyer
2. Three categories for union representatives (lawyer, regional representative, local representative) and four categories for employer representatives (outside lawyer, inside lawyer, outside nonlawyer, inside nonlawyer), omitting three combinations with less than ten cases (see table 13)
3. Two dichotomies coded lawyer versus nonlawyer for unions and outside lawyer versus other for employers
4. A simple dichotomy with one category as union lawyer opposing an outside lawyer for the employer and all other combinations as the other category

In the discussion below, I report analyses using all four approaches, but then focus on just two of them (numbers 2 and 3).

Table 16 details the logistic regression results using each of the measures of type of representative. While for all of the analyses the set of predictors accounts for some variation in outcomes in grievance arbitration (as indicated by what I have labeled as the "Model χ^2"),[64] none of the models is particularly strong. Two statistics show the lack of strength of these models. One is R^2 statistic in the table; this is one crude indicator, which ranges from 0 to 1, of how much of the variation in outcome the model explains.[65] The other is the PRE (for "proportional reduction in error") statistic; this statistic indicates how well the model improves the prediction of winning or losing, and ranges from 0 (if the model provides no improvement) to 1 (if the model eliminates all error in prediction). Both the R^2 and PRE statistics are around .05 for most of the models, indicating that the model accounts for something on the order of five percent of the uncertainty in outcome.

The predictor that stands out in all four analyses is the log appearance ratio, with values ranging from .23 to .32. From my explication of the interpretation of the impact of appearance ratio on the odds of winning, this suggests that the appropriate power for the appearance ratio is somewhere between 1/4 and 1/3. There is also some evidence that both type of issue and type of local might make a difference. Generally, locals in a non-public setting seem to be less successful, particularly in comparison with public health care locals and perhaps teachers, with the odds of a public health care local winning a grievance as much as three times the odds of a

TABLE 16. Logistic Regression Results

Effect	Model 1 β	Model 1 χ²	Model 2 β	Model 2 χ²	Model 3 β	Model 3 χ²	Model 4 β	Model 4 χ²
Constant	−2.30	—	−2.95	—	−2.04	—	−1.84	—
Type of union	—	6.87	—	6.07	—	9.02	—	6.38
Private sector employees	0.00		0.00		0.00		0.00	
	—		—		—		—	
Police/Fire	0.33	1.09	0.34	0.90	0.50	2.45	0.37	1.43
	(.32)		(.36)		(.32)		(.31)	
Health	**0.96**	6.45	**0.90**	4.27	**1.05**	7.52	**0.85**	5.26
	(.38)		(44)		(.38)		(.37)	
Teachers	0.53	2.30	**0.80**	3.93	**0.75**	4.31	0.61	2.98
	(.35)		(.40)		(.36)		(.35)	
Other	0.44	2.63	0.51	2.46	**0.59**	4.75	0.46	3.08
	(.27)		(.33)		(.27)		(.26)	
Type of issue	—	11.89	—	12.08	—	11.92	—	10.86
Work assignments and duties	0.00		0.00		0.00		0.00	
	—		—		—		—	
Dismissal	0.36	0.77	0.55	1.63	0.42	1.02	0.40	0.92
	(.42)		(.43)		(.42)		(.41)	
Other discipline	0.66	2.51	0.81	3.47	0.73	3.02	0.66	2.49
	(.42)		(.44)		(.42)		(.42)	
Compensation	**0.97**	5.42	**1.10**	6.41	**1.03**	6.05	**0.97**	5.49
	(.42)		(.43)		(.42)		(.41)	
Hours	0.78	3.33	**0.97**	4.79	**0.85**	3.91	0.73	2.96
	(.43)		(.44)		(.43)		(.42)	
Seniority	0.07	0.03	0.25	0.31	0.15	0.12	0.07	0.03
	(.43)		(.45)		(.43)		(.43)	
Other	**0.79**	4.68	**0.92**	5.65	**0.83**	4.96	**0.74**	4.07
	(.37)		(.39)		(.37)		(.37)	
Log of experience ratio	**0.28**	12.07	**0.32**	12.90	**0.27**	10.12	**0.23**	7.69
	(.08)		(.09)		(.09)		(.08)	
Representation 1	—	7.51						
Lawyer (U)/ lawyer (E)	1.14	2.64						
	(.70)							
Lawyer (U)/ nonlawyer (E)	0.00							
	—							
Nonlawyer (U)/ lawyer (E)	0.57	0.70						
	(.68)							
Nonlawyer (U)/ nonlawyer (E)	0.55	0.61						
	(.70)							

TABLE 16.—Continued

Effect	Model 1 β	Model 1 χ^2	Model 2 β	Model 2 χ^2	Model 3 β	Model 3 χ^2	Model 4 β	Model 4 χ^2
Representation 2			—	14.17				
Lawyer (U)/			**1.81**	4.76				
outside lawyer (E)			(.83)					
Lawyer (U)/			1.24	2.12				
inside lawyer (E)			(.85)					
Lawyer (U)/			0.00					
inside nonlaw. (E)			—					
Regional rep (U)/			0.81	1.01				
outside lawyer (E)			(.81)					
Regional rep (U)/			1.15	1.94				
inside lawyer (E)			(.82)					
Regional rep (U)/			1.11	1.76				
inside nonlaw. (E)			(.84)					
Local rep (U)/			1.49	2.32				
outside lawyer (E)			(.98)					
Regional rep (U)/			0.71	0.52				
outside nonlaw. (E)			(.98)					
Locval rep (U)/			0.72	0.63				
inside nonlaw. (E)			(.92)					
Representation 3					—	9.70		
Lawyer (U)/					0.21	0.41		
other (E)					(.33)			
Lawyer (U)/					**0.95**	9.54		
outside lawyer (E)					(.31)			
Nonlawyer (U)/					0.23	0.95		
other (E)					(.24)			
Nonlawyer (U)/					0.00			
outside lawyer (E)					—			
Representation 4							0.40	3.50
(special effect)							(.21)	
Model χ^2	37.75		46.62		40.34		34.14	
	14 df, $p < .001$		19 df, $p < .001$		14 df, $p < .001$		12 df, $p < .001$	
pseudo-R^2	.051		.064		.055		.046	
PRE	.052		.019		.047		.057	
n	557		551		556		556	

Note: Figures in parentheses are standard errors of logistic regression coefficients; coefficients shown in bold type are statistically significant at the .05 level or higher. Coefficients for reference categories have been set equal to zero to facilitate comparisons.

private-employer local winning.[66] Unions appear to be two to three times more successful (in terms of odds) in winning grievances dealing with compensation, hours, and discipline short of dismissal than they are in grievances concerning work assignments and duties.[67]

Turning to the results for the various specifications of type of representative, keep in mind that all of the results discussed here control for the impact of log appearance ratio, type of local, and type of issue. As in the bivariate analysis, the simple lawyer/nonlawyer dichotomy (Model 1) does not produce any statistically significant differences. At first glance, the coefficients look reasonably large—for example, the one for lawyer versus lawyer is 1.14, which converts to an odds effect of over 3—but these effects reflect that the category with the lowest success for unions, union lawyer versus employer nonlawyer, has only fourteen cases. Using the most complex categorization, shown in Model 2, suggests some differences based on representation. The base category here also has a small number of cases (12), but even using an alternative base category with more observations produces some evidence of significant variation. Using the third approach to categorizing representation (lawyer versus nonlawyer for unions and outside lawyer versus other for employers) produces the clearest and strongest effects for representation: the odds of a union winning when it has a lawyer and the employer does not have an outside lawyer is about double that of situations when the employer does not have an outside lawyer,[68] and two and one-half times that in the situation when the union has a nonlawyer and the employer has an outside lawyer.[69] Lastly, collapsing the representation variable into a simple dichotomy (union nonlawyer against an outside lawyer versus the other situations) produces less sharp results, with the difference between the two situations only multiplying the odds of the union winning by about one and one-half.[70]

We can get more of a sense of the impact of representation by using the logistic regressions to estimate the expected win rates for various situations. I used two of the models, Models 2 and 3, to do this estimation. For all of the estimates, I assumed a log appearance ratio of zero (which means that the two representatives appeared in the data set an equal number of times). I computed three estimates.

1. Best case for union (a compensation grievance involving a health care local)
2. Best case for employer (a duties or work assignment grievance involving a private employer local)
3. A mid-level estimate, controlling only for log appearance ratio

I computed the first two estimates by obtaining the predicted log odds for each representational situation, and converting that back to a percentage. To get the third estimate, I did additional logistic regressions using only representational situation and experience as predictors; I used the estimates from those regressions to obtain the predicted log odds for each cell. Tables 17 and 18 display the results; the first entry in each cell is the original percentage without any controls; the second entry (in italics) is the best-case employer estimate. The third entry (underlined) is the best-case union estimate, and the fourth entry (in bold) is the mid-level estimate.

The two sets of best-case estimates provide a good idea of the range of likelihood of success for each representational combination. Of most interest, however, is the comparison of the original union success rate without controlling for the appearance ratio and the estimate controlling for appearance ratio. Looking at the row in table 17 for union regional representatives, one sees that while the success rate of these representatives when opposed by outside lawyers does not change upon controlling for the appearance ratio, that success ratio goes down vis-à-vis other types of employer representatives. In fact, the predicted union success rate generally goes down after introducing this control, except when the union is pitted against an outside lawyer. Looking at table 18 shows a similar pattern: the success rate for unions does not change when the employer has an out-

TABLE 17. Predicted Union Success (Model 2) (in percentages)

Type of Union Representative	Type of Employer Representative			
	Outside Lawyer	Inside Lawyer	Outside Nonlawyer	Inside Nonlawyer
Lawyer	46	42		17
	24	*15*	—	*48*
	<u>70</u>	<u>57</u>		<u>28</u>
	45	**37**		**14**
Regional nonlawyer	31	45	34	43
	11	*14*	*10*	*14*
	<u>47</u>	<u>55</u>	<u>44</u>	<u>54</u>
	31	**39**	**28**	**37**
Local nonlawyer	28			27
	19	—	—	*10*
	<u>63</u>			<u>44</u>
	34			**19**

Source: Estimated based on logistic regression model 2 shown in table 16.

Note: Figures in roman type are observed success rates; italics show the best-case employer estimates; underlined show the best-case union estimates; bold shows the midlevel estimate.

side lawyer as a representative, but the union success rate goes down vis-à-vis the other types of employer representatives regardless of whether the union representative is a lawyer or a nonlawyer.

What is this pattern telling us about the impact of type of representative on the outcome of grievance arbitration? A large proportion of the cases in this data set were handled by union representatives who did a lot of cases. In 54 percent of the cases, the union's representative appeared eight or more times; in 26 percent of the cases, the union's representative appeared thirteen or more times. While some of the employer's representatives appeared frequently as well, fewer were regular or high-volume players. In only 28 percent of the cases was the employer's representative someone who appeared eight or more times, and in only 15 percent of the cases thirteen or more times. At the other end of the spectrum, 19 percent of the employer's representatives made a single appearance, compared to only nine percent of the union representatives; two-thirds of the cases involved an employer representative who appeared five or fewer times, compared to one-third of the cases on the union side. Clearly, experience makes a difference, and an experienced nonlawyer has a high likelihood of success against an inexperienced lawyer. In this sample, the regional union representatives opposing inside lawyers appeared on average 11.9 times in the data set; the inside lawyer appeared on average only 3.7 times.[71]

In summary, this statistical analysis indicates that type of representative does appear to be associated with a measurable difference in the like-

TABLE 18.   Predicted Union Success (Model 3)
(in percentages)

Type of Union Representative	Type of Employer Representative	
	Outside Lawyer	Other
Lawyer	46	38
	25	*14*
	<u>73</u>	<u>56</u>
	45	**34**
Nonlawyer	31	42
	11	*14*
	<u>51</u>	<u>57</u>
	31	**36**

Source: Estimated based on logistic regression model 3 shown in table 16.

Note: Figures in roman are observed success rates; italics show the best-case employer estimates; underlined show the best-case union estimate; bold shows the midlevel estimate.

lihood of a union winning a grievance arbitration. However, it is not the simple lawyer/nonlawyer distinction that accounts for the difference. Rather, it appears to be more a function of specialization. Specialist nonlawyers and specialist lawyers appear to be better advocates than nonspecialist lawyers. This pattern is consistent with what I reported for the other venues: effectiveness of representation is closely linked to specific experience, both advocacy experience and substantive experience. Many of the inside lawyers appearing for employers handle a range of matters, with labor-related issues generally and grievance arbitration more specifically a small part of their responsibilities. The regional representatives for unions are career labor representatives and advocates. Most have substantial specific expertise, plus considerable experience as advocates in the grievance setting. Interestingly, as shown in tables 17 and 18, when the legal professional nonspecialist is pitted against the nonlawyer specialist, the nonlawyer does quite well, in large part due to the experience that the nonlawyer brings to his or her advocacy.

Selective Use of Representatives

What about the issue of whether parties in grievance arbitration strategically choose the type of representative they will employ? Might it not be possible that the union will let the regional representatives handle the less important, less strong cases, while employing a lawyer for the more important, stronger grievances? Recall my earlier observation that there is often something going on beyond the immediate grievance. In situations where the local wants to pursue a grievance viewed by the regional council as weak or of marginal significance, the council could choose to let the regional (or local) nonlawyer representative handle it, saving the council's funds for hiring a lawyer for the stronger, more important cases.

There were 95 locals that appeared more than one time in my data set. Only 10 of these locals employed a mix of lawyers and nonlawyers to handle their grievances. Of the remaining 85, 73 were always represented by nonlawyers, and 12 were always represented by lawyers. There did not appear to be any clear relationship between the number of times a local appeared and whether it used a mix of lawyers and nonlawyers. Conversations with arbitrators and representatives indicated that the type of representative a local had was more a matter of practice than strategic behavior. Interestingly, of the four locals that had a large number of cases and used a mix of lawyers and nonlawyers, three used predominantly lawyers and one used predominantly nonlawyers.[72] Overall, it is difficult to square the general pattern here with careful, strategic decision making.

On the employer side, there may be a bit more strategic choice of representatives, although, overall, it too appears to be governed more by standard operating procedures. In the sample, there were 116 employers appearing two or more times; 100 used all lawyers or all nonlawyers. Of that 100, 15 used a mix of inside and outside lawyers. Again, for most employers, the pattern seemed to be largely a question of standard operating procedures, with a small number of employers making more strategic choices. One employer appeared in the data set 22 times, every time with a nonlawyer representative; there was one employer appearing 11 times, always with an inside lawyer, and there were two appearing 10 times, one always with an inside lawyer and one with a combination of inside (8) and outside lawyers (2). One interpretation for the employers is that some of the smaller employers might be making strategic choices, while larger employers with substantial numbers of cases rely upon in-house expertise. This is probably the case, although for most employers it still appears to be largely a question of standard operating procedures, particularly for those that always use outside lawyers, and perhaps for many of those that always use inside lawyers.

Overall, one cannot dismiss the possibility that the selection of type of representative is in part a strategic choice, particularly on the employer side. However, both the statistical patterns here and the conversations with participants in the process suggest that standard practices are the primary determinants. Moreover, given the dominance of standard practices, it would be difficult to draw conclusions about systematic differences among cases across employers and unions based on the nature of the representation employed.[73]

Nonlawyers Doing the Most Lawyerly Things

I have one further piece of evidence from the grievance arbitration setting on the ability of nonlawyers to provide legal representation in specialized settings. As noted earlier in this chapter, one frequent element of the grievance arbitration process is the filing of post-hearing written briefs by the representatives. The question I consider here is to what degree do the briefs of the lawyers differ from those of the nonlawyers?

To answer this question, I took a sample of twenty-four briefs from the closed-case files of the WERC: six were union briefs written by lawyers, six were union briefs written by nonlawyers, six were employer briefs written by lawyers, and six were employer briefs written by nonlawyers.[74] I then drew samples of labor lawyers, arbitrators, law professors who taught labor law, law students in labor law courses, and advanced undergraduates in law-related courses.[75] Each of these individuals received a randomly chosen set of four briefs (the set an individual received could be all written by lawyers, all written by nonlawyers, or any combination in between) and was asked to try to identify the type of author for each of the four briefs.[76]

Table 19 summarizes the results of the experiment. On a pure guessing basis, one would expect that 50 percent of the briefs would be correctly identified. Interestingly, for undergraduates, this was almost precisely the result: they identified 50.3 percent of the briefs correctly. In contrast, those most directly involved in the day-to-day work of grievance arbitration—labor lawyers and arbitrators—identified almost 70 percent correctly.[77] Of more interest, however, is that even this most experienced group misidentified about 30 percent of the briefs they received.

Let me focus on just the law professors, arbitrators, and lawyers. This group identified 68 percent of the briefs correctly. Interestingly, they were more successful in identifying the briefs written by lawyers (74 percent correct) than by nonlawyers (63 percent correct; $\chi^2 = 7.78$, $p < .01$). More importantly, the gap in correct identifications was notably larger for employer briefs (76 percent lawyer vs. 59 percent nonlawyer; $\chi^2 = 9.41$, $p < .01$) than for union briefs (71 percent vs. 66 percent; $\chi^2 = 0.85$, $p > .25$).[78] What this means is that the respondents were most likely to mistake nonlawyer employer briefs as having been written by lawyers. One simple

TABLE 19. Identifying Briefs Written by Lawyers and Nonlawyers

	Number of Respondents	Number of Correct Responses				Percent Correct
		One	Two	Three	Four	
Undergrads	40	26%	44%	18%	8%	50.3
	(39)					(159)
Law students	13	15%	23%	38%	15%	59.6
	(13)					(52)
Law professors	31	17%	28%	21%	31%	63.9
	(29)					(122)
Arbitrators	34	9%	31%	31%	28%	69.7
	(32)					(132)
Lawyers	82	4%	37%	40%	20%	69.1
	(81)					(327)
All respondents	200	12%	35%	31%	20%	64.0
	(194)					(792)

Source: Data collected by the author.

Note: The number in parentheses in second column is the number of respondents with usable information regarding four briefs. The number in parentheses in the last column is the total number of briefs with usable information; the percentage in this column is based on this number. The "number of correct responses" columns rely upon only those with usable information regarding four briefs.

explanation might be that, as was true for the data analyzed in the previous section, employers are more likely to be represented by lawyers, and many respondents erred on the side of "lawyers" when they were unsure about an employer brief (which side had filed the brief was readily apparent from its text). It is also possible that employer nonlawyer representatives were more able and likely to consult with inside legal staff in preparing their briefs.

One can also look at the authors of the individual briefs that were most frequently misidentified and most frequently identified correctly. As it turns out, there is no clear pattern here. For example, the two lawyers whose briefs were most frequently misclassified as written by nonlawyers are both individuals who handle a significant number of grievance arbitrations (one appeared twelve times in my sample of WERC decisions, and one appeared fifteen times). Furthermore, one of these lawyers (brief correctly classified by 40 percent of the respondents), who represented employers, was from one of the most widely used management-oriented firms; the other, who represented unions (brief correctly classified by 21 percent of the respondents), was a solo practitioner. The briefs of several lawyers were classified correctly by 90 percent or more of the respondents; one of these handled twenty cases in my WERC decision sample, while another handled only one.

On the nonlawyer side, one author's brief was correctly classified by every respondent, and that author handled twenty-eight cases for one of the large union regional councils. The brief written by another nonlawyer, who handled fifteen cases for this same council, was mistakenly identified as written by a lawyer by 78 percent of the respondents. On the employer side, the brief of one outside nonlawyer representative who handled seven cases in my sample was classified correctly by 73 percent of the respondents. It is difficult to find any clear pattern in this information. Some nonlawyers write very "lawyer-like" briefs, but this would seem to be more a matter of personal style than of the amount of experience handling cases. Likewise, some lawyers write briefs that are not recognized as written by lawyers, but this does not appear to be a function of inexperience.

To get some additional idea of what might explain the classification of briefs, I went back to a subset of my original respondents, again sending them a set of four briefs. This time, however, the briefs were not randomly selected. One set was designed to include briefs identified as written by lawyers, and another consisted of briefs written by nonlawyers; both of these sets contained a mix of lawyer and nonlawyer briefs. Additional sets were mixed, some with sharply contrasting briefs and some less contrasting. The respondents were told,

All four of these briefs tended to be identified as written by the same type of author (all by lawyers or all by nonlawyers). In fact, the authorship varied (some written by lawyers and some by nonlawyers).

This was true only for the first two sets, but was intended to try to get the respondents to think about what distinguished one from another. I asked the respondents to read the briefs, then to supply this information.

1. Give your assessment as to how most people would evaluate these briefs. (Would people tend to think that all were written by lawyers or that all were written by nonlawyers?)
2. Indicate what it is about the briefs (e.g., form, language, nature of argumentation, etc.) that you believe would lead people to label them all as lawyer-written or as nonlawyer-written.
3. For each of the individual briefs, indicate your best guess as to the nature of the authorship.
4. Tell me on what basis you distinguish among the briefs.

The answers to these questions are, at best, suggestive. Recall that one brief was correctly identified by all respondents as written by a nonlawyer; those respondents who received this brief on the second round pointed to the author's poor writing as a primary factor for labeling it a nonlawyer brief. I included this brief in a set of briefs that tended to be labeled non-lawyer in the first round; two of them were by lawyers and two by non-lawyers. Five people got this set in the second round: two thought overall the set would be identified as written by lawyers, two thought it would be nonlawyers, and one wasn't sure. Interestingly, one of those who thought that most professionals would think they were by nonlawyers (because of "imprecise use of language, grammar and syntax errors, and absent legal reasoning") thought that three of the four were in fact by lawyers.

Looking at the opposite set, the one that tended to be identified as written by lawyers, even when the author was not a lawyer, fourteen respondents got this set on the second round. All but two thought that "most professionals" would think they had been written by lawyers. There was clearest agreement on two of the briefs. In evaluating the one that was actually written by a lawyer, the respondents noted its reference to prior cases, statutes, and the like, plus its well-focused argument. Many respondents faulted the two nonlawyer briefs for poor writing; however, while they described one as lacking citations or legal research, one respondent described it as "very disciplined, but somehow more like a social scientist's."

In summary, respondents expected lawyers to be able to write reasonably well, and when they found a poorly written brief they tended to label it as having been written by a nonlawyer. Second, respondents expected briefs to follow a fairly standard format (particularly with regard to citation style), and those that deviated from this style were labeled as written by nonlawyers. Third, and last on the list of criteria, was substance: briefs with citations to case law, statutes, and so on, were seen as written by lawyers. These factors were most clear when a respondent mislabeled a brief and described it as having the characteristics associated with the category they chose.

This experiment shows that there are differences in the aggregate in the nature of the briefs written by lawyers and nonlawyers. At the same time, the experiment makes it very clear that one need not be a lawyer to write a lawyerly brief, and that having completed law school by no means guarantees that the briefs a lawyer writes will be recognizable as a lawyer's work product.

Conclusion

The analysis in this chapter again points to the importance of experience and substantive expertise. In some circumstances, legal training does make a marginal difference. However, the most consistent predictor of success is my very crude indicator of the relative system-specific experience of the advocates for the union and the employer. It is possible that some of the importance of this experience variable reflects the specific features of the WERC, particularly the small number of arbitrators and the repeated appearance of advocates before those arbitrators. For this reason, it may be that my analysis of the WERC does not apply to other arbitration venues.

Nonetheless, of the four settings I have considered, labor grievance arbitration before the WERC bears the most similarity to the courtroom: it is clearly adversarial rather than inquisitorial. Two key factors differentiate grievance arbitration from civil litigation: the absence of juries (although a significant portion of civil cases are, in fact, tried to judges rather than juries)[79] and the centrality of the continuing relationship between the two parties.[80] Both of these factors serve to complicate the advocate's role by requiring a more subtle approach to developing and presenting cases to the adjudicator. Overzealous advocacy can damage the longer term relationship between the two parties. I also suspect that such advocacy might lead at least some arbitrators to question the competence of the advocate, given that the arbitrators are fully conscious of the continuing relationship into which they must intervene.

With this in mind, it is striking that formal legal training does not make a greater difference. Various elements of the law school curriculum are geared to training future lawyers to understand their duties to their clients, and the need to look for outcomes that are in the best interest of those clients. Effective advocacy requires an ability to see the big picture that includes both the instant dispute and the longer term. In labor grievance arbitration, that longer term is the ongoing relationship between union and management. I find no evidence that formal legal training makes any difference in this regard. One point of speculation, to which I will return in the final chapter, is that legal training itself may have relatively little direct impact. Rather, it may be that the small differences I observe reflect more of a screening effect. That is, those who go to law school tend to be more inclined to be competitive and adversarial (after all, that is our image of lawyers). Success as an advocate may require little of the type of skills and knowledge law school imparts. Rather it may require a combination of specific knowledge, specific experience, and a desire to win. While law school is a common way station on the path to specific knowledge and experience, it need not be the only one. In the words of one of the arbitrators who participated in my experiment in identifying lawyer and non-lawyer briefs, "In twelve years as an arbitrator it has been my experience that there were few qualitative differences between briefs submitted by lawyers and nonlawyers. The big differences in what is submitted are between people who are smart and experienced, and those who are not."

CHAPTER 6

Advocacy Today and Advocacy in the Twenty-first Century

Explaining Advocate Effectiveness

What do we learn by looking at the four venues discussed in the preceding chapters? The simplest answer to this question is that there are no simple answers in the debate about whether nonlawyers can be effective advocates. The closest we can come to a simple answer is that "it depends."

Nonlawyers are effective in three of the four disparate settings I considered. Interestingly, the venue where the nonlawyers are least effective is the one in which many of the nonlawyers are members of another recognized profession (accountancy). Furthermore, legal training by no means guarantees that an advocate is effective: I observed a number of lawyers who provided, at best, marginal representation although they were probably better than no representation at all.

Assessing the Dimensions of Advocacy Representation

The framework I described in chapter 1, summarized in table 1, helps in understanding the patterns reported in chapters 2 through 5, both in terms of when nonlawyers are effective and when lawyers are not. The framework has three primary dimensions.

> Nature of expertise
> Representative–client relationship
> Accountability and control

Each of these has a series of three subdimensions. All three of the primary dimensions explain something about how advocates perform, although the subdimensions of representation differ in their usefulness.

While one naturally expects effectiveness to be associated with success (and my analysis clearly assumes this connection), it is important not to equate the quality of performance entirely with outcomes. Ineffective advocates win many cases, and effective advocates regularly lose;[1] the factual and legal quality of a case limits the impact the advocate can make. With a weak case, an advocate can be very effective and still lose; and with a very strong case, an ineffective advocate can win, even when confronting a highly expert, experienced opponent.[2] In the discussion that follows I consider effectiveness in the broader senses I outlined in chapter 1.

Expertise

The expertise dimension is the most telling in explaining effectiveness. For example, why did the accountants (and other tax specialists, whom I will simply lump with accountants in order to simplify the discussion)[3] perform so poorly in the appeals before the Wisconsin Tax Appeals Commission (TAC)? The accountants presumably possessed *substantive* expertise; they knew the tax law and regulations as well as, perhaps even better than, the lawyers appearing before TAC. Accountants may well be very effective in resolving questions about tax returns by negotiating with tax authorities. However, in the formal hearing setting, accountants were clearly out of their element; they lacked *process* expertise. Accountants did not know how to present a case to the Tax Appeals Commission, and they often failed to understand the prehearing process (such as the importance of formal requests for documents made by the attorney for the Department of Revenue, or the necessity of making a timely request for subpoenas for witnesses needed to make their case).

To understand further the role of process expertise in advocacy, we need to consider the second subdimension of expertise: general versus specific. General process expertise involves knowing

> how to examine and cross-examine witnesses,
> how to prepare written arguments, and
> how to develop and present a case.

The model for this expertise is the courtroom. Specific process expertise involves knowing how a particular forum differs from the general model.

> how appellate advocacy differs from trial advocacy,
> how civil advocacy differs from criminal advocacy, and
> how advocacy in a Social Security hearing or an unemployment compensation hearing differs from that in the trial courtroom.

Lawyers with extensive experience in one setting often encounter difficulty in adjusting to the expectations or procedures of another setting. For example, a lawyer with substantial experience in trial work, but little or no experience in Social Security hearings, may not understand the procedural or evidentiary conventions used by the administrative law judges. A lawyer might be accustomed to presenting a generalist trial judge with suggested case citations on a specific point of law; this same lawyer might be surprised when the specialist Social Security administrative law judge (who has just told the lawyer that he will find the lawyer's client to be disabled) responds skeptically, or even in a hostile manner, to the lawyer's offer of some case citations "that would help the judge in writing his decision." The experienced Social Security lawyer knows that citations are of no interest once the judge has made up his or her mind in your favor; the citations are useful only when the lawyer needs to convince a judge who does not seem to be going the lawyer's way or who seems to be undecided.

A similar problem of specialized process expertise is evident in the unemployment compensation (UC) case (described in chap. 2) where the lawyer made a motion for summary judgment.[4] The employer's lawyer believed that he had gotten the claimant to acknowledge a factual point (i.e., the claimant had almost immediately started working at another job) that totally undercut the claimant's case. The reaction of the administrative law judge was surprise, almost stunned silence. The UC hearing process does not make provisions for a motion for summary judgment.

This last example also illustrates the importance of substantive expertise, not just in the law generally, but also in the specific area under consideration. The lawyer was experienced and knowledgeable, probably in many areas. However, he clearly was not conversant with the rules governing unemployment compensation. As discussed in chapter 2, the fact that a UC claimant has another job does not disqualify the claimant from receiving benefits. One does not have to be unemployed to get benefits; if the new job pays less than the UC benefit, then the claimant may be entitled to at least a partial payment of benefits. In this case, the claimant had taken a job that paid entirely on a commission basis, but had not earned any commissions during the period in question.

The remaining subdimension of expertise is formal training versus insider knowledge. The formal side of this dimension reflects the ability to prepare and make legal arguments. The briefs experiment reported in chapter 5 shows that formal training does makes a difference (at least in terms of the skills required to prepare such arguments—how much impact the briefs have is less clear), but that nonlawyers can often do a good job with such tasks. Another aspect of formal skills is the ability to recognize subtle interlinkages across issues or areas of law. The bar commonly argues against permitting nonlawyer practice by pointing to the risk that a nonlawyer who is knowledgeable in only one area might fail to recognize some subtlety or interlinkage (e.g., a tax implication in a divorce case, or a potential product liability claim in a workers' compensation case). In the words of one lawyer: "People don't show up with a nice, simple legal problem in a small, neat box. They usually show up with a legal problem with one or two cans tied on its tail."[5] Nothing in my research was clearly directed to detecting this specific problem, but I saw no evidence that in fact the routinized problem frequently came with cans on its tail in the settings I considered. Furthermore, in some settings, such as labor grievance arbitration, regular nonlawyers intimately familiar with an ongoing set of issues and relationships can be more cognizant of the multiplicity of attached "cans" than would be a specialist lawyer brought in on a one-shot or intermittent basis.

The informal side of this dimension did show up repeatedly in my analysis, primarily in terms of people knowledge. Those with experience in a forum, regardless of their formal training, are acquainted with the decision makers and are often able to tailor their presentations to what they believe would be most persuasive to a particular person. This is least evident in cases before the Tax Appeals Commission, simply because none of the petitioners' advocates handled large numbers of cases before TAC. On the other hand, the attorneys for the Department of Revenue (DOR) are regulars before TAC and clearly understood the expectations of the commissioners. I did note some major differences in style among the DOR attorneys, with some coming across as considerably more aggressive than others. I suspect that a petitioner's advocate who knew the DOR attorneys from prior cases might have been able to respond to these differences more effectively than an advocate unfamiliar with the DOR attorneys. I doubt that this would make a big difference, if any, in outcomes, but it could well be important in preparing clients to be cross-examined during the hearing.

In the UC cases, the people knowledge is clearly important to the small group of advocates who regularly appear. My conversations with some of those advocates indicated that they differentiate among the administrative law judges and tailor their presentations, stylistically rather than substantively, based on their prior contact with a particular judge. Most often this involves knowing when to end the presentation of a client's case (i.e., being able to read the signals from the judge that the judge has the information needed to decide a case). This people knowledge goes both ways, because the administrative law judges know the regular advocates and differentiate among those who know what they are doing and those who do not. Of particular importance here is the judges' perceptions as to the care that advocates use in screening cases, with the judges believing that the best advocates are the most selective.[6] This, in turn, probably means that if a judge's initial inclination is to rule against one of these advocates (and these advocates do lose some proportion of their cases), the judge may be inclined to give the case a closer look.

In the Social Security setting, the regular advocates differentiate between sympathetic and unsympathetic administrative law judges. The advocates gear their preparation to their knowledge of the individual judges. This is illustrated by the use of networking to get information about unfamiliar judges who are visiting from other hearing offices; regular advocates report both making calls to get information when they are scheduled to appear before a visitor and receiving calls from regulars in other locales when one of the local judges is temporarily hearing cases away from home. As I described in chapter 4, this people knowledge can extend beyond the administrative law judges to include other regulars in the process, such as the medical and vocational experts. I described an example of how a lawyer used his knowledge of one such expert to try to undercut that expert's damaging testimony. As with the UC administrative law judges, at least some of the Social Security judges use their knowledge of individual advocates as some indicator of the strength of a claimant's case or the likelihood of an appeal if the judge denies the claim.[7] Interestingly, my informal interviews with the regular advocates suggested that there may not be a strong relationship between how frequently the advocate appears in Social Security appeals and the advocate's selectivity.

Of the settings I considered, the most thorough people knowledge probably occurs in the grievance arbitration cases, simply because of the ongoing nature of the relationships involved in these cases. In my analysis in chapter 5, I differentiated among a variety of types of representatives; however, most of these representatives have extensive interaction with the system, including the arbitrators and opposing advocates. In fact, it is common for a particular employer–union combination to specify a small panel of arbitrators that they will use in a rotating fashion. Recall that the most important distinction I drew in my analysis of grievance arbitration was between the employer's inside staff (both law-trained and lay) that handled a mix of issues, and outside lawyers (for both employers and unions) and union regional representatives. There may be a subtle difference in the people knowledge of these two broadly defined groups. The former group interacts with the other players in a very limited set of cases (those involving the inside advocate's employer); in contrast, the latter group interacts with the other players in a broader range of cases. This may allow the outside players to develop a fuller understanding of how both arbitrators and opposing advocates deal with cases and issues; seeing the world only from within a particular employer–union context may limit an advocate's perspective on the other actors.

Representative–Client Relationship

The various settings I looked at involve a variety of types of representative–client relationships; these relationships' connection to outcomes and effectiveness is complex. Take the first subdimension I described in chapter 1: is the relationship preexisting or ad hoc? In the labor and tax settings, virtually all of the lawyer–client relationships I observed existed before the particular case arose. No doubt there are occasions in which a tax appellant or a party in a labor grievance will retain a representative on an ad hoc basis, but I have no empirical means of assessing what difference this would make in practice.

In the Social Security setting, virtually all of the lawyer/client relationships are ad hoc. Lawyers and advocates seldom know their clients before the client comes in the door with the denial of a claim. While an individual who has an ongoing relationship with a general practice lawyer might turn to that lawyer when denied a claim for Social Security disability, the general practice lawyer is unlikely to have significant expertise in Social Security law, and there is little from the ongoing relationship that is likely to assist the lawyer in handling a client's Social Security appeal.[8] Occasionally, a lawyer might handle a set of issues arising out of single injury: a personal injury suit, a workers' compensation claim, and a Social Security disability claim; however, this involves not a preexisting relationship, but a multiple-case relationship.

The only setting in which advocates with and without preexisting relationships appeared regularly was UC appeals. While this could be the case for both claimants and employers, I observed no examples involving claimants (this would have most likely involved a union official appearing on behalf of the claimant).[9] The primary example that I did observe involved employer advocates such as those from the hypothetical UC, Inc. described in chapter 1. Interestingly, there were variations in the types of advocates provided by firms like UC, Inc. Some of the advocates were freelancers hired on a per-hearing basis; while they tended to have experience relevant for handling a hearing (e.g., former police officers), they had no prior knowledge of their client's personnel policies or discipline system. Others of these advocates were full-time employees of a UC consulting firm; they both provided assistance to the client in setting up and operating its personnel and discipline system and also appeared on behalf of the client when the client became involved in a UC appeal. The difference in the representation is striking. The former tended to first meet the client outside the hearing room; consequently, preparation for the hearing was limited to a brief conversation. In the hearing, the representative was able to ask questions, both of the claimant and the client, but usually did little to orchestrate the client's case. In contrast, the latter type of representative knew the client's personnel procedure, reviewed the specifics of the instant case, and decided what witnesses and evidence should be presented at the hearing based upon both the specifics of the case and the broader context.

The representatives that I observed covered the full range along the subdimension I labeled "broker vs. alter ego." Fee-for-service providers included both lawyers and nonlawyers, as did "inside" representatives. However, as I will discuss in more detail below, my analysis indicates that the lawyers that prior research would predict to have interests in potential conflict with those of their clients—contingency-fee lawyers in Social Security disability cases—in fact, have interests in close alignment with the client. The result is that these lawyers function very clearly and effectively as alter egos of their clients. In the setting with the clearest "inside/outside" distinction—labor grievance arbitration—this distinction is thoroughly confounded with expertise in a way that makes any assessment of impact of the lawyer–client relationship impossible. Situated between the inside representatives and the outside fee-for-service representatives on this sub-dimension are outside representatives who are salaried employees of advocacy or service organizations; again, with these representatives, there is no clear connection between the nature of their relationship to their clients and the quality of representation they provide.

The last subdimension of representative–client relationship concerns the understanding of the representational role the advocate is supposed to take: Should the advocate serve simply as the agent of the client (follow the client's instructions), or should the advocate serve as more of a trustee, exercising independent judgment concerning the client's interests? Even though this is a conceptually distinct aspect of the relationship, it turns out to be closely tied to whether or not the relationship is ongoing.[10] Those advocates who regularly work with a client seem much more inclined to consult with the client as the hearing progresses, while those who are handling the case on an ad hoc basis appear more inclined to make evidentiary and tactical decisions without consultation. There are two reasons for this pattern. First, the clients involved in the ongoing relationship are more likely to be sophisticated in the process involved; this is true in tax cases involving business clients, labor grievances, and the employer side of UC cases. In at least some situations, there is clearly pressure on the advocate to do things that the advocate might not choose to do. This is most evident in labor grievance arbitrations: an advocate might believe that a case has little or no chance of success, but senses that the "client" nonetheless wants the matter pursued for reasons not related to the case itself (e.g., demonstrating to supervisors or to union members that the employer or union stands behind them).

Accountability and Control

One of the standard arguments of the legal profession in defending the exclusion of nonlawyers from representational activities is the accountability of lawyers through a regulatory process. Typically, the lawyer discipline system is under the formal control of a state's supreme court, although the operation of that system is often delegated to a body within the state bar association or to some independent agency. Interestingly, only one of the types of nonlawyer advocates that I observed is subject to a formal licensing and disciplinary system, and that is the accountants who were, as a group, one of the least effective types of advocate I observed.[11] None of the other types of advocates are subject to a formal licensing or disciplinary system, and their effectiveness does not seem to be affected in any discernible pattern.

Those players in the forums that I looked at who are repeat players clearly exercise some control over their advocates. This is normally anticipatory rather than active; that is, advocates perform in certain ways because of what they believe they need to do to maintain the goodwill of their clients. Where it is evident, this pattern is true for both lawyers and nonlawyers. It is most explicit among those handling grievance arbitrations; the relationships between the representatives and their clients are long-term, as are the relationships between the principals in the arbitration. Participants made a number of comments to me suggesting that particular actions reflected not so much the effect it would have on the outcome of the case as on the expectations of their principals.

There is very little in the way of forum-centered control that I could see. Some of the forums had the power to exclude advocates who failed to perform at some minimum standard, but I heard nothing to indicate that such powers are used regularly. For example, administrative rules governing advocates in UC appeals hearings were created some years ago because of one advocate who was a problem, but those rules have never actually been invoked since, as far as anyone could remember.

Very few of the advocates I observed were "shareholders" in the cases they were handling. Importantly, the setting where such advocates are common, Social Security disability, seems to demonstrate the potential of share holding to create a positive incentive that can make some difference, at least at the margin. One of the major differences between lawyer and nonlawyer advocates handling Social Security cases is the manner of compensation. The lawyers tended to work on a no-win, no-fee basis, while the nonlawyers tended to be salaried employees of advocacy agencies. Consistently, even after controlling for some major differences in the types of cases handled by lawyers and nonlawyers, lawyers have a marginally higher success rate. In my observation, the best of the lawyers I observed seemed more confident, more thorough, and more creative than did the best of the nonlawyers. It did not seem that the lawyers knew the regulations better or had better legal analyses of their cases. Rather, the lawyers had a clear incentive to win, because "no win, no fee." Furthermore, the nature of the Social Security cases prevented conflicts of interest between the lawyers and clients that can arise in matters where the process involves strategic interaction of adversaries or where the amount at stake is uncertain (creating opportunities for negotiated settlements that are in the advocate's interest at the cost of the client).

Summary: Understanding Effectiveness in Advocacy

My observations make it clear that expertise is central to effective advocacy. The other dimensions serve at most to modify the effectiveness of advocates (although not always in ways that prior research would predict). In those settings where various types of advocates have similar levels of expertise, the differences among the advocates are, at best, small. The striking differences in effectiveness tend to appear where there are clear differences in specialized technical expertise, both process and substantive. Advocates with specialized process and substantive expertise almost invariably also bring insider knowledge about the key players that helps them in presenting a client's case.

The presence or absence of formal legal training is less important than substantial experience with the setting. It is almost certainly the case that lawyers are more able to move across settings, particularly if the settings differ both substantively and procedurally. That is, while formal legal training may not directly prepare a lawyer to be an advocate in a specific setting, it can give the lawyer the general knowledge needed to prepare to handle cases in an unfamiliar setting. Two caveats regarding lawyers' ability to move across different settings should be noted. First, the lawyer's advantage may be less clear if two settings are closely related, such as in labor grievance arbitration and UC appeals. A nonlawyer unfamiliar with court processes but experienced in grievance arbitration and knowledgeable about workplace disciplinary processes might be more effective walking in to handle a UC appeal than would a lawyer experienced in trial process but without substantial experience in workplace-related issues. Second, I was struck by the seeming willingness of some lawyers to come into an unfamiliar setting and proceed as if it were exactly the same as a traditional courtroom. This was most evident in UC appeals, where lawyers frequently seemed oblivious to the needs and expectations of the administrative law judges, or the procedures that typically governed the hearings. A lawyer who had little or no familiarity with UC hearings could easily have spent a couple of mornings watching hearings (which are public); this would have given the lawyer at least some idea what to expect and how to prepare for the hearing. To my knowledge, none of the lawyers engaged in this kind of preparation.[12]

Rethinking Barriers to Legal Practice: It Is Time to Repeal Unauthorized Practice of Law Statutes

Vocal critics of the legal profession maintain that the only *real* reason for restrictions on who can provide legal services is the protection of lawyers from competition.[13] One witness at a public hearing of the ABA Commission on Nonlawyer Practice referred to the profession as a "greedy lawyer cartel" that sells justice to the highest bidder.[14] More thoughtful and careful analyses have made similar, though less strident, observations. For example, law professor Richard Abel develops a strong case that historically the profession sought to limit both the "production of producers" of legal services (i.e., entry into the profession) and the "production [of legal services] by producers" (i.e., who provides services and the nature of what is provided).[15] While the profession has largely lost control of the production of producers,[16] lawyers continue to work hard to limit the opportunities for nonlawyers to compete in providing the kinds of services upon which lawyers rely for their livelihoods. The profession continues to fall back on the standard rhetoric about "protecting the public" from incompetent providers,[17] even in the absence of systematic evidence that the quality of routine services delivered by nonlawyers is substantially below that delivered by lawyers. While lawyers can provide anecdotal evidence of errors by nonlawyers, professional disciplinary bodies can provide similar evidence of errors by lawyers. There is *no* evidence that the presence of a disciplinary body actually reduces the number of errors of legal service providers.

Does this mean that absolutely anyone should be permitted to hang out a shingle and offer legal services? In fact, some countries allow anyone to do exactly this, subject to some very specific exclusions in the types of services offered. In England, for example, one of the biggest providers of legal advice is the Citizens' Advice Bureau (CAB).[18] The CABs are locally funded dispensers of a wide range of advice, much of which would, at least in the United States, be labeled legal advice. Interestingly, while the managers of most CABs are salaried employees, trained volunteers handle most of the actual client contacts, with professionals (including volunteer solicitors) often available for backup or more specialized advice. I have, on a number of occasions, described CABs to persons in the United States interested in increasing access to legal services. When I am asked about the unauthorized practice of law issues raised by the CAB, I often see reactions of surprise, if not incredulity, when I explain that this is not an issue, because anyone in England may dispense legal advice or assist with a claim pursued outside the courts.

What my analysis shows, and what the experience of a variety of specialized agencies reinforces,[19] is that formal legal training is only one path to the skills and knowledge necessary for competent legal assistance and representation. Part of the issue is that the image of legal services still revolves around the general practitioner who is there to help individuals with the full range of legal needs. If one thinks of legal practice in terms of specialized areas rather than as a generalist practice, it is clear that a person can acquire specialized representational competency, both in terms of the legal substance and the legal process/procedures, through a variety of avenues. Furthermore, it is also clear that traditional legal training in the United States equips a person with only some parts of this competency, and that training primarily serves to prepare the practitioner to acquire specialized competency.

Specialized experience and training other than law school can probably be just as effective in preparing a person to provide representation in a narrow, specific area. For the kinds of contexts I have examined, the key is the combination of the three types of expertise: knowledge about the substance of the area, an understanding of the procedures used, and familiarity with the other regular players in the process. The latter element can come only with experience, but the first two (substantive and procedural expertise) could be imparted through one-year, specialized training programs for paralegals, legal technicians, and licensed advocates. The expertise necessary to handle specialized proceedings or tasks could also be acquired experientially, either through an apprentice-like process or by parallel experience.

There are two questions one might still ask about the idea of opening up specialized legal services to nonlawyers. First, would the nonlawyers be more prone to error than are lawyers? Second, in what ways should the nonlawyers be regulated, particularly with regard to avenues of recourse for dissatisfied clients? In discussing the possibility of nonlawyer practice with lawyers, I have regularly been told of experiences with a client who had first gone to a nonlawyer who made errors that the lawyer now had to try to clean up.[20] The assumption of such observations is that a lawyer would not have made such a mistake. Interestingly, we know almost nothing about the frequency of "legal error," a phrase that I use to parallel the idea of "medical error." One striking finding from the medical arena in recent years is the frequency of errors in medical treatment.[21] How frequent is error in the provision of legal services?[22]

Over the last twenty years, I have used lawyers for a variety of tasks: purchasing a home, drafting a will and a trust agreement, handling a personal injury claim, and probating an estate (a different lawyer for each matter). All of the lawyers were experienced, and all produced satisfactory results or work products. Probably unlike many individual users of legal services, I read most documents produced by the lawyers with some care. In virtually every case, I picked up some error in at least one of the documents the lawyer prepared: the failure to note the removal of a lien in a title opinion, an error in describing the nature of an injury, listing the wrong people in a petition to close an estate. One of the errors resulted from the lawyer's failure to consult his file, one resulted from not closely reading the title abstract, and one probably resulted from a miscommunication between me and the lawyer handling the matter. While none of the errors were consequential in the end, it is conceivable that one or more of the errors could have led to substantial legal expense if they had gone undetected.

My experience is purely anecdotal, but it raises the question of whether errors by nonlawyers are, in fact, more frequent than errors by lawyers. We simply do not know the answer to this question.[23] One might speculate that if one compared three groups—nonlawyer specialists, lawyer specialists, and lawyer generalists—the latter would be the most likely to make an error. If this speculation is correct regarding the rate of errors, then the logic of excluding nonlawyers (assuming their error rate to be higher than that for lawyer specialists) would also dictate allowing only lawyer specialists to handle matters within their area of specialization.

How might nonlawyer practitioners be regulated? Can the regulation of lawyers provide one or more models for regulating nonlawyers? David Wilkins has identified three separate mechanisms currently used to regulate lawyers.[24]

> Institutional controls, in which institutional forums within which the lawyers work take some responsibility for uncovering and sanctioning lawyer misconduct (in the federal courts this type of control is exemplified by Rule 11 sanctions for filing frivolous cases, unsupported claims, motions, etc.)[25]
> Liability controls, in which disgruntled clients can seek compensation by bringing a claim for professional malpractice
> Disciplinary controls, in which independent agencies (often a part of the state bar) investigate and prosecute violations of rules of professional conduct (with the final disciplinary authority typically resting with the state supreme court)[26]

All three of these are currently or potentially applicable to nonlawyer advocates.

As I noted earlier in this chapter, many of the agencies before which representatives appear already have the power to regulate both lawyers and nonlawyers who appear before them. For example, within the federal arena, many administrative agencies, including the Social Security Administration,[27] have broad latitude to regulate advocates (both in permitting nonlawyers to appear and in disciplining advocates who appear before them);[28] state agencies often have similar powers. Of the three state agencies I looked at in Wisconsin—the Unemployment Compensation Division, the Wisconsin Tax Appeals Commission, and the Wisconsin Employment Relations Commission—only the former has disciplinary powers in this sense, while the other two do not.[29] In the case of the Tax Appeals Commission, there are relatively few advocates who appear before the commission more than once or twice a year; consequently, commissioners are unlikely to recognize a pattern of problems for an individual advocate. The federal Internal Revenue Service does have mechanisms for regulating and/or disciplining the taxpayer representatives who would be potential advocates before the Tax Appeals Commission. I expect that if the commission felt that a representative was creating problems, it could request, and almost certainly would receive, powers to regulate advocates.[30] In the arbitration arena, because of the voluntary, contractual nature of the arbitration process, there is no obvious mechanism for institutional control of advocates; furthermore, the continuing nature of relationships, both between the parties and between advocates and their principals, make it likely that the parties are in a position to monitor the performance of the advocates without institutional intervention.

The experience of the agencies with such disciplinary power is interesting. I previously noted that the Wisconsin Unemployment Compensation Bureau's administrative rules were put into place some years ago because of problems with one nonlawyer advocate, and that no one at the bureau could recall a single incident in which the rules had actually been invoked to discipline an advocate. The Social Security Administration initiates "only a few dozen cases each year,"[31] and there is no indication that there are more problems with nonlawyers than with lawyers. As of the mid-1980s nonlawyers constituted 16.5 percent of the persons registered to practice before the Trademark and Patent Office, and about a sixth of the disciplinary matters initiated during that period pertained to nonlawyer practitioners.[32] The New York State Workers' Compensation Board,[33] which requires nonlawyers to pass an examination covering workers' compensation law and procedures before being allowed to appear as representatives, initiates disciplinary proceedings against "very few" nonlawyers; one official remarked to me that there are probably more complaints about nonspecialist lawyers—any lawyer licensed in New York can handle a workers' compensation matter, and the Workers' Compensation Board has no regulatory authority over lawyers appearing before it—than about nonlawyers who have passed the board's examination. Thus, where there is experience with institutional regulation, there is no evidence that it is used disproportionately to discipline nonlawyers.

In principle, liability controls ought to be available in any venue for any type of representative, on simple consumer-protection grounds. In the same way that one would have recourse against a plumber who made a faulty repair that led to substantial expense, one could seek damages against an advocate who failed to provide competent services. The dilemma here is that of standards against which to measure performance, but this is also a problem in legal malpractice because of the difficulty in separating performance of the advocate from the outcome of the matter. Obvious things, such as missing filing deadlines and the like, can be applied just as easily to nonlawyer advocates as to lawyer advocates. The major reason that liability controls are not frequently used with regard to nonlawyers (except, perhaps, with regard to accountants) is the question of available sources of compensation for damages. Lawyers (and many other professionals) typically carry professional liability insurance, and this insurance provides a source of potential compensation. In fact, many states require at least some types of service providers to carry insurance or to be bonded, although only one state—Oregon—requires that lawyers carry liability insurance.[34] Licensing often provides a mechanism for enforcing an insurance requirement (and in fact, it may well be the most important aspect of some licensing systems).[35] Devising some type of licensing system for nonlawyer advocates who offer their services to the public could be justified on the grounds of providing an insurance mechanism (but this would probably also require imposing an insurance requirement on attorneys). With an insurance mechanism in place covering the work of nonlawyer advocates, there is no reason that the liability system would work any less well for nonlawyers than it currently does for lawyers.

The last mechanism, disciplinary controls, goes hand in hand with licensing. Here, however, the licensing authority assumes responsibility for discipline, while the liability system relies entirely upon the dissatisfied client/customer. The central component of this system is some mechanism for identifying possible problems, investigating and prosecuting problems, and imposing disciplinary sanctions upon proof that the problems are real. As with the liability mechanism, disciplinary controls rely upon the existence of some type of standards to be enforced. For most professions and occupations subject to licensing and regulation, it is executive agencies of the various states that handle the licensing and disciplinary process (in Wisconsin a Department of Regulation and Licensing handles this for a number of professions and occupations).[36] In most states, the state supreme court oversees the licensing of legal professionals because they are deemed to be "officers of the court."[37] One can imagine a variety of ways of organizing the licensing and disciplining of nonlawyer advocates, either through some central agency or through venue-specific offices. One might complain that such mechanisms would be costly for the public, but there is no reason that the license fees could not be set at a level that covers the cost of administration. Nonlawyer advocates might object to bearing this cost on the grounds that it would make their costs of practice so high that they could not compete with lawyers. If this is true, it in effect means that their current costs fail to reflect the "real costs" of their practice, because it does not take into account the need to protect clients from unethical behavior or to compensate clients for practitioner errors.[38]

In summary, the need to regulate and control nonlawyer advocates is real, but also feasible. The same types of mechanisms and protections for clients available with regard to legal professionals would work (and in some settings already exist) for nonlawyer advocates. The failure of these mechanisms to be further developed to date reflects a variety of factors: the relatively small stakes involved in large numbers of cases, the absence of apparent and recurring problems with nonlawyer advocates, and continuing unwillingness of the legal profession to accept and deal with the reality of nonlawyer practice. The latter of these may be the most important: the continued focus on the idea that the work of nonlawyer advocates represents the unauthorized practice of law results in the pursuit of traditional responses (i.e., seeking to suppress such work), rather than systematically investigating the nature of problems created by such activities and designing mechanisms to regulate the providers and protect their clients.

As discussed in chapter 1, beginning in the late 1980s and continuing into the 1990s various groups within the legal profession have considered the issue of nonlawyer practice. Starting with California, bar committees have studied the problems and potential of nonlawyer provision of legal services. Those committees have generally concluded that it is time to recognize both that such practice now exists and that it should, and probably will, expand. The response to these reports from the bar associations that spawned them have generally been hostile. In California, when the Commission on Legal Technicians developed proposals that would permit limited practice by nonlawyers and provide for the regulation of those practitioners, segments of the bar opposed to permitting any nonlawyer practice succeeded in blocking the commission's proposals both before the bar and in the legislature.[39] In 1992, the American Bar Association created a Commission on Nonlawyer Practice. In 1994, the commission published a document summarizing its findings that nonlawyer practice was already widespread and that there was no support for the traditional contention that such practice resulted in widespread abuse.[40] In response to this document, and in anticipation of a formal report and recommendation, ABA members hostile to the direction the commission was moving mobilized in opposition. Led by the former president of the State Bar of New Jersey, Thomas Curtin, the National Caucus of State Bar Associations adopted a resolution against any plan that would permit legal technicians to offer their services to the public.[41] The commission's final recommendations were relatively tame.[42]

> The range of activities of traditional paralegals should be expanded, with lawyers remaining accountable for their activities.
>
> States should consider allowing nonlawyer representation of individuals in state administrative agency proceedings. Nonlawyer representers [sic] should be subject to the agencies' standards of practice and discipline.
>
> The activities of nonlawyers who provide assistance, advice and representation authorized by statute, court rule or agency regulation should be continued, subject to review by the entity under whose authority the services are performed.
>
> With regard to the activities of all other nonlawyers, states should adopt an analytical approach in assessing whether and how to regulate varied forms of nonlawyer activity that exist or are emerging in their respective jurisdictions. Criteria for this analysis should include the risk of harm these activities present, whether consumers can evaluate providers' qualifications, and whether the net effect of regulating the activities will be a benefit to the public. State supreme courts should take the lead in examining specific nonlawyer activities within their jurisdictions with the active support and participation of the bar and public.

Two additional recommendations reflected the commission's recognition that the core issue was access by the citizenry to the legal services needed to achieve justice.

> The American Bar Association, state, local and specialty bar associations, the practicing bar, courts, law schools, and the federal and state governments should continue to develop and finance new and improved ways to provide access to justice to help the public meet its legal and law-related needs.

The American Bar Association should examine its ethical rules, policies and standards to ensure that they promote the delivery of
affordable competent services and access to justice.

These recommendations recognize the current reality, but refrain from
strongly advocating major extensions of that reality, with one exception.
The commission apparently was impressed that nonlawyer practice permitted under the federal Administrative Procedures Act had shown that
nonlawyers could effectively practice in administrative agencies; their
recognition of this fact seems to have led to their recommendation that
state administrative agencies be similarly opened to nonlawyer practice.
Beyond this one area, the commission stated its view that nonlawyers
could be effective, but recommended no action other than that the states
take an "analytical approach" in considering whether to extend rights of
nonlawyer practice and how to regulate that practice. Despite calls that the
ABA act upon and adopt the commission's recommendations,[43] no action
has been taken, and none appears contemplated. The commission's recommendations are quickly being forgotten, although a fairly large number
of states have been considering proposals to modify (or in some cases, to
enhance) existing limitations on nonlawyer practice.[44]

I completed my research and a first draft of this book, including the
core policy conclusions, before the release of the commission's final report.
The thrust of the commission's findings are consistent with my own analysis. I go somewhat beyond the commission's position regarding opening
up nonlawyer practice, but I am not subject to the political constraints and
lobbying the commission faced. I suspect that in the absence of the political assault, the commission would have taken a much stronger stand in
support of finding ways to permit a wide range of providers to offer legal
services to the public. Undoubtedly, just as I have suggested, the commission would want such providers to be subject to appropriate regulation
and discipline; the public can be well served by nonlawyer providers, but
must have suitable recourse should the services fall below some established
standard. In this regard, nonlawyer providers are no different than are
members of the legal profession, with the exception that my proposal
would require third-party insurance protection for consumers, which only
Oregon requires of the practicing bar.

Implications for Legal Education and the Structure of the Legal Profession

The strongest defense that the legal profession might mount against my
analysis is to come to grips with the issue of specialization, both in legal
practice and in legal training. While "expertise" and "specialization" are

conceptually distinct (one can have significant expertise in a particular area without being a specialist in that area), the interconnection between expertise and specialization has increased as the legal system has become more complex to meet the growth of legal and regulatory institutions. As specific expertise becomes more important in an area of legal practice, the relevance of specialization increases.[45] Recognizing the relevance of specialization is central to accepting the need for specific expertise that goes beyond the general expertise imparted by the contemporary American law school. One need only note the common linguistic roots of *specialization* and *specific* expertise.

The issue of specialization within the bar is almost as controversial as the issue of nonlawyer practice.[46] The legal profession clings to the image of the general practitioner, and there are many such practitioners at work across the country, particularly in smaller cities and towns. Through experience, the general practitioner develops the expertise and competence to handle a range of recurring matters. This broad range of competency builds upon the legal education provided by American law schools.

American legal education is best described as a professional liberal education.[47] That is, a law school is not a trade school.[48] The goal of legal education is to provide the future lawyer with a set of intellectual orientations and tools rather than the specific legal knowledge and skills necessary to provide legal services to real, live clients. It is not surprising that a common complaint of law school graduates is that law school failed to prepare them adequately for the real life world of law practice.[49] Legal academics freely acknowledge this problem, describing the role of law school as that of preparing students for the later process of learning how to handle legal practice by actually practicing.[50] The defenders of legal education argue that law school teaches the future lawyer how to analyze a case, how to do legal research, and, most importantly, how to "think like a lawyer."[51] The actual practice of law draws upon these skills but involves much more— things that can only be learned by doing.

At least some law schools have responded to criticisms about the lack of practical training by increasing the resources devoted to skills-oriented courses.[52] Schools have added courses on legal writing, beefed up attention to legal ethics and other important aspects of professionalism, and created both credit and noncredit clinic programs where students interact with clients who have real legal needs. However, these developments have brought no evidence of a decrease in the complaints of graduates that the reality of actual law practice comes as a shock.

In 1989, in response to various concerns about legal education, the ABA's Section on Legal Education and Admissions to the Bar created a Task Force on Law Schools and the Profession. The report of this Task

Force, known as the MacCrate Report,[53] discusses in detail the "skills and values" that lawyers should possess. The report does recognize that "changing law and new complexities have put an increasing premium on specialization to maintain competence and to keep abreast of subject matter."[54] However, strikingly absent from the MacCrate Report is the question of what "expertise" lawyers should possess and how lawyers should obtain that expertise. The report's authors recognize that lawyers should have expertise (or, to use the report's term, "competence"),[55] but they express this in terms of values:

> As a member of a profession dedicated to the service of clients, a lawyer should be committed to the values of:
>
> > Attaining a Level of Competence in One's Own Field of Practice;
> > Maintaining a Level of Competence in One's Own Field of Practice;
> > Representing Clients in a Competent Manner.[56]

The burden of obtaining this competence—which relates directly to specialization ("one's own field of practice")—lands squarely on the lawyer as an individual. In fact, possessing competence is not a requirement for accepting a case if the lawyer believes that he or she can obtain a "requisite level of competence . . . by reasonable preparation."[57] The judgment as to whether the lawyer has, or can obtain, the necessary competence lies solely with the lawyer, subject to the client deciding to retain the lawyer and the client having the option of bringing a disciplinary or malpractice action if the client believes the lawyer's performance demonstrated a lack of competence.

My research makes it clear that lawyers are not always the best judge of their own competence, and that competence is relative, not absolute. On a surprising number of occasions I saw lawyers representing clients in situations where the lawyer clearly lacks either the process expertise or the substantive expertise, or both, to do an effective job of serving the client. A personal anecdote, unrelated to this research, starkly illustrates this problem. My father decided to sell his house, and because he could not be present for the closing employed a lawyer recommended as someone knowledgeable about real estate to represent him. After the sale was completed, my father realized that he needed to make some changes in his will to reflect that he was no longer a homeowner, and to adjust some other provisions related to his personal situation. Having been satisfied with the services of the lawyer who handled the closing, he contacted that lawyer about handling the changes to the will. The lawyer indicated that he could handle that, and my father took him his existing will, explained the changes he wanted, and said something like "keep it simple." In fact, the existing will was not simple (for important reasons), and the key provision my father wanted to add shouted for something more than a simple bequest. The lawyer could not understand the need for the various complexities in the existing will, nor did he appear to make any efforts to find out if there were good reasons for those complexities; it never even occurred to him that a provision making a simple bequest was not what my father actually wanted. The result was that the lawyer produced a will that was inappropriate to my father's circumstances, which had to be completely rewritten. The lawyer may have been an excellent real estate lawyer, but he was a poor judge of his own competence to draft a will that required something more than standard clauses.

If minimal competency simply means that a client is better off being represented by a minimally knowledgeable lawyer than by no one at all, then lawyers do, in the venues I examined, usually bring at least this minimal competence. In many settings or situations, the only choice may be to use the services of a lawyer who has no more than this minimal competence (particularly if the matter is such that the lawyer cannot afford or is unwilling to invest considerable time in obtaining greater competence). However, my research shows that an expert nonlawyer is preferable to a minimally competent lawyer, and it may well make sense to facilitate the availability and use of expert nonlawyers where specialist lawyers are not available.

In a modern law-oriented society such as the United States, the skills–values duality is not sufficient. Much as in contemporary medical practice, the general practitioner can provide basic types of general services, but is not able to develop and maintain a high level of expertise in the range of matters brought by actual and potential clients. Specialists are able to provide higher-quality services, and to do so more efficiently, than is the generalist.

The issue of specialization is one that has been on the legal profession's agenda for some time.[58] Some areas, most clearly tax and intellectual property, have long been the province of specialists. In the arena of corporate legal services, the large corporate law firm has been organized around the idea of specialization for most, if not all, of the twentieth century.[59] However, only in the last twenty or thirty years has the issue of specialization begun to produce any formal developments, with the California bar adopting the first state-level system for certifying at least some specialists in 1973,[60] and private groups such as the National Board of Trial Advocacy creating their own specialist certification systems. In significant part, the specialization issue has been closely tied up with the question of lawyer advertising: under what circumstances should a lawyer be permitted to hold him- or herself out as a specialist in a particular area?[61] The

ABA Model Rules of Professional Conduct prohibit lawyers from claiming specialization except in officially recognized categories.[62] In the wake of the Supreme Court's 1977 decision striking down absolute bans on lawyer advertising, *Bates v. State Bar of Arizona,*[63] the ABA moved to create model standards for specialty areas, adopting a plan developed by the Standing Committee on Specialization in 1979.[64]

Surprisingly, only a minority of states have actually adopted systems for certifying specialists,[65] and proposals for such systems have often been controversial.

> Would recognizing specialities advantage some lawyers over others in getting clients?
> Would uncertified lawyers who actually practice in an area be more at risk for claims of malpractice in the event of a negative outcome?
> Would specialization drive up fees?[66]

Added to the controversy over the impact of recognizing specialization is the dilemma of which *dimensions* of specialization to recognize. In addition to substantive areas of law (tax, admiralty, real estate), there is the question of task-oriented specialities (litigation, administrative process, etc.) or venue-oriented specialties (Internal Revenue Service, Securities and Exchange Commission, federal court, U.S. Supreme Court, etc.). These are essentially the same as my distinctions among the three types of expertise: substantive, process, and insider expertise.[67]

Generally the developments with regard to specialization have been experience-related rather than training-related.[68] Unlike the medical profession, where one enters a formal training program (a residency) to become a specialist, a lawyer works in the field to become certified as a specialist. Only after a number of years of experience can the lawyer seek such certification. One can argue that training for a specialization today is where legal training was ninety years ago: it is essentially an apprentice system (but often without the guidance of an experienced mentor).[69] Just as legal training moved from the law office to the law school, it may be time that specialized training made a similar move.

Given that the profession has been reluctant to move forward in a major way to deal with the reality of specialization, it is not surprising that formal legal education has almost nothing to say about specialization. Law schools offer myriad specialized courses, but within the traditional three-year LL.B. or J.D. program, there is no structure to either permit or encourage specialization. There are increasing numbers of specialized masters' (LL.M.) programs in fields such as tax, real estate, agricultural law, banking law, securities regulation, and even government procurement law. The growth in LL.M. programs, which at one time were primarily aimed at persons who wanted to become law teachers, is in part a response to the MacCrate Report, but also a source of income for law schools.[70]

The idea that formal legal education should train specialists as well as generalists is not new. In 1990, several law professors published a proposal that envisioned a multitrack legal education in which a student could train to be a "generalist," a "generalist with designated speciality," a "complex specialist with a generalist base," or a "limited specialist."[71] This proposal received relatively modest attention, perhaps in part because it was appended to an attack on the contemporary prestige hierarchy of law schools, and in part because it had a very strong "trade school" flavor. The legal academy is unlikely to move in the trade school direction, given the status structure of the American university. However, even within this educational context, there are many professional programs that succeed in preparing students for the practice of their profession while maintaining academic legitimacy. Furthermore, it is not clear that including an element of specialization in legal education is inconsistent with the legal academy as we now know it.

One of the interesting comments I have heard from my law school colleagues is that it is most fun to teach the general education, first-year courses. At most schools these courses include the big five: criminal law, civil procedure, torts, contracts, and property. Law faculty see the first-year students as the most highly motivated. This motivation comes from the newness and uncertainty of the environment and from the fact that these courses serve to create the student hierarchy within each year's entering class (i.e., who will be at the top of the class, on law review, be most sought after, etc.). After the first year, the challenge decreases, and for those outside the class elite the motivation for grades is less. One might also speculate that within the range of elective courses students take in years two and three, it may not be clear what will actually be important for their future careers.

One could imagine a three-year law school program that retained the current first-year model, in which students learn how to read a case, how to do basic legal analysis, and how to use basic legal research tools. The third semester could easily consist of a number of electives, plus one of the remaining required or general courses (e.g., professional responsibility/ethics, evidence, constitutional law, etc.); semesters four and five could consist of the balance of the required/general courses, plus intensive study in an area of specialization. The final semester could include a combination of limited course work plus some clinic-oriented activities giving the students supervised, hands-on experience within the area of specialization. Alternately, one could imagine a joint LL.B./LL.M. program that required four years of study;[72] in this model, the third and fourth years would involve a combination of specialized course work and clerkship in a practice in the student's specialty or a relevant clinical experience.

Many other common-law countries require a period of clerkship in which a prospective lawyer must work in a legal office for six months to a year before obtaining a law license. In England, Canada, and Australia, this clerkship is referred to as "articling," shorthand for working for a period as an "articled clerk." Historically, articling is a remnant of the apprenticeship system for training lawyers (particularly solicitors). Articling receives mixed reviews from those who have gone through the system. A 1979 survey of then-recent Ontario law graduates, where prospective lawyers are required to complete a twelve-month articled clerkship,[73] found that 76 percent rated their articling experience as excellent or good "preparation for a career in law"; the remaining 24 percent rated the experience as fair (17 percent), not very good (5 percent), or not good at all (2 percent).[74] Despite an apparent surface satisfaction, various commentators have noted a variety of important dissatisfactions and have proposed alternative practical training experiences embedded in a clinical, as opposed to apprentice model.[75] English and Australian commentators have also noted dissatisfaction with articling as a training experience, reflecting problems with the apprenticeship model of the clerkships and changing structure of (and economic pressures on) legal practice.[76]

The clinical model, another type of hands-on training, has grown in favor.[77] Originally the intention of clinical legal education was to provide a mechanism for giving law students some hands-on experience while at the same time increasing the availability of legal services to disadvantaged groups. While many clinical programs still target the needs of those who otherwise might go without legal assistance, the concept of clinical programs has become more amorphous, covering virtually "any educational experience other than classroom discourse and library research."[78] In this broader sense, the model I am suggesting could be said to have a clinical component. The difference, however, is that the hands-on aspects of specialized training must have a more prominent role than clinical education currently has in most law school curricula. In effect, it probably needs to take the best of both the articling system (which involves working within private practice) and the clinical model (which typically is run through the law school itself) and combine them into a system where law schools work systematically with practitioners to provide students with needed practical experience.[79] This may involve rethinking and reworking current informal systems of summer (and academic year) clerkships in law firms so that more focused experiences are available. Where the goals of many of these programs and experiences today are to expose students to a setting or type of practice, the specialized clinical/clerkship model would have to involve more directed experiences, perhaps planned jointly by law faculty and practitioners who will directly work with and/or supervise students.

One of the questions that would have to be confronted in the development of a working model of legal education that included a significant element of specialization is the definition of specialties. In fact, before a system of specialized education could be put into operation, the profession must confront the reality of legal specialization as it has come to exist at the end of the twentieth century.

Legal Advocacy in a Postprofessional World

While the central focus of my analysis has been on the practical question of whether nonlawyers can be effective advocates, the results of that analysis raise intriguing theoretical issues regarding the study of professions and their role in society. While I hesitate to add another "post-word" to a lexicon now overflowing with "posts" (postmodernism, poststructuralism, postmaterialism, postindustrialism, post-Soviet, post-this, and post-that), my analysis suggests that it would be useful to begin to think about *postprofessionalism* as a concept that encapsulates many of the developments described by my analysis.[80]

In his influential book, *The Coming of Post-Industrial Society,* Daniel Bell advances the argument that the late twentieth and the early twenty-first centuries will be marked by sharp shifts in the nature of social and economic organization. Bell argues that these turn on the decline in importance of heavy manufacturing and the increasing significance of high-end services and technical expertise.[81] Much of his analysis ties directly to the role of professions in society, so much so that Bell at one point notes that it would not have been inaccurate to label the phenomenon he was describing as the "professional society,"[82] although he seems to have been thinking more in terms of scientific and technical professions than of some of the traditional professions such as law and the clergy.

Carroll Seron draws heavily on the concept of postindustrialism as a vehicle for developing her analysis of solo and small firm attorneys. She is particularly interested in the ways that postindustrialism shapes the opportunities for and the structure of the segments of legal practice geared to serving the needs of individuals and small businesses.[83] Seron observes that

> Legal entrepreneurs push the boundaries of the norms of professionalism and incorporate a diversity of postindustrial designs. The leeway they enjoy, however, is protected only *absent a change in policy*

by the profession at large or the successful demand for a change in policy by outside and marginal groups [emphasis in the original]. For example, these findings suggest that the expansive use of paralegals ... pose[s] an institutional challenge to a delicate balance across occupations ... A movement for professional autonomy for paralegals upsets the balance between occupational domains.[84]

Seron very briefly describes the movement to permit independent paralegals to offer services directly to the public. What she does not see is that this movement is part of the phenomenon of postprofessionalism.

What do I mean by postprofessionalism? Obviously, the starting point to answer that question is a definition of *profession.* Within the extensive literature on the professions scholars have suggested a variety of definitions.[85] This is not the place to delve into an extensive review of the professions literature, and for my purposes the least restrictive definition is adequate: "professions are exclusive occupational groups applying somewhat abstract knowledge to particular cases."[86] There are two key elements to this definition: exclusive occupational groups and the application of abstract knowledge. Postprofessionalism refers to the loss of exclusivity combined with routinizing the application of knowledge through a combination of increased specialization and reliance on information technology. The result is that services previously provided only by members of professions can now be delivered by specialized nonprofessionals.

One of the intriguing developments regarding professions in recent years has been the loss of control over the marketplace for their services. In an essay entitled "The Decline of Professionalism," Richard Abel argues that the legal profession's control over both the production of producers (i.e., entry into the profession) and production by producers (by whom and how legal services are delivered) has declined in the latter decades of the twentieth century. One result is that the number of lawyers has increased sharply; a second is that traditional controls such as limits on advertising, mandatory fee schedules, and the like have either disappeared or have been greatly relaxed. More generally, the role of professional organizations as the guardians of the profession's rights and privileges has declined.[87] Abel argues that the development, and now the decline, of the professions reflected a historical "trajectory of professionalism"; that is, professions are "historically specific institutions for organizing the production and distribution of services."[88] Recent developments reflect changes in the production and distribution of services. While part of the loss of control is due to things such as increasing access to education,[89] much of it reflects changes in how knowledge is developed and distributed in society.

One of the elements of emphasis in Daniel Bell's analysis of the coming postindustrial society is the role of knowledge. While he sees the most apparent change in the shift from production of goods to production of services, Bell argues that it is the growth in the professional and technical occupations that is the "most startling change."[90] The work of these occupations revolves around knowledge, and it is around knowledge that postindustrial society is organized. Bell observed that knowledge has been "necessary for the functioning of any society," but went on to argue that what distinguishes knowledge in the postindustrial society is the centrality of "theoretical knowledge—the primacy of theory over empiricism and the codification of knowledge into abstract systems of symbols."[91]

Bell fails to see one implication of the codification of knowledge which has served to undercut the role of professions in much of day-to-day life (even while they may remain central to scientific and technological advances). The codification of knowledge makes possible the subdivision of expertise in ways that allow persons with much less than traditional professional training to deliver services that rely upon knowledge previously the province of professionals. The codification and general systematization of knowledge and information make it possible to develop new ways of imparting and accessing that knowledge. In addition, the more that knowledge can be converted to or expressed in terms of information and decision-making rules, the more the tools of information technology can be brought to bear in using that knowledge.

One observable sign of codification of knowledge is increasing differentiation within many professions in terms of specialization. Where we once thought of doctors or lawyers, we now have doctors who describe themselves as allergists, cardiologists, dermatologists, endocrinologists, nephrologists, neurologists, pediatricians, obstetricians, oncologists, ophthalmologists, orthopedists, otorhinolaryngologists, radiologists, rheumatologists, urologists, and a whole host of surgeons; and lawyers who are legal specialists in criminal defense, divorce and family, elder law, insurance defense, labor law, litigation, patents and trademarks, personal injury, real estate, workers' compensation, and wills and estates. As the professionals have recognized the quality and efficiency gains of specialization, they have built on the identification of specialized tasks within their already specialized areas of work to delegate to nonprofessionals or lesser professionals. Many of these tasks are extremely routine, but this is not always the case. In fact, in some of the areas of practice, the professionals are able to design the practice so that relatively little of the client or patient contact is with the professional him- or herself. In a sense, the professionals have themselves created many of the conditions for postprofessionalism to take hold.

Given the very close linkage between information and knowledge, the rapidly improving tools for accessing information reduce the need to rely upon highly trained individuals who have acquired extensive information as part of their training. Take for example the ways of delivering support for complex technological tools such as computer hardware and software. At one time, most sellers of these tools hired experienced professionals to provide user consulting; support staff needed to have a thorough understanding of the software (and frequently the hardware it ran on) to be able to diagnose and solve user problems. Over time, information technology has emerged that allows technology companies to build sophisticated data bases of information that persons with small amounts of training and experience can access to deal with many, if not most, user questions and problems.

Among providers of legal services, the traditional tools for accessing legal information (i.e., case law) was a sophisticated set of categories closely tied to a variety of legal concepts. These categories, developed by the West Publishing Company, form the West "Key Number" system, which in turn is integrated into the West Digests. To effectively access case law, one needed training in the central concepts that lie at the core of the category system. Modern information technology has led to an alternative system for accessing case law: free text searches using massive electronic data bases (most prominently Westlaw and Lexis). The result is to make it possible for persons with a much less sophisticated understanding of legal categories and principles to perform at least rudimentary legal research. For example, lawyers regularly delegate research tasks to paralegals and legal assistants.

As tasks become specialized and it becomes possible for persons to acquire the limited set of knowledge necessary to deliver highly specific services traditionally the domain of a member of a recognized profession, it becomes increasingly difficult for the profession to maintain any exclusivity over those tasks. A common claim by professionals seeking to protect their domain is that someone without the level of training required to be a full member of the profession will not be able to recognize the complex interrelationships and subtle issues raised in a specific case. This argument is used by lawyers seeking to ban nonlawyers from handling real estate closings, and by ophthalmologists seeking to limit the tasks that can be carried out by optometrists. Yet, at each point when previously restricted tasks have been opened to new providers, the problems predicted by the profession opposing relaxation of restrictions have failed to materialize in significant numbers (if at all).

The transition to postprofessionalism is similar in some ways to the transition from a craft-based to an industrial-based mode of production of products. Prior to the modern factory, craftspeople produced most non-agricultural goods for sale. Becoming a craftsperson was typically a process that involved many years, usually achieved by serving an apprenticeship. The craftsperson typically possessed a number of interrelated skills that together were necessary to produce a type of product. The development of the factory revolved around isolating the individual tasks needed for production and then hiring semiskilled workers each with just enough skill to carry out one (or several) of those tasks. The result was cheaper production of products, a shift from human capital (in the form of skilled craftspeople) to industrial capital, the destruction of livelihoods for large numbers of craftspeople, and the effective end of many crafts (except for highly specialized or artistic applications).

Postprofessionalism is a similar phenomenon, but rather than the production of specialized goods it involves the production of specialized services. Much as craftspeople were displaced by early technological developments and the division of tasks into relatively simple elements, professionals are being displaced by service providers organized around highly specialized tasks who may, when needed, draw upon modern technological tools to access information. Just as craftspeople viewed this new form of goods production as a threat to their livelihood, members of modern professions are having to deal with the economic threats posed by specialized service providers. Where industrialization shattered the traditional economic role of persons skilled in the use of their hands, postprofessionalism is an equivalent development for those skilled in the use of their heads.

To date, the medical profession, at least in the United States, has succeeded in maintaining control over most nonprofessionals who might be potential competitors for routine service delivery. Health maintenance organizations (HMOs) and other organizational providers of medical care use specialized paraprofessionals for an increasing number of tasks. While it still at least appears that the professional physician is formally in control, that control is shifting from the physician to the organization. As part of this, the paraprofessional providers may be achieving elements of autonomy (from physicians if not from the organization), which they had not previously enjoyed. Where before the paraprofessional was limited to roles that supplemented physicians, they are increasingly supplanting physicians, which in turn reduces the number of physicians needed.[92] These changes reflect the health care providers' needs to obtain economies. As physicians begin to lose jobs within these organizational medical providers, they will begin to have to deal with the pressures of postprofessionalism.

For lawyers, postprofessionalism is real and immediate. Over the last several years, whenever a group has been appointed to examine the issue of whether it is time for the legal profession to come to grips with the reality of nonlawyers providing a wide range of legal services, the resulting report has recommended finding a way to accommodate (and regulate) the competing providers. In every case, elements of the bar have opposed the proposals, usually successfully. This has delayed their coming to grips with the brave new world of postprofessionalism, but it has not prevented that world from emerging. For the legal profession, the task of holding back the pressures of postprofessionalism is complicated by the political unpopularity of the profession. How long the profession can succeed in retaining substantial control over the provision of legal services is a question I cannot answer. This study, however, shows that many of the customary arguments cannot be justified by systematic empirical research.

Was there ever any validity to the arguments used by the legal profession in support of limits on who could provide legal services, or did the success of the profession in asserting a broad monopoly simply reflect the political power of the profession? Many observers have pointed out that American legislatures are relatively unique in the high proportion of lawyers among their members. One might argue that lawyers have only maintained their control over delivery of legal services because of their political strength. However, this argument neglects the fact that professional monopolies have involved fields other than law.

Furthermore, the conflicts within the legal profession are deep and long-standing; given those conflicts, there is no reason to expect that the profession itself would be united over the issue of what constitutes legal practice. Similarly, there are deep conflicts within the profession over the issue of specialization, and it is precisely those conflicts that have prevented significant movement on the specialization issue. Interestingly, while the question of what constitutes the practice of law is an issue that might be seen as dividing the profession between those who serve individual or small-business clients and those who serve large organizations,[93] my analysis shows that the issue of specialization is one that cuts across the client base. The nature of expertise involved in many areas is not so esoteric as to be relevant only to the large consumer of legal services; it is just as important for lawyers serving individuals as it is for lawyers serving corporations.

Is it only politics that is holding back the postprofessional tide, or might there be other structural factors that help maintain the role of professionals who serve individual and organizational clients? For example, it might be that clients value the professional–client relationship in ways that will make moving toward paraprofessionals difficult. Seron argues that the solo and small-firm lawyers she studied perceived that the relationship they had with a client was very important from the client's perspective.[94] Interestingly, in the area where this is probably the most true, divorce cases, many of the practitioners are uncomfortable with the nature of client expectations for the lawyer–client relationship. They see the client as expecting a relationship that the lawyer either cannot guarantee to deliver (the knight-in-shining-armor advocate) or is not trained to deliver (the social worker/therapist).[95]

While many clients do want a "relationship" with the provider of "professional" services, others see the professional simply as a service provider from whom they want an efficiently delivered service. Expectations vary among clients and patients just as expectations vary among consumers generally. Keep in mind that some consumers value the product of the craftsperson and will choose that over the more standard industrial product despite the increased cost. Some consumers may prefer a relationship with a professional and be willing to pay for it. This pattern exists in today's medical marketplace. There is a lot of discussion of the breaking of the traditional doctor–patient relationship (although what most people are actually referring to is the general practitioner–patient relationship; few people had long-standing relationships with their surgeon!). While many people are forced by employers or others to obtain medical services through one of the new types of organizations, others have a choice. Typically that choice involves paying a premium for the traditional fee-for-service medical service; just as some fraction of consumers of products pay for the handmade or custom-made item produced by a craftsperson, some people are willing to pay a premium to maintain a traditional doctor–patient relationship (and to increase their flexibility of choice among medical service providers). In a hundred years, it will be interesting to look back and see if the expectations associated with the doctor–patient relationship have disappeared as those who remember (probably in somewhat idealized terms) "the way it used to be" pass from the scene.

Finally, while I may be overstating the changes that are occurring, it is also very possible that I have grossly underestimated the changes that will be coming in the organization of work as applied to service providers. The origins of the rise of professions lay in significant part in the nature of the knowledge base that existed at the time the professions came into prominence. My image of postprofessionalism revolves largely around the way that service providers segment and deliver services that draw on that knowledge base. However, it may well be that the nature of knowledge is much more fluid than I have imagined, and that the future organization of occupations will not turn on the kinds of expertise that we see today. If knowledge becomes increasingly accessible in ways that require less and less specialized training and experience, we may see forms of organization delivering services that we cannot at this time readily imagine. Such a development would radically alter the way that work is organized, particularly in what we call the service sector of the economy. Perhaps there will be a post-service economy in the year 2100, and doctors, lawyers, and other professionals as we know them today will have largely disappeared from our social and occupational structure.

Notes

Chapter 1

1. William L. F. Felstiner, "Influences of Social Organization on Dispute Processing," *Law & Society Review* 9 (1974): 81.

2. There is a popular perception that contingency fees start at one-third and go up from there. A survey of Wisconsin contingency fee practitioners shows that only about half of the cases those lawyers described for the survey involved a fee fixed as one-third of the recovery; see Herbert M. Kritzer, "Investing in Justice: Making Money from Contingency Fee Work," *Wisconsin Lawyer* 70, no. 8 (Aug. 1997): 12.

3. As I will explain below, in some types of cases, the precourt aspects might be handled by a nonlawyer advocate. I could identify only three types of cases in which nonlawyers do appear as advocates for clients (other than themselves—i.e., other than *pro se,* or other than police officers "prosecuting" traffic offenses in justice of the peace or traffic courts) in a "court" proceeding.

The U.S. tax court (which is actually not part of the judiciary)
Tribal courts situated on lands reserved to Native Americans
Some domestic and sexual violence cases

See *Nonlawyer Practice in the United States: Summary of the Factual Record Before the American Bar Association Commission on Nonlawyer Practice,* Discussion Draft for Comment (Chicago: American Bar Association, April 1994), 19–20.

4. In fact, the organized legal profession, which is dominated by private practitioners, has been hostile to competition even when it comes from within the profession. The bar opposed the creation of services for the poor funded by the federal government out of fear that it would draw off clients and shift control from the profession to the government; see Earl Johnson Jr., *Justice and Reform: The Formative Years of the American Legal Services Program* (New York: Russell Sage Foundation, 1974), 18–19, 43–64. More recently, the private practice bar in some states has tried to find ways to prevent insurance companies from having in-house counsel represent insureds in tort actions; see Michael A. Macc, "Insurance Companies Move Defense In-House," *National Law Journal* (Nov. 13, 1995), sec. C, 38.

5. *Nonlawyer Activity in Law-Related Situations: A Report with Recommendations* (Chicago: American Bar Association Commission on Nonlawyer Practice, 1995).

6. A parent who attended her daughter's undergraduate commencement at Stanford in 1995 reported this to me: at the university-wide graduation ceremonies, the audience booed when the law students were asked to stand up and be recognized. A source I spoke with at the university said that there was something of a good-natured tradition of students booing some of the professional graduates (law and business), but that source did not realize that the audience had joined in the booing of the law graduates.

7. See Z. Bankowski and G. Mungham, "Laypeople and Lawpeople and the Administration of the Lower Courts," *International Journal of the Sociology of Law* 8 (1981): 89.

8. See Frederick H. Zemans, "The Non-lawyer as a Means of Providing Legal Services," in *Lawyers and the Consumer Interest,* eds. R. G. Evans and M. J. Trebilcock (Toronto: Butterworths, 1982), 277–85.

9. Advocates appearing in the magistrates' courts, which deal with minor criminal matters, have been quoted as acknowledging the limited requirements for handling work in that venue: "It's a matter of acclimatisation, not skill . . . Anybody can tackle criminal advocacy; just learn the mumbo-jumbo, that's all"; quoted in Roger Cotterrell, *The Sociology of Law: An Introduction,* 2d ed. (London: Butterworths, 1992), 195.

10. Until the mid-1980s, English solicitors held a monopoly on handling property transfers ("conveyancing"); they now share the work with licensed conveyancers.

11. The primary work of many loss assessors is not negotiating personal injury settlements; rather, they assist persons (or organizations) who have experienced a loss in negotiating settlements with their own insurance companies (e.g., if a house burns down, a loss assessor might be employed by the homeowner to provide an independent assessment of the loss). The parallel group in the United States would be public insurance adjusters; see "The Professional Public Insurance Adjuster: Working for You . . . On Your Side!" (Washington, DC: National Association of Public Insurance Adjusters, 1988). In at least one state, Massachusetts, some of these public adjusters do handle third-party personal injury claims; see *Nonlawyer Practice,* 21, A.MA-2.

12. In 1995 it became permissible for English solicitors to offer their clients the option of paying on a no-win, no-pay basis. However, this fee system, called "conditional fees," does not work on a percentage of recovery basis as do contingency fees in the United States (the American system of percentage fees is really a commission fee system). The new English system allows solicitors to charge a premium on their normal fee of as much as 100% to clients who opt for the conditional arrangement. See "Conditional Fees Implemented," UK Goverment Press Release, Reuter Textline (Nexis), July 4, 1995.

13. As noted previously, some public insurance adjusters in Massachusetts (and perhaps other states) provide this type of service. One such adjuster reported that he learned how to handle claims by working for an insurance company; see *Nonlawyer Practice,* 21.

14. Malcolm Dean, "Victims Told to Avoid Assessors," *Guardian,* March 3,

1987, 2; "Maintenance and Champerty: Claims Assessors and Contingency Fees," Memorandum by the Council of the Law Society (March 1970), 1–6.

15. Hazel Genn and Yvette Genn, *The Effectiveness of Representation at Tribunals* (London: Lord Chancellor's Department, 1989), 243–44.

16. For the more legalistic tribunals, many presiding officers believed that a law-trained specialist was needed; ibid., 245–46.

17. Ron W. Ianni, *Report of the Task Force on Paralegals in Ontario* (Toronto, Ontario: Ministry of the Attorney General, 1990), 64–69.

18. W. A. Bogart and Neil Vidmar, "Empirical Profile of Independent Paralegals in the Province of Ontario." Report prepared for the Ontario Task Force on Independent Paralegals (Windsor: University of Windsor Law School, 1989), 73.

19. Ibid., 47–48.

20. Nelly Zoric-Kappos, "Pointts: Customer Survey" (Mar. 1994); appended to John G. Kelly, "Client Centered Legal Services" (mimeo by author, Toronto, n.d.).

21. Computed by the author from machine-readable data set, Terance D. Miethe, *Public Attitudes Toward Lawyers and Legal Disputes, 1993* (Ann Arbor, MI: Inter-university Consortium for Political and Social Research, 1995). The percentage did not vary appreciably by the type of matter the lawyer handled (one of the coded types was traffic offenses).

22. Gary A. Hengstler, "Vox Populi: The Public Perception of Lawyers: ABA Poll," *ABA Journal* 79, no. 9 (September 1993): 60–61.

23. Computed by the author from data collected for West Publishing/National Law Journal by Penn & Schoen Associates; a general discussion of the results of the survey can be found in Randall Samborn, "Poll: Image of Lawyers Around Country Grows Worse," *New York Law Journal,* April 2, 1993, 1.

24. *Nonlawyer Activity,* 159; the contexts considered by the commission went well beyond the advocacy settings I will be examining.

25. As late as 1996, elements of the Virginia bar were pushing legislation to ban title insurance underwriters and settlement agents from conducting real estate closings. See Ann Davis, "Virginia Bar Wants to Be There at Closings," *National Law Journal* (Sept. 6, 1996), sec. A, 6.

26. R. Bucher and A. Strauss, "Professions in Process," *American Sociological Review* 66 (1961): 325–34; Robert Dingwall, "Accomplishing Profession," *Sociological Review* 24 (1976): 331–49; Gerald L. Geison, *Professions and Professional Ideologies in America* (Chapel Hill: University of North Carolina Press, 1983); Everett C. Hughes, "Professions," *Daedalus* 92 (1963): 655–68; Talcott Parsons, "Professions," in *International Encyclopedia of the Social Sciences,* ed. David Sills (New York: Macmillan, 1968), 12:536–47.

27. Deborah Chalfie, "Lawyers Not Only Source of Good Legal Advice," *Milwaukee Journal* (Dec. 23, 1989), sec. A, 9.

28. Richard L. Abel, *American Lawyers* (New York: Oxford University Press, 1989), 246.

29. Herbert M. Kritzer, *The Justice Broker: Lawyers and Ordinary Litigation* (New York: Oxford University Press, 1990), 170–76.

30. Carroll Seron, *The Business of Practicing Law: The Work Lives of Solo and Small-Firm Attorneys* (Philadelphia: Temple University Press, 1996), 82.

31. Marc Galanter; "The Day After the Litigation Explosion," *Maryland Law Review* 46 (1986): 3–39; Deborah R. Hensler, "Reading the Tort Litigation Tea Leaves: What's Going On in the Civil Liability System?" *Justice System Journal* 16 (1993): 139–54; Thomas B. Marvell, "Tort Caseload Trends and the Impact of Tort Reforms," *Justice System Journal* 17 (1994): 193–206.

32. One must be careful not to overstate this inclination given that the United States has long looked to the courts for a wide range of issues; to quote the famous line from Alexis de Tocqueville's nineteenth-century classic *Democracy in America,* "Scarcely any political question arises in the United States that is not resolved, sooner or later, into a judicial question"; ed. P. Bradley (New York: Alfred Knopf, 1945), 280.

33. Erhard Blankenberg, "The Infrastructure for Avoiding Civil Litigation: Comparing Cultures of Legal Behavior in The Netherlands and West Germany," *Law & Society Review* 28 (1994): 789–808.

34. See Abel, *American Lawyers,* 112–15; Willard Hurst, *The Growth of American Law* (Boston: Little, Brown, 1950), 319–25; Barlow F. Christensen, "The Unauthorized Practice of Law: Do Good Fences Really Make Good Neighbors—or Even Good Sense?" *American Bar Foundation Journal* (1980): 159–216.

35. I base my discussion on the work of Corinne Lathrop Gilb, "Self-Regulating Professions and the Public Welfare: A Case Study of the California Bar" (Ph.D. thesis, Radcliffe College, 1956), 220–55. Unless otherwise indicated, I have based my description of specific events and developments on Gilb's account; for the most part, I have omitted specific page citations.

36. *California Code of Civil Procedure* v. 1 (1872), 281, 145 (cited in ibid., 230).

37. *People v. Merchants Protective Corp.* 189 Cal. 531 at 535 (1922).

38. These independent adjusters are much like the current-day "loss assessors" in England; the position of the Law Society is that it is unethical for solicitors to handle cases referred to them by loss assessors. Nonetheless, I was told by both assessors and insurers that the assessors have no trouble finding a solicitor to handle cases that the assessors are not able to settle. Interestingly, nonlawyers are permitted to appear in workers' compensation proceedings before the administrative body that handles such cases; *Eagle Indemnity Company v. Industrial Accident Commission* 217 Cal. 244 (1933).

39. Starting in 1937, the American Bar Association entered into agreements with the national organizations of a number of competitors; see Quintin Johnstone, "The Unauthorized Practice Controversy: A Struggle Among Power Groups," *University of Kansas Law Review* 4 (1955), 22–29.

40. Quoted in Gilb, "Self-Regulating Professions," 234.

41. This agreement generated some controversy with several local bar associations that had persuaded local title companies to agree to even greater restrictions.

42. While the fact that this was limited to "gratuitous" advice might seem like a minor threat to the bar, "gratuitous" could be interpreted as any advice not specifically charged for (i.e., the legal services would be bundled into other services for a single price).

43. *Agran v. Shapiro,* 127 Cal. App. 2d Supp. 807 (1954).

44. See "Agran Case in Perspective," *Unauthorized Practice News* 22 (December 1956): 37–41.

45. *Zelkin v. Caruso Discount Corporation,* 186 Cal. App. 2d 802 (1960).

46. For a summary of the current status in California, see *Nonlawyer Practice,* A.CA–1ff.

47. Christensen, "Unauthorized Practice," 190.

48. This estimate is based on figures reported by Deborah Rhode, "Policing the Professional Monopoly: A Constitutional and Empirical Analysis of Unauthorized Practice Prohibitions," *Stanford Law Review* 34 (1981): 29, 33. She reports a figure of 1,188 "inquiries, investigations, and complaints" for a subset of states that does not appear to include California. I arrived at the 1,600 figure by adding together the 1,188 and 395 and rounding; the 2,000 is a guesstimate.

49. Ibid., 36–38.

50. Ibid., 33–34. The role of unauthorized practice of law enforcement as more of a protection of lawyers than a protection of consumers was noted empirically as long as 40 years ago; see Johnstone, "Unauthorized Practice Controversy," 3–4.

51. But see, "Bar: Bean Counters Are Doing Our Work," *National Law Journal* (Oct. 13, 1997), sec. A, p. 5; "Attorney-Client Privilege for Bean Counters?" *National Law Journal* (Nov. 10, 1997), sec. A, p. 12.

52. 5 U.S.C. §555(b) (1994).

53. Donald J. Quigg, "Nonlawyer Practice Before the Patent and Trademark Office," *Administrative Law Review* 37 (1985): 409–11.

54. David B. Holmes, "Nonlawyer Practice Before the Immigration Agencies," *Administrative Law Review* 37 (1985): 417–19.

55. Jacob M. Wolf, "Nonlawyer Practice Before the Social Security Administration," *Administrative Law Review* 37 (1985): 413–15; Jerry L. Mashaw et al., *Social Security Hearings and Appeals: A Study of the Social Security Administration Hearing System* (Lexington, MA: Lexington Books, 1978), 92–96; William D. Popkin, "The Effect of Representation in Nonadversary Proceedings—A Study of Three Disability Programs," *Cornell Law Review* 62 (1977): 1029–30.

56. See *Nonlawyer Practice,* 18; in *Sperry v. Florida ex rel Florida Bar,* 373 U.S. 379 (1963), the U.S. Supreme Court ruled that the Administrative Procedures Act provisions preempt any state action to enforce unauthorized practice rules against nonlawyers appearing before federal agencies.

57. Rhode, "Policing the Professional Monopoly," 78.

58. Ibid.

59. For example, between 1973 and 1982, the State Bar of Wisconsin devoted substantial time and effort to trying to block Peter Anderson, an environmental activist who served as public affairs director for the organization Wisconsin's Environmental Decade, from appearing before the state's Public Service Commission.

60. Richard Lempert and Karl Monsma, "Lawyers and Informal Justice: The Case of a Public Housing Eviction Board," *Law and Contemporary Problems* 51 (1988): 135–80; Karl Monsma and Richard Lempert, "The Value of Counsel: 20

Years of Representation before a Public Housing Eviction Board," *Law & Society Review* 26 (1992): 627–67.

61. William Simon, *An Innovative Model Providing High Quality Legal Assistance for the Elderly in Wisconsin* (Madison: Center for Public Representation, 1989).

62. *Report of the Public Protection Committee* (San Francisco: State Bar of California, 1989), 2.

63. Rosalind Resnick, "Looking at Alternative Services," *National Law Journal* (June 10, 1991), 32.

64. Victoria Slind-Flor, " 'No' to Legal Technicians in California," *National Law Journal* (Sept. 9, 1991), 19.

65. See Deborah R. Hensler and Marisa E. Reddy, *California Lawyers View the Future: A Report on the Future of the Legal Profession and the State Bar* (Santa Monica: RAND Corporation, 1994), 11, 17.

66. Rosalind Resnick, "Legal Techs Face Regulation," *National Law Journal* (June 22, 1992), 3.

67. Randall Samborn, "So What Is a Lawyer, Anyway?" *National Law Journal* (June 21, 1993), 42.

68. Mike France, "Bar Chiefs Protect the Guild," *National Law Journal* (Aug. 7, 1995), sec. A, 1, 28.

69. *Nonlawyer Activity,* 4–12.

70. Hope Viner Samborn, "Shades of Regulation: State Bills Apply Sundry Standards to Independent Paralegals," *ABA Journal* 83, no. 6 (June 1997): 26.

71. Interestingly, the most extensive systematic comparison of lawyers and nonlawyers has focused on their performance as judges in limited jurisdiction courts rather than as representatives. A study that compared lay and law-trained town and village justices in New York state found little to distinguish the work of the two groups. See Doris Marie Provine, *Judging Credentials: Nonlawyer Judges and the Politics of Professionalism* (Chicago: University of Chicago Press, 1986). Similarly, a study carried out in England that compared the sentencing patterns of law-trained and lay magistrates (judges of the lower criminal courts) found only minimal differences; see Shari Seidman Diamond, "Revising Images of Public Punitiveness: Sentencing by Lay and Professional English Magistrates," *Law & Social Inquiry* 15 (1990): 191–221.

72. In a recent U.S. study of the impact of representation in public housing eviction hearings, the authors chose to simply group lawyers and paralegals under the label "legal representation"; see Monsma and Lempert, "The Value of Counsel."

73. One part of a study of the legal needs of the elderly in Wisconsin examined a program of legal assistance to the elderly that uses nonlawyer "benefit specialists." As described by Simon, *An Innovative Model,* the primary function of benefit specialists is to assist elderly persons in obtaining the benefits to which they are entitled (Social Security, Medicare, Medicaid, various tax credits, etc.). As part of this work, benefit specialists will appear as advocates on behalf of clients in administrative hearings. The legal needs report provides an extensive description of the organizational framework in which benefit specialists work (including training and

attorney backup) and the kinds of caseloads handled by benefit specialists in terms of the kinds of issues dealt with and number of clients served, but no more than a brief mention of their more formal advocacy work; see Spangenberg Group, *Wisconsin Elder Legal Needs Study* (Madison: Wisconsin Bureau on Aging, 1991).

74. The authors are not able to give a specific estimate of the percentage of cases in which legal counsel fail to provide adequate representation, but they note that "everyone in the offices we surveyed seemed to agree that it was a significant part of the whole. Our direct observations were consistent with the perceptions of the people involved in the [hearing] process"; Mashaw et al., *Social Security Hearings,* 91–92.

75. Ibid., 92. In a study of representation in nonadversary proceedings, Popkin reports one comparison of attorney versus nonattorney representatives: attorneys are no more likely to request a hearing than are nonattorneys (96% versus 93%) but they are more likely to introduce new evidence at the hearing than are nonattorneys (67% versus 47%); see Popkin, "Effects of Representation," 1029–30.

76. Legal Services Corporation, *Special Legal Problems and Problems of Access to Legal Services of Veterans, Migrant and Seasonal Farm Workers, Native Americans, People with Limited English-Speaking Abilities, Individuals in Sparsely Populated Areas* (Washington, DC: Legal Services Corporation, 1979).

77. Frank Kochman, "Investigation into the Present State of Special Legal Representation of Veterans." Appendix A in *Special Legal Problems and Problems of Access to Legal Services of Veterans, Migrant and Seasonal Farm Workers, Native Americans, People with Limited English-Speaking Abilities, Individuals in Sparsely Populated Areas* (Washington, DC: Legal Services Corporation, 1979), A-56. While the success percentage for attorneys is based on a total of only 44 cases (compared to 263 cases for service organization representatives), the gap is so large that the difference is statistically significant.

78. Ibid., A-32.

79. Derby suggests a somewhat similar set of categories—competency, attorney–client relationship, disciplinary proceedings, solicitation of business, expense and access—as criteria for evaluating the appropriateness of nonlawyer representatives; see Lloyd P. Derby, "The Unauthorized Practice of Law by Laymen and Lay Associates," *California Law Review* 54 (1966): 1334–43.

80. There is a fourth dimension that I will not consider in my research: *representational context.* This dimension can also be thought of as having three subdimensions.

> *Case-oriented vs. policy-oriented.* Is the representation provided for specific cases, disputes, or problems, or is it focused on the formulation of policy before legislative or administrative agencies?
> *Locus of decision-making.* Is the ultimate decision made by the parties and their representatives, or is the decision made by some third-party adjudicator, rule-maker, or legislator? Is the third party a facilitator of some type (e.g., a mediator) or an ultimate decision maker (e.g., an adjudicator)?
> *Process control.* Is the presentation of issues, facts, arguments, and so forth

controlled primarily by the parties and their representatives, or is it controlled by the third party?

81. Committee on the Future of the Legal Profession (The Marre Committee),
A Time for Change (London: The General Council of the Bar & The Law Society,
1988).

82. See Kritzer, *The Justice Broker.*

83. H. Laurence Ross, *Settled Out of Court* (New York: Aldine Publishing
Company, 1980); Jerome Carlin, *Lawyers on Their Own: A Study of Individual
Practitioners in Chicago* (New Brunswick, NJ: Rutgers University Press, 1962).

84. Austin Sarat and William L. F. Felstiner, "Law and Strategy in the Divorce
Lawyer's Office," *Law & Society Review* 20 (1986): 93–134; see also Austin Sarat
and William L. F. Felstiner, *Divorce Lawyers and Their Clients* (New York: Oxford
University Press, 1995).

85. Another similar area, where nonlawyers are generally *excluded,* is bankruptcy; see *In re Matter of Arthur* 15 B.R. 541 (1981).

86. This dimension is probably the most closely linked to political discussions
of representation; the alternate definition above (*delegate* versus *trustee*) is trace-
able directly to the writings of Edmund Burke (*Reflections on the Revolution in
France,* 1790), who first discussed these two contrasting images of the role of the
representative.

87. See Amy B. Chasanov and Eileen Cubanski, "Understanding Denials and
Appeals in the United States," paper presented at Second Research Conference on
Reform of the Unemployment Insurance System (sponsored by the Advisory
Council on Reform of the Unemployment Insurance System), Colchester, VT,
Aug. 17–18, 1995, 44.

88. See Douglas E. Rosenthal, *Lawyer and Client: Who's in Charge* (New York:
Russell Sage Foundation, 1974); Geoffrey P. Miller, "Some Agency Problems in
Settlement," *Journal of Legal Studies* 16 (1987): 189–215; Earl Johnson Jr.,
"Lawyer's Choice: A Theoretical Appraisal of Litigation Investment and Deci-
sions," *Law & Society Review* 15 (1980–81): 567–610; Herbert M. Kritzer, William
L. F. Felstiner, Austin Sarat, and David M. Trubek, "The Impact of Fee Arrange-
ment on Lawyer Effort," *Law & Society Review* 19 (1985): 251–78.

89. I take the term *broker* from my earlier work; see Kritzer, *The Justice Broker.*

90. See particularly Johnson, "Lawyer's Choice."

91. See Rosenthal, *Lawyer and Client;* Milton R. Wessel, *The Rule of Reason: A
New Approach to Corporate Litigation* (New York: Addison-Wesley, 1976).

92. The literature on political representation recognizes that the reality faced by
the representative may dictate some pragmatic combination of the trustee and delegate roles. This hybrid rule is customarily referred to as the *politico;* see the essays
in John C. Wahlke and Heinz Eulau, eds., *Legislative Behavior: A Reader in Theory
and Research* (Glencoe, IL: The Free Press, 1959).

93. James Eisenstein and Herbert Jacob, *Felony Justice: An Organizational
Analysis of Criminal Courts* (Boston: Little, Brown, 1977).

94. Jonathan D. Casper, *American Criminal Justice: The Defendant's Perspective* (Englewood Cliffs, NJ: Prentice-Hall, 1972).

95. Kenneth Mann, *Defending White-Collar Crime: A Portrait of Attorneys at Work* (New Haven: Yale University Press, 1985).

96. In rural settings, professional colleagues rather than clients may provide the locus of expectations and control; see Donald D. Landon, "Clients, Colleagues, and Community: The Shaping of Zealous Advocacy in Country Law Practice," *American Bar Foundation Research Journal* (1985): 81–112.

97. See John Morison and Philip Leith, *The Barrister's World and the Nature of Law* (Milton Keynes: Open University Press, 1992).

98. Robert L. Nelson, "Ideology, Practice and Professional Autonomy: Social Values and Client Relations in the Large Law Firm," *Stanford Law Review* 37 (1985): 503–51; Robert L. Nelson, *Partners with Power: Social Transformation of the Large Law Firm* (Berkeley: University of California Press, 1988); John P. Heinz and Edward O. Laumann, *Chicago Lawyers: The Social Structure of the Bar* (New York: Russell Sage Foundation, 1982); John P. Heinz, "The Power of Lawyers," *Georgia Law Review* 17 (1983): 891–911.

99. In Michigan, where there is no such limit, the legal profession sought to block nonlawyer advocates from appearing in unemployment compensation appeals; see Eric Freedman, "Non-Lawyers May Represent Clients at Michigan Job Hearings," *National Law Journal* (July 29, 1985), 11.

100. See my earlier work in *Let's Make a Deal: Understanding the Negotiation Process in Ordinary Litigation* (Madison: University of Wisconsin Press, 1991).

101. Federal appeals court judge Frank M. Coffin describes such a case involving the late Edward Bennett Williams, whom Coffin describes as "one of the ablest advocates in the Age of Tungsten"; see *On Appeal: Courts, Lawyering, and Judging* (New York: W. W. Norton, 1994), 145–47.

102. My conceptualization of "advocate effectiveness" builds on Williams's notion of "negotiator effectiveness," which he defines in a rich, multifaceted way.

Comprehensiveness of resolution
Satisfaction of the parties
Quality of the outcome
Nature of resources utilized
Observance of the rules of the game
Costs of the negotiations

See Gerald R. Williams, *Legal Negotiations and Settlement* (St. Paul: West Publishing, 1983), 9.

103. Robert K. Yin, *Case Study Research,* rev. ed. (Beverly Hills, CA: Sage Publications, 1989), 53–58.

104. While some of the specifics of the various venues may be unique in Wisconsin, there is no reason to expect that the types of patterns I am looking for or looking at would not generalize nationally.

105. For one of the venues, I wrote a complete draft of my observational conclusions before even starting the data collection. For two others, I outlined my

observational analysis first. For the fourth, I avoided looking at the published data until after I had completed the observations.

106. Only twice did a claimant deny me permission to be present, and none of the advocates I contacted refused outright.

Chapter 2

1. For background on the adoption of the system in Wisconsin, and then as part of the Social Security Act of 1935, see Paul A. Raushenbush and Elizabeth Brandeis Raushenbush, *Our "U.C." Story* (Madison, WI: privately published, 1979). Another useful historical study is Saul J. Blaustein, *Unemployment Insurance in the United States: The First Half Century* (Kalamazoo, MI: W. E. Upjohn Institute for Employment Research, 1993), 107–216. Regarding recent developments and issues, see Blaustein, 217–64; and W. Lee Hansen and James F. Byers, *Unemployment Insurance: The Second Half-Century* (Madison: University of Wisconsin Press, 1990).

2. For a contemporary "state of the system" overview, see *Unemployment Insurance in the United States: Benefits, Financing, and Coverage* (Washington, DC: Advisory Council on Unemployment Compensation, 1995). Discussions of many of the issues confronting the system in the 1990s can be found in "Special Issue, Unemployment Compensation: Continuity and Change," *University of Michigan Journal of Law Reform* 29 (1995–96): 1–611.

3. Ken Morris, "On Appeal: Claimant Advocacy and Full and Fair Hearings," *Unemployment Compensation: Studies and Research* (Washington, DC: National Commission on Unemployment Compensation, 1980), 665.

4. In fact, the unemployment compensation system maintains accounts for each employer paying unemployment taxes, and payments to former employees are deducted from these accounts.

5. A claimant is monetarily eligible if he or she earned enough wages in covered employment during the requisite time period.

6. Wisconsin denial rates for separation and nonseparation issues were 46% and 58% respectively. Nationally, the corresponding denial rates were 56% and 61%; see Wayne Vroman, "Disputes Over Unemployment Insurance Claims: A Preliminary Analysis," paper presented at Second Research Conference on Reform of the Unemployment Insurance System, Colchester, VT, Aug. 17–18, 1995, tables 2 and 3.

7. These figures were provided by Karla Kelekovich from the Wisconsin Department of Industry, Labor and Human Relations (DILHR), Division of Unemployment Compensation; they are from U.S. Department of Labor forms ES-218 and ES-207, plus internal reporting forms used by DILHR.

8. While the Wisconsin statutes refer to the hearing officers as the "appeal tribunal" (Wis. Stat. 108 [1994]), the administrative rules refer to them as "administrative law judges" (Wis. Adm. Code ILHR 140.001(1) [1994]).

9. In Wisconsin UC judges also decide disputes over UC taxes paid by employers. For example, a small business may try to avoid paying UC taxes by arranging for what it characterizes as contracts with persons who then describe

themselves as independent contractors. There are complex rules governing who is an employee for UC tax purposes, and disputes that arise under these rules go to the same judges who decide appeals about UC benefits. In these tax cases, a lawyer normally appears to represent the state, and the result is a very different dynamic. I do not consider tax cases in my discussion in this chapter.

10. In some states, a three-person panel decides UC appeals; see Amy B. Chasanov and Eileen Cubanski, "Understanding Denials and Appeals in the United States," paper prepared for the Second Research Conference on Reform of the Unemployment Insurance System (sponsored by the Advisory Council on Unemployment Compensation), Colchester, VT, Aug. 17–18, 1995, 5.

11. States that fail to meet federal mandates risk losing federal funding for administration costs.

12. Wisconsin is on the low side of "average" in terms of the rate of appeals; see Chasanov and Cubanski, "Understanding Denials and Appeals," table 4.

13. Federal mandates do not require that there be a second-level appeal; however, most states include such a mechanism in their system. See Robert I. Owen and Edward A. Wood, "Timeliness in Deciding Second-Level Appeals," *Unemployment Compensation: Studies and Research* (Washington, DC: National Commission on Unemployment Compensation, 1980), 643.

14. Claimants have less success when they appeal (winning only 5% of their appeals to LIRC) than do employers (who win 17%); figures provided by Bureau of Legal Affairs, Unemployment Compensation Division, Wisconsin Department of Industry, Labor and Human Relations (computer run entitled "BOLA Tribunal Hearings Report, 01/01/94 to 12/31/94," dated 01/17/95).

15. There are provisions for suspending an agent who "has engaged in the solicitation of a claimant solely for the purpose of appearing at a hearing as the claimant's representative for pay"; *Wis. Stat.* 108.105 (1994); the Wisconsin Administrative Code (*Wis. Adm. Code* ILHR 140.18(2)(a) [1994]) extends the power of suspension to include failure to comply with standards of conduct established in the code (*Wis. Adm. Code* ILHR 140.18(1)[1994]).

16. Murray Rubin, "The Appeals System," *Unemployment Compensation Studies and Research* (Washington, DC: National Commission on Unemployment Compensation, 1980), 630.

17. *State Bar of Michigan v. Galloway,* 71983 (1985); *Michigan Hospital Association v. Employment Security Board of Review,* 72029 (1985). Interestingly, the nominal victor in this case was an employer that used the services of an unemployment compensation cost control management firm (which, in turn, relied primarily on nonattorneys to appear as advocates); see Eric Freedman, "Non-Lawyers May Represent Clients at Mich. Job Hearings," *National Law Journal* (July 29, 1985), 11.

18. See Rick McHugh, "Lay Representation in Unemployment Insurance Hearings: Some Strategies for Change," *Clearinghouse Review* 16 (1983): 867.

19. The data used to obtain these figures, and which are used in the statistical analysis that follows, were supplied to me by BOLA from BOLA's management information system. Strictly speaking, these are cases in which a decision was issued in 1991; consequently, a few cases were heard in December 1990, and some

of those cases heard in December 1991 are not included because the decisions were not issued until 1992.

20. *Wis. Stat.* 108.09(8)(a) [1994]; see also *Wis. Adm. Code* ILHR 140.17(2).

21. In some circumstances a claimant may receive "supplemental" benefits that extend the 26-week maximum, which increases the fee that a lawyer representing the claimant may receive.

22. In fact, these firms often contract with individuals, mostly nonlawyers, and pay fees on a per-case basis that fall well below the effective $500 cap for claimant representatives.

23. National Commission on Unemployment Compensation, *Basic Structure of a Federal-State Unemployment Insurance Program and Related Supporting Provisions: Responses to the National Commission on Unemployment Compensation* (Washington, DC: National Commission on Unemployment Compensation, 1979), 13.

24. See Marc Galanter, "Why the 'Haves' Come Out Ahead: Speculations on the Limits of Legal Change," *Law & Society Review* 9 (1974): 95–160.

25. "The Standard for Appeal Promptness—Unemployment Compensation," 20 CFR 650. This standard has existed for over 20 years; the Department of Labor adopted it in response to a U.S. Supreme Court decision, *California Department of Human Resources* v. *Java,* 403 U.S. 121 (1971); for background on this case, and its aftermath, see Murray Rubin, *Federal-State Relations in Unemployment Insurance* (Kalamazoo, MI: W. E. Upjohn Institute for Employment Research, 1983), 215–25. The success of states in meeting this standard has been mixed; see Unemployment Insurance Service, *Leadership in Appellate Administration: Successful State Unemployment Appellate Operations* (Washington, DC: U.S. Department of Labor, Employment and Training Administration, 1989), 4–5.

26. John Henry Merryman, *The Civil Law Tradition: An Introduction to the Legal Systems of Western Europe and Latin America,* 2d ed. (Stanford, CA: Stanford University Press, 1985), 111–18. For more detail on Germany see Benjamin Kaplan, Arthur T. von Mehren, and Rudolf Schaefer, "Phases of German Civil Procedure," *Harvard Law Review* 71 (1958), 1234–35; John H. Langbein, "The German Advantage in Civil Procedure," *University of Chicago Law Review* 52 (fall 1985): 830–32.

27. The prior employer is liable for unemployment compensation only if the claimant worked in the new job for at least four weeks.

28. Unemployment Compensation Appeals Clinic, *A Worker's Guide to Unemployment Compensation* (Madison, WI: Unemployment Compensation Appeals Clinic, n.d.), 10–11.

29. Rubin, "The Appeals System," 628.

30. An evaluation of the unemployment insurance appeal system in Canada at about this same time (the early 1980s) included a consideration of the impact of representation. Nationally, claimants achieved at least some measure of success rate in 57% of cases with representation compared to 42% without (there generally are no employer appeals in Canada because the employers do not have a direct interest in the payment of unemployment compensation); Hélène G. Royer, *Eval-*

uation of the UI Appeal System (Ottawa: Employment and Immigration Canada, Program Evaluation Branch, Strategic Policy and Planning, 1995), 45.

31. Maurice Emsellem and Monica Halas, "Representation of Claimants at Unemployment Compensation Proceedings: Identifying Models and Proposed Solutions," *University of Michigan Journal of Law Reform* 25 (1995–96): 292. This study makes no differentiation among types of representatives, reason for separation from employment, or whether the employer or the claimant appealed.

32. See ibid., 293–304.

33. In the 1979 study, 65% were attorneys, 11% were paralegals or law students, and 24% were union representatives; Rubin, "The Appeals System," 628.

34. Ibid., 629; Rubin also suggests that that "the hiring of an attorney is often itself a reflection of confidence in the likelihood of a favorable decision."

35. Something like this also happens on the employer side, but in a different form. If the employer goes to its representative (such as a lawyer or its UC management firm), and, after reviewing the case, the representative tells the employer that it's a loser, the employer may choose to not even show up at the hearing (i.e., let the claimant win essentially by default).

36. Throughout my analyses in this chapter, I treat most employers who use an inside staff person as "unrepresented." The key exceptions are those employers who are represented by someone from the inside legal staff; these employers are coded as "represented." In later tables where I break out types of representatives, the category labeled "inside or none" does not include inside lawyers.

37. Cases were dropped from the analysis for the following reasons: 4,371 because neither side appeared; 4,597 because the employer did not appear; 2,064 because the claimant did not appear; 717 because the decision was not clearly for one side or the other (mostly dismissals or withdrawals); and 11 because both sides had appealed the initial determination.

38. See Chasanov and Cubanski, *supra* note 10, 41–43.

39. The figures for the employer are obtained by simply subtracting from 100 the percentages won by the claimant that are shown in the table.

40. This may in part reflect which appeals are included in the various analyses. I restricted my analysis to separation cases where both sides appeared for the appeal.

41. These figures all assume that both sides appeared at the hearing.

42. This latter figure is computed from the lower right-hand corner entry of table 3, which shows that claimants won 67.2% of the cases appealed by the employer (100% – 67.2% = 32.8%).

43. In 1991, there were 524 employer appeals of misconduct cases where the claimant failed to appear; in 80 of these appeals, the judge affirmed the initial determination in favor of the claimant, and in another 47 the judge affirmed with modifications or amendments such an initial determination; in fact, the employer obtained outright reversals in only 231 (44%). I should note that the failure of the employer to appear does not guarantee that a claimant appealing a denial for benefits because of a discharge will win a reversal. In 1991 there were 666 cases in which a claimant appealed a denial due to a misconduct discharge and where the

employer failed to appear at the hearing; the judge affirmed the denial in 11.8% of those cases.

44. State of Wisconsin, Department of Industry, Labor and Human Relations, Unemployment Compensation Bureau form UCL-4616MA (R. 02/88).

45. Merryman, *The Civil Law Tradition,* 112.

46. See Benjamin Kaplan, "Civil Procedure—Reflections on the Comparison of Systems," *Buffalo Law Review* 9 (1960): 410.

47. This and other "transcripts" are reconstructions based on my observational notes.

48. The claimant also brought a friend to serve as a witness, but the friend did not testify.

49. I also had a residual "other" category that included family members and representatives I could not otherwise classify (i.e., the title information was missing). I omitted this category from the following tables, which is why the numbers in the tables are less than the total number of representatives shown in prior tables.

50. There are too few cases where both sides have agents to allow any conclusions to be drawn.

51. I observed this judge in a number of cases, and I never saw him allow an advocate to take the primary role, even advocates who had reputations as being very good.

52. The employer's advocate told me after the hearing that this contention by the claimant came out of the blue; it had not been raised in any meetings or discussions.

53. Most, if not all, of the students I saw were volunteers with the UC Clinic that operated out of the Labor Temple in Madison. This program is not formally part of the UW-Madison clinic program, but is advertised to students as a means of getting advocacy experience. It was originally set up by members of the local bar and is modestly funded (its annual budget is about $4,000), largely by the Dane County Bar. The South Central (Wisconsin) Federation of Labor provides a rent-free office, and a United Way–funded referral agency (First Call for Help) assists in scheduling clients.

54. This was one of the few cases I observed where the judge "sequestered" the witnesses by asking them to wait in the hall until it was time for their testimony; the usual practice was for all persons to be in the hearing room during the entire hearing.

55. This student realized that he was having problems and at the end of the case expressed to the judge a concern that his client, a young woman who had been discharged from the optical department at a large discount store, might have been better off without a representative. Given the employer's evidence, I doubt that this would have been the case.

56. The alleged misconduct included tardiness, absence without notifying the employer, neglecting and/or mistreating customers, and excessive personal use of the store telephone. There was no doubt the the employee had problems that accounted for much of what had happened. She apparently was in an abusive relationship with an alcoholic boyfriend, who had actually had the claimant arrested at one point under Wisconsin's mandatory arrest law for domestic violence (she

had hit her boyfriend when he arrived home at 3 A.M. and started verbally abusing her); the absence without notifying the employer was when she was in jail from this arrest.

57. The employer presented testimony and documentation of having gone through the various steps in the disciplinary process; there was some question whether the claimant had been fully informed of the disciplinary process, although it was stated in the employee handbook.

58. The employer brought a sample of the subquality product to the hearing.

59. The most extreme example of this I saw involved a claimant who was discharged for failing to get an insurance license, which was one of the conditions of her employment (i.e., she was hired on the condition that she obtain the license). There was no dispute over that being a condition of employment or over her failure to get the license (although the claimant asserted that she had been told she was "being laid off due to lack of work"). The claimant even acknowledged that the employer had given her the books to study from and had allowed her to spend time on the job during slow periods studying the material. The advocate asked no questions of the employer, and only three questions of his client: how much education she had had (high school graduate plus one year at the local technical school), did she seek help from teachers in high school when she had difficulty (yes), and whether there had been a relationship between the claimant and the employer before being hired (yes, they were friends).

60. *A Worker's Guide,* 11.

61. One judge commented to me after hearing my description of the law students, "Although I definitely have experienced plenty of situations rivaling those you observed, at least lately my law student representatives have not made such pathetic showings [as you describe]." This same judge went on to note that "some [law students] just do not understand the relevance or proper framing of a question, no matter how many times you tell them, even if you are nice."

62. Overall, the judge was unusually "laid back" in how she handled the case; when it became clear that there was not enough time to present the entire case, and that it would be necessary to continue the hearing at a later date, the judge remarked that she was leaving to take another job, and they needed to reconvene before she left. Due to other commitments, I was unable to observe the continuation.

63. In response to questions by the judge, the claimant mentioned other factors such as verbal abuse from the supervisor and questionable business practices.

64. During the brief recess, while everyone else was out of the hearing room, the judge (whom I had observed a number of times on previous occasions) whispered to me regarding the attorney: "He doesn't know what he is doing."

65. One account manager for a large national UC firm was listed as the representative for 56 Wisconsin appeals in 1991; he may have also appeared at appeals in Illinois.

66. One of these advocates was listed as the representative for 201 appeals in 1991; another was listed for 61 appeals.

67. Recall that if both sides have lawyers or if neither side has any advocate, the

claimant win rate in these appeals is 39 to 40%. Recall also that the 19% and 54% are based on very few cases, but the difference is statistically significant.

Chapter 3

1. The governor appoints the members of the commission, subject to confirmation by the state senate. The three commissioners serve staggered six-year terms. There is no limit on the number of terms that a commissioner may serve.

2. *1991–1993 Biennial Report of the Tax Appeals Commission* (Madison: Wisconsin Tax Appeals Commission, 1993), 10.

3. Ibid., 8–9.

4. For a summary of the commission's procedure, see Thomas M. Boykoff, "Procedures Before the Wisconsin Tax Appeals Commission," *Wisconsin Bar Bulletin* 54, no. 10 (Oct. 1981): 31–34.

5. *Biennial Report,* 8; TAC staff provided the figures for 1993–94. Counting cases here is slightly deceptive because the commission's procedure requires the filing of separate cases for each year and each party, even if there is, in fact, a single issue to be decided. For example, the peak in dispositions was 617 in 1992–93, but 149 of these were handled together as a single matter, and 43 were handled together as a second matter. If one counts each of these sets as a single matter, the number disposed drops to 427.

6. One appeal, from a case that started before the commission, eventually found its way to the U.S. Supreme Court as *Wisconsin Department of Revenue v. Wrigley* 60 U.S.L.W. 4622 (1992).

7. The commission rules have specific time deadlines, and the Department of Revenue is aggressive in moving for dismissals of petitions that fail to meet those deadlines; see Boykoff, "Procedures," 32.

8. Ibid., 34.

9. Ibid.

10. A few of these did not involve full hearings; when the parties could stipulate to all of the factual issues, the commission could decide the case based upon the stipulated facts and written briefs.

11. This figure hides the substantial year-to-year variation that occurs. For the three years I looked, the percentages of cases disposed of by "Decision and Order" were 24%, 11%, and 16%. These variations reflect, in part, large blocks of related cases being disposed of together. For example, in 1991–92 (the 24% year), of the 120 cases disposed by decision and order, 45 were actually a single case with 45 separate docket numbers; in 1992–93 (the low year), of the cases disposed of by means other than decision and order, 192 were in two sets.

12. Commission staff normally designate any cases involving $2,500 or less as a small-claims matter; commission records indicate this designation by appending SC to the case's docket number. If either the Department of Revenue or the commission itself believes that the case presents an issue of statewide significance, the commission will treat the case as a non-small-claims matter.

13. These figures are from my own count from the commission records. As with

the other figures from the commission's caseload, there is substantial year-to-year variation due to the occasional large set of cases.

14. This difference is statistically significant by standard criteria; $\chi^2 = 5.465$ (1 df), $p = .0175$. When I look year by year, there is actually one year (1991–92) in which the proportion of non-small-claims cases disposed of by decision and order (25%) was greater than the proportion of small claims so disposed (22%); however, that was a year in which there was a large set of cases disposed of by decision, and if I drop out that set, the proportion of non-small claims disposed of through a decision drops to 14%. Similarly, there is another year (1992–93) when two large sets of non-small-claims cases (one of 149 cases and one of 43 cases) were disposed of without a formal decision; that year the proportion of non-small claims so disposed is only 8% with those cases included, but rises to 16% without, which is higher than the 15% figure for small claims disposed of by decision that year.

15. Prior to the hearing on the merits, there are usually one or more prehearing conferences or hearings on motions (related to such things as discovery, or the timeliness of filing). Prehearing conferences and motion hearings are often (usually in the case of conferences) done by telephone; in cases where a petitioner is out of state or unable to travel, the commission may, with DOR consent, conduct an evidentiary hearing by telephone.

16. One exception to this concerns certain penalties imposed by DOR, in which case the DOR must show that the penalty is justified; see Boykoff, "Procedures," 34.

17. Normally only one commissioner is present at a hearing even if the entire commission will ultimately decide the case.

18. These combinations occur when the case presents multiple issues, such as in the car wash case discussed later in this chapter.

19. There is no real difference in attorneys' success rate depending upon whether the case involved a hearing or the parties agreed upon a stipulated set of facts; attorneys secured some relief for their clients in 65% of cases with hearings and 60% without (a difference that is not statistically significant).

20. I should note that because of the small n's here the differences do not achieve statistical significance; however, this is counterbalanced by the fact that the pattern controlling for small claims is the same as that without the control, and without the control the difference is significant ($\chi^2 = 7.59$, 1 df, $p = .006$).

21. As in the prior chapter, the quotations are approximations based on my observational notes.

22. That Ms. A might make a mistake in how she handled her income from unemployment compensation is not surprising given the 10-step worksheet (buried in the tax instruction booklet) one must first find and then complete.

23. Of the 23 decisions with no hearing, 16 involved attorney representatives. Put another way, only 8% of the cases without an attorney representative resulted in decisions based upon stipulated facts in contrast to 29% of the cases with an attorney representative.

24. The commissioner had mentioned this to me in the hall before the hearing began.

25. 71.11(7m) Wis.Stats. (1985–86).

26. Mr. N ran a bookkeeping service. While his client referred to Mr. N as "my accountant," it was not clear whether Mr. N was a CPA.

27. Mr. S introduced as an exhibit the department's "First Request for Production of Documents," the department having made this request under the formal procedural rules of the Circuit Court which governed the commission's procedure.

28. The commission affirmed the Department of Revenue's assessment in this case.

29. This was the only case that I observed involving a nonlawyer representative in which that representative indicated a desire to file a brief. I did not see the brief, but despite or regardless of what the accountant said in it, the commission affirmed the assessment of the Department of Revenue.

30. At the beginning of his closing argument, the accountant commented that the delay in the mailing of the permit reflected a misunderstanding in the office.

31. The commission affirmed the department on the issue related to the date the permit was returned.

32. I base this description of the listing on the dockets as they existed at the time of the hearing. The Tax Appeals Commission maintains its docket using a word processor, and new versions get printed as new events occur. When I rechecked the docket sheets for these cases after the decision, I discovered that they no longer listed a representative for either case.

Chapter 4

1. My description of the programs and the appeals process draws heavily on Thomas E. Bush, *Social Security Disability Practice* (Santa Ana, CA: James Publishing Group, 1992). Supplemental sources include William D. Popkin, "The Effect of Representation in Nonadversary Proceedings—A Study of Three Disability Programs," 62 (1977) 989–1048; Jerry L. Mashaw et al., *Social Security Hearings and Appeals: A Study of the Social Security Administration Hearing System* (Lexington, MA: Lexington Books, 1978); and Jerry L. Mashaw, *Bureaucratic Justice: Managing Social Security Disability Claims* (New Haven: Yale University Press, 1983).

2. Claimants with limited DI insurance coverage may obtain both DI and SSI.

3. Programs such as standard Social Security retirement benefits can produce disagreements arising from things such as the claimant's age or the claimant's past payment of Social Security taxes; however, such disputes are much less common than under the disability programs.

4. *Social Security Bulletin, Annual Statistical Supplement 1994*, 266.

5. "Process Reengineering Program; Disability Reengineering Project Plan," *Federal Register* 59, September 19, 1994, 47891.

6. Prior to 1979 OHA was known as the Bureau of Hearings and Appeals.

7. Other benefits administered by the Social Security Administration can lead to denials and appeals; however, the vast majority of appeals involve DI and SSI. For example, in fiscal year 1993, 94% of the appeals disposed of by the Office of Hearings and Appeals involved DI and/or SSI, with the balance involving Old Age

and Survivor Insurance (OASI), Medicare, and black lung; Social Security Administration, *Annual Report to Congress* (Washington, DC: GPO, 1994), 44. My discussion and analysis essentially ignores the non-DI/non-SSI appeals.

8. The data series in figure 2 stops at 1993. Since then there has been a substantial increase in the number of appeals, and growing conflict between the Social Security Administration and the federal courts to which OHA decisions can be appealed; see Robert Pear, "U.S. Challenges Courts on Disabilities," *New York Times,* April 21, 1997, sec. A, 12, and accompanying brief item and figure, "Busy Times in Disability Courts."

9. This may be due in significant part to SSI cases involving children; these cases have arisen in response to the Supreme Court decision in *Sullivan v. Zebley* (493 US 521 [1990]) which broadened the eligibility for such benefits. According to one 1994 report, "at least 750,000 requests for SSI for children . . . have been rejected in the last two years"; "Parents 'Crazy' for Federal Cash," *Newsweek* (Oct. 31, 1994): 54–55.

10. Data on representation and outcomes are from tables obtained from the Office of Hearings and Appeals. Some of the tables were initially provided to me by the National Organization of Social Security Claimants' Representatives (NOSCCR).

11. See Jacob M. Wolf, "Nonlawyer Practice before the Social Security Administration," *Administrative Law Review* 37 (1985): 413–15. One advantage that lawyers have over nonlawyers is that in DI cases, the Social Security Administration will withhold 25% (up to a fixed maximum) of the back benefits which it will pay directly to an attorney representative; no such withholding will be done for nonattorney representatives (id., 414). In 1995, the Social Security Administration proposed doing away with this system of direct payment to attorneys; see "Social Security Fee Proposal Draws Protest," *National Law Journal* (Sept. 11, 1995), sec. A, 12.

12. OHA counts as nonattorney representatives persons such as legal assistants, paralegals, social workers, etc.; it does not count family members who speak on behalf of a claimant.

13. In 2 to 3 percent of cases, both an attorney and a nonattorney appear; consequently, the percentage of claimants who have no representative is slightly higher than what would be indicated by simply adding together the lawyer and nonlawyer cases.

14. Popkin, "The Effect of Representation," 1023–24.

15. As figure 3 shows, this rate of representation was consistent with the pattern in the mid-1970s.

16. Popkin also reports success rate by representation at the reconsideration stage; 23% of those without representatives win at this earlier stage, compared to 20% of those with a representative.

17. "Report of the Disability Claims Process Task Force," reprinted in Subcommittee on Social Security of the Committee on Ways and Means, *Recent Studies Relevant to the Disability Hearings and Appeals Crisis* (Washington, DC: GPO, 1975), 101. The figure for nonlawyer representatives is based on only 33 cases, but even so, it differs significantly from either of the other two figures.

18. The gap between those with and without representatives is not surprising. As one judge put it, "the big difference is not between lay and attorney representatives, but between the represented and the unrepresented"; there are "serious evidentiary problems with the unrepresented because they don't bring the documents we need to find in their favor." While it is clear that representation helps for cases that get to a hearing, the situation is somewhat less clear for cases decided without a hearing. In recent years OHA has adopted procedures to identify quickly cases that can be easily decided on the available record. If one omits from consideration appeals that are dismissed (most commonly either because of untimely filing or failing to follow through), in the aggregate the gap between represented and unrepresented claimants has disappeared in the last few years. As it turns out, the largest proportion of unsuccessful appeals for unrepresented claimants are those that are dismissed. The procedures being used in some OHA regional offices grants benefits in a large number of clear-cut cases before an attorney or other representative becomes involved.

19. See "SSA Profile Screening Project," *Social Security Forum* 17, no. 2 (Feb. 1995), 11–13.

20. See M. Wade Baughman, "Reasonable Attorney's Fees Under the Social Security Act: The Case for Contingency Agreements," *University of Illinois Law Review* 1997 (1997): 253.

21. Table entitled "Attorneys and Non-Attorney Representatives in Total Dispositions, National Data, Fiscal Year 1993" provided to the author by OHA. In concurrent SSI/DI cases, attorneys appeared in 54% of cases.

22. Ibid. Nonattorneys appeared in 14.4% of concurrent DI/SSI claims.

23. This figure is based on data contained in quarterly computer tabulations provided to the author by the Office of Hearings and Appeals.

24. 20 C.F.R §404.1520.

25. This description of the five steps is adapted from Bush, *Social Security Disability Practice,* §112.

26. An additional requirement in finding disability relates to the duration. The impairment must either be expected to last for a continuous period of at least 12 months or to result in death (20 C.F.R §404.1522(b); see also Bush, *Social Security Disability Practice,* §115). However, for purposes of my study of disability appeals, this criterion is not particularly important because the delays in the system usually push the period from application to hearing well beyond 12 months, and so it should be readily apparent by the time the case gets to a hearing whether or not the duration requirement is met.

27. Bush, *Social Security Disability Practice,* §113; appropriate work-related and medical expenses can be deducted from the gross figure.

28. Ibid., §100.

29. The regulations introduce further discretion by permitting a finding of disability under the listings for a medical condition that "equals" the listing; see Mashaw, *supra* note 1, 109. For example, such an equivalence might be considered met if a claimant has multiple conditions none of which actually meet the listings' criteria for that disability but that taken together are deemed to be equal to the listings.

30. Only the prior 15 years are relevant with regard to work experience.

31. 20 C.F.R. §404.15774(a)(1); obviously, it is in the interest of SSA to encourage workers to try to go back to substantial gainful activity, and the purpose to the "unsuccessful work attempt" rule is to avoid creating disincentives for such attempts.

32. In cases involving psychological impairments, evidence may be supplied by psychologists. In my discussion above, I use "physician" or "doctor" as a generic reference to medical professionals of the level of physicians, osteopaths, optometrists, and psychologists.

33. Bush, *Social Security Disability Practice,* §210–19.

34. Ibid., §151.

35. Heart or respiratory conditions can also limit exertional capacity.

36. See Patrick D. Halligan, "Credibility, Chronic Pain, and Converted Mental Conflict: Some Distinctions for Adjudicators," *West's Social Security Reporting Service* 38, no. 6 (Dec. 3, 1992): 3–78

37. Information from tabular data provided to the author by the Office of Hearing and Appeals, table entitled "Participants per Hearing Held, National Data, Fiscal Years 1977 Through 1993." Through 1991, less than 1% of the hearings involve testimony by the claimant's physician; for some reason this jumped to 15% in 1992, but dropped back to 3.2% in 1993.

38. Ibid. Both of these figures increased in 1992 and 1993, with about 44% of hearings involving a vocational expert and 13% medical experts; the trend of an increase appears to have started around 1989 or 1990. On rare occasions the claimant may have his or her own vocational expert come to testify.

39. Donna Price Cofer, *Judges, Bureaucrats, and the Question of Independence: A Study of the Social Security Administrative Hearing Process* (Westport, CT: Greenwood Press, 1985), 144.

40. The Appeals Council, on its own initiative, may review OHA cases resulting in an award of benefits. In fiscal year 1993, there were 2,532,841 initial determinations, 746,425 reconsiderations, 346,423 administrative law judge dispositions, 68,253 Appeals Council decisions, and 5,030 federal court decisions on DI and SSI applications/cases; Committee on Ways and Means, U.S. House of Representatives, *Overview of Entitlement Programs: 1994 Green Book: Background Material and Data on Programs within the Jurisdiction of the Committee on Ways and Means* (Washington, DC: GPO, 1994), 57.

41. The names in the following transcript, and all others, are pseudonyms assigned arbitrarily.

42. In fact, the MVV criterion was dropped right around the time this case came to hearing.

43. In one of the later cases, the advocate had a lot of experience with Social Security cases. Most of his questions were not leading, but some, particularly toward the end of his questioning of the claimant, were. For example:

A: Who referred you to Dr. Y?

C: The surgeon?

A: Dr. Y has been more optimistic than the other doctor?

C: Yes.
A: That's why you are no longer with [former employer]?
C: Yes.

44. It is interesting to note that in the statistical data made public by the Federal Judicial Center and the Administrative Office of the U.S. Courts, two agencies of the federal judiciary, the identities of the judges involved in individual cases are withheld. Unlike the administrative law judges who are part of the executive branch, the judges of the judicial branch are not subject to FOIA.

45. This element is also important in various court settings. Regarding criminal courts, see James Eisenstein, Roy B. Flemming, and Peter F. Nardulli, *The Contours of Justice: Communities and Their Courts* (Boston: Little, Brown, 1988); regarding divorce practice, see Austin Sarat and William L. F. Felstiner, *Divorce Lawyers and Their Clients* (New York: Oxford University Press, 1995).

46. This view appeared to be at least in part due to the claimant's not taking pain medication. When asked if he took any medications for the pain, the claimant had replied, "No, what's the sense of taking pain pills."

47. I observed two consecutive hearings involving the same representative, VE, and judge. Essentially, the same kinds of job availability questions came up in the second case, which involved a Hmong woman in her late forties (no one knew her exact age) who spoke no English and had no schooling. Her only work experience was on the family farm in Laos, plus housework and care of her twelve children. The disability claimed in her case was mental depression (although her language had no term for such a condition), plus possible mental retardation. The VE identified some of the same types of jobs as in the other case, plus "lens matcher," "tooth inspector," counter supply worker, "brusher" in the shoe industry. In questioning the VE, the representative again raised questions about the requirements of each of these jobs and the claimant's ability to meet those requirements. The representative also explicitly brought out the VE's experience working in sheltered workshop settings so that the judge would be aware of "where the VE was coming from."

48. One can identify three archetypical screening practices: take everything (i.e., screen out no cases), take only those that are sure winners, screen out only those that are clear losers.

49. One element of preparation that might make a difference in a small number of cases is the amount of advanced notice a representative has. Because a large proportion of nonlawyers work for advocacy agencies, they might encounter a larger proportion of last-minute walk-ins. At one hearing involving a nonlawyer, it was immediately clear to the judge that the advocate was not on top of what was going on; however, the representative explained her lack of knowledge by the fact that she had "never received a hearing notice because [she] came in at the last moment." Actually, this is less a problem of lawyers versus nonlawyers than it is a problem of fee-for-service practice versus more of a social service practice. A very similar thing happened in a case involving a private-practice lawyer handling the matter pro bono on behalf of a legal services agency. He did not learn of the hearing until a few days before it was scheduled, because the Social Security office

either had never received or had lost his notice of appearance. The lawyer was not able to see the file before the hearing or make arrangements for his client to travel from the town where she lived (which was about 35 miles from the hearing site).

50. I would like to thank Carrie Menkel-Meadow for suggesting this line of explanation.

51. I should note that the advocates in question generally represented SSI claimants, who were precisely the potential clients that many fee-for-service lawyers were very reluctant to take on.

52. The lawyer explained to me later that his reluctance to accept the judge's suggestion at the hearing was actually more of an issue of client relations than a disagreement with the judge. He viewed the judge's suggestion as a clear signal that the judge would not grant an earlier onset date. However, the lawyer did not want to agree to it on the spot, on the chance that the later date would result in significantly lower benefits and his client would later be upset that the lawyer had not insisted on the earlier date.

53. Through the 1980s, some of these lawyers would obtain statistical reports from OHA that showed, on a quarterly basis, the reversal rates for individual judges. OHA stopped compiling such reports in the late 1980s, and as a result, the lawyers now rely entirely on reputation and experience.

54. Some months after completing my observations of Social Security hearings, I had occasion to talk to several of the specialist lawyers. Two or three of them spontaneously mentioned to me that they had been getting calls from lawyers in Indianapolis, because a retired judge from Milwaukee had just been assigned 200 or so hearings in Indianapolis.

55. Kevin M. Clermont and John D. Currivan, "Improving on the Contingent Fee," *Cornell Law Review* 63 (1978): 529–639; Patricia M. Danzon, "Contingent Fees for Personal Injury Litigation," *Bell Journal of Economics* 14 (1983): 213–24; Earl Johnson, "Lawyers' Choice: A Theoretical Appraisal of Litigation Investment Decisions," *Law & Society Review* (1980–81): 567–610; Herbert M. Kritzer, "Rhetoric and Reality, Uses and Abuses, Contingencies and Certainties: The American Contingent Fee in Action," paper presented at Conference on the Law and Economics of Litigation Reform, Georgetown University Law Center, Washington, DC, Oct. 28–29, 1994; Herbert M. Kritzer, William L. F. Felstiner, Austin Sarat, and David M. Trubek, "The Impact of Fee Arrangement on Lawyer Effort," *Law & Society Review* 19 (1985): 251–78; F. B. MacKinnon, *Contingent Fees for Legal Services* (Chicago: Aldine, 1964); Geoffrey P. Miller, "Some Agency Problems in Settlement," *Journal of Legal Studies* 16 (1987): 189–215; Douglas E. Rosenthal, *Lawyer and Client: Who's in Charge?* (New Brunswick: Transaction Books, 1974); Daniel L. Rubinfeld and Suzanne Scotchmer, "Contingent Fees for Attorneys: An Economic Analysis," *RAND Journal of Economics* 24 (1993): 343–56; Murray L. Schwartz and Daniel J. B. Mitchell, "An Economic Analysis of the Contingent Fee in Personal-Injury Litigation," *Stanford Law Review* 20 (1970): 1125–62; and Timothy M. Swanson, "The Importance of Contingency Fee Agreements," *Oxford Journal of Legal Studies* 11 (1991): 193–226.

56. This may have shifted somewhat in recent years. In the early 1980s the average OHA processing time was in the range of five to six months; by the early 1990s

it had edged up to seven and one-half months, and by the mid-1990s it may be up to close to nine months. See *Social Security Forum* 15, no. 2 (Feb. 1993): 22.

57. The nonlawyer specialists may have less discretion in the cases that they take. In particular, they may work in agencies that have policies that preclude the kind of screening that a fee-for-service lawyer can undertake. Judges are quite aware of the case acceptance policies of such agencies, and this affects the message conveyed by the appearance of such representatives.

58. This is one clearly distinguishing feature between specialist lawyers and specialist nonlawyers. The end of the line for the latter is the Appeals Council; if the Appeals Council denies benefits, a nonlawyer must turn the case over to a lawyer to take to federal court.

Chapter 5

1. See David Lewin and Richard B. Peterson, *The Modern Grievance Procedure in the United States* (New York: Quorum Books, 1988).

2. Arnold M. Zack, *A Handbook for Grievance Arbitration: Procedural and Ethical Issues* (New York: Lexington Books, 1992); Robert Coulson, *Labor Arbitration—What You Need to Know,* 3d rev. ed. (New York: American Arbitration Association, 1988).

3. In the setting I observed, something between one-third and one-half of the hearings have court reporters present. In contrast, the Federal Mediation and Conciliation Service reported that in fiscal 1994 only 10.6% (527) of the 4,949 cases arbitrated (i.e., in which arbitrators issued awards) under its auspices had transcripts; "Arbitration Statistics, Fiscal Year 1994" (Washington, DC: Federal Mediation and Conciliation Service, 1995).

4. In fiscal year 1994, briefs were filed in 98% of the Federal Mediation and Conciliation cases in which awards were issued; ibid.

5. In the setting I observed, the arbitrators did have substantial experience in mediation.

6. Based on my survey of representatives, described later, it appears that the employer may be more likely than the union to perceive the presence of underlying issues; 54% of employer representatives reported such issues compared to only 27% of union representatives.

7. An analysis of 601 published arbitration awards (all published in 1985 or 1986 in either *Labor Arbitration Reports* or *Labor Arbitration Awards*) found that about two-thirds of the arbitrators had law degrees; see Perry A. Zirkel and Philip H. Breslin, "Correlates of Grievance Arbitration Awards," *Journal of Collective Negotiations in the Public Sector* 24 (1995): 49. A survey of labor arbitrators on the Federal Mediation and Conciliation roster as of summer 1980 found that 51% were trained in law; John Smith Herrick, "Profile of a Labor Arbitrator," *Arbitration Journal* 37, no. 2 (1983): 20. Smith cites a study from about a decade earlier that found that 54% of labor arbitrators had law degrees; ibid., 21.

8. These schedules are seldom met, but since the parties have ongoing relationships, the norm is for one party to agree to an extension of time when the other

party requests one. Because the arbitrator is there to serve the parties, he or she will go along with such requests.

9. Herbert J. Heneman III and Marcus H. Sandver, "Arbitrators' Backgrounds and Behavior," *Journal of Labor Research* 4 (1983): 115–24; Nels E. Nelson and Earl M. Curry Jr., "Arbitrator Characteristics and Arbitration Decisions," *Industrial Relations,* 20 (1981): 312–17; Brian Bemmels, "Arbitrator Characteristics and Arbitrator Decisions," *Journal of Labor Research* 11 (1990): 181–91; Zirkel and Breslin, "Correlates of Awards," 50.

10. Bemmels, "Arbitrator Characteristics"; Heneman and Sandver, *supra* note 9; and Perry A. Zirkel, "A Profile of Grievance Arbitration Cases," *Arbitration Journal* 38 (Mar. 1983), 35–38; and Zirkel and Breslin, "Correlates of Awards," 50.

11. Bemmels, *supra* note 9; Heneman and Sandver, "Arbitrators' Backgrounds"; Zirkel and Breslin, "Correlates of Awards," 50.

12. Bemmels, *supra* note 9; Heneman and Sandver, *supra* note 9.

13. Marsha Katz and Helen Lavan, "Arbitrated Public Sector Employees Grievances," *Journal of Collective Negotiations in the Public Sector* 20 (1991): 293–305; Brian Bemmels, "The Effect of Grievants' Gender on Arbitrators' Decisions," *Industrial and Labor Relations Review* 41 (Jan. 1988): 251–62; Zirkel, "Profile of Grievance Cases"; Zirkel and Breslin, "Correlates of Awards," 51.

14. Ken Jennings, Barbara Sheffield, and Roger Wolters, "The Arbitration of Discharge Cases," *Labor Law Journal* 38 (1987): 33–47; Brian Bemmels, "Gender Effects in Discharge Arbitration," *Industrial and Labor Relations Review* 41 (Oct. 1988): 63–76.

15. Bemmels, "Effect of Grievants' Gender"; Bemmels, "Gender Effects in Discharge Arbitration," 14; Richard N. Block and Jack Stieber, "The Impact of Attorneys and Arbitrators on Arbitration Awards," *Industrial and Labor Relations Review* 40 (1987): 543–55; Zirkel and Breslin, "Correlates of Awards," 50.

16. K. Dow Scott and G. Stephen Taylor, "An Analysis of Absenteeism Cases Taken to Arbitration," *Arbitration Journal* 38, no. 3 (Sept. 1983): 61–69.

17. Katz and Lavan, "Public Sector Grievances"; Bemmels, "Effect of Grievants' Gender"; and Block and Stieber, "Impact of Attorneys and Arbitrators."

18. Scott and Taylor, "Analysis of Absenteeism Cases."

19. Jennings, Sheffield, and Wolters, "Arbitration of Discharge Cases."

20. Katz and Lavan, "Public Sector Grievances"; Bemmels, "Effect of Grievants' Gender"; Block and Stieber, "Impact of Attorneys and Arbitrators"; Zirkel, "Profile of Arbitration Cases"; and Zirkel and Breslin, "Correlates of Awards," 50.

21. Bemmels, "Arbitrator Characteristics"; and Heneman and Sandver, "Arbitrators' Backgrounds."

22. Jennings, Sheffield, and Wolters, "Arbitration of Discharge Cases"; and Bemmels, "Gender Effects in Discharge Arbitration."

23. Joseph P. Cain and Michael J. Stahl, "Modeling the Policies of Several Labor Arbitrators," *Academy of Management Journal* 26 (1983): 140–47.

24. Block and Stieber, "Impact of Attorneys and Arbitrators"; Zirkel, "Profile of Arbitration Cases"; and Zirkel and Breslin, "Correlates of Awards," 50.

25. For an early study of commercial arbitration that considered the impact of

lawyer representatives, see Soia Mentschikoff, "Commercial Arbitration," *Columbia Law Review* 61 (1961): 859, 864.

26. Zirkel, "Profile of Arbitration Cases," 37–38.

27. Zirkel and Breslin, "Correlates of Awards," 50.

28. The reports of neither of these studies show the actual tabulations from the analyses concerning representation; they only describe the results of relevant statistical tests.

29. Block and Stieber, "Impact of Attorneys and Arbitrators."

30. An unpublished study also looks at discipline and discharge cases. That study finds some effect when the employer had an attorney and the union did not; T. H. Wagar, "The Impact of Legal Representation on Discipline and Discharge Arbitration Decisions: Evidence from Nova Scotia," paper presented at the 43d Annual Meeting of the Industrial Relations Research Association, Washington, DC, 1990 (described in Zirkel and Breslin, "Correlates of Awards," 47).

31. Orley Ashenfelter and David Bloom, "Lawyers as Agents of the Devil in a Prisoner's Dilemma Game," National Bureau of Economic Research Working Paper No. 4447 (Sept. 1993).

32. This lack of effect is not just a question of statistical significance. Using "no attorneys" as the reference category, Block and Stieber, "Impact of Attorneys and Arbitrators," found probit coefficients in the .25 to .47 range when only one side had an attorney (positive for union attorneys and negative for employer attorneys); the coefficient for both having an attorney was always less than .06, and frequently .01 to .02.

33. Even here, there is a substantial range. An inside lawyer for an employer with contentious labor relations might have a substantial number of arbitrations (one a month, or more). In a law firm with a large labor law practice, there might be one or more arbitration specialists who do one or more arbitration hearings a week.

34. Public sector employers and unions may agree to use private arbitrators and mediators rather than using arbitrators who work for WERC; however, because the services of WERC are essentially free (the only charge being a $25 filing fee), WERC staff handle many, if not most, public sector cases.

35. The WERC also enforces the state's labor relations statutes by adjudicating "prohibited practice" and "unfair labor practice" cases.

36. WERC staff arbitrators are permitted to hear cases in Wisconsin only under the auspices of WERC; however, staff arbitrators can free-lance on cases outside Wisconsin, and several individuals have significant private practices doing this work.

37. As of 1995, only three of the twenty were not lawyers.

38. *Employment Relations Commission Biennial Report, July 1, 1991–June 30, 1993* (Madison: Wisconsin Employment Relations Commission, n.d.), 4, 10, 18–19.

39. Some employer–union contracts create their own "closed panels" by naming a group of arbitrators who will be used on a rotating basis.

40. My original goal had been to observe several times this number of arbitration hearings. However, the volume of hearings, particularly in the summer

months when my schedule permitted a lot of flexibility, was not very large. In several cases, I arrived to observe a hearing, only to have the case settle or the entire day be devoted to unsuccessful settlement negotiations.

41. The end date was the date of the last award filed at the WERC offices at the time I did the coding.

42. WERC keeps the files in its office for about one year before sending them off to the record center.

43. The sampling frame was drawn from about six months of public sector cases decided by WERC arbitrators. The 54 representatives in the sample appeared a total of 142 times in that set of cases.

44. While I interpret the hospital's attorney's performance as reflecting less detailed knowledge, an alternative interpretation was that he was doing the best he could with a weak case.

45. The hospital's attorney appeared four times in the sample, winning the other three of his cases.

46. Another issue that came up during the union's case was whether one aspect of the grievance had been filed in a timely fashion. The testimony made it fairly clear that it had not been, and the arbitrator eventually so ruled.

47. While this may have been a surprise that could have been avoided, some unplanned or unexpected happenings cannot be fully anticipated. The best example of this was reported by one of the union lawyers who responded to my mail survey; when asked whether she had been surprised by anything in the testimony of the union's witnesses, she reported, "no, although the grievant's arrival twenty minutes late for the hearing probably did not help, given that two of the disciplinary charges against him regarded his failure to report for duty on time."

48. The arbitrator actually rejected the *district's* argument regarding the applicability of the overtime agreement, but the outcome did not turn on the applicability of that agreement.

49. Interestingly, the presence of the court reporter might have been intended as a form of intimidation in itself. At the close of the hearing, the union's representative expressed concerns about the cost of having transcripts of the hearing prepared (the labor contract called for the union and the district to split any transcript costs), noting that the union had not been informed by the district's lawyer that he (the lawyer) had arranged for a court reporter to be present.

50. This city showed up five times in my sample of cases from the WERC files; in every one, it employed an outside lawyer to represent it at the arbitration hearing.

51. The discharge was on the grounds that the employee was not available for work due to an injury. The appeal dealt with the question of whether the arbitrator relied upon contract language or something outside the contract language in deciding the case. The court found that the arbitrator improperly went beyond contract language.

52. Of the 19 nonlawyer union representatives who responded to my survey, 18 had attended such a course.

53. From my survey of representatives, I had a small amount of information on preparation time, but not enough to allow for inclusion in the analysis reported

below. I should note one interesting pattern in the effort data from the survey: the average number of hours devoted to case preparation and brief writing was virtually the same for the union nonlawyer representatives and the outside employer lawyers, 26.5 and 25.5 hours respectively (17 and 18 respondents respectively). The numbers of responding union lawyers and inside employer lawyers were much smaller (six of each), but the mean amount of time for both of these types of representatives was a bit lower, 15 and 18 hours respectively. Lowest, but with only four respondents, was the category of nonlawyer employer representatives with a mean of 12.5 hours. A one-way analysis of variance across all five subgroups just misses statistical significance ($p = .062$), but an analysis of just the different types of employer representatives is statistically significant ($p = .005$).

54. Herbert M. Kritzer, "Using Categorical Regression to Analyze Multivariate Contingency Tables," in *New Tools for Social Scientists: Advances and Applications in Research Methods,* ed. William D. Berry and Michael S. Lewis-Beck (Beverly Hills, CA: Sage, 1986), 157–201.

55. Table 12 showed patterns for all cases, discipline cases only, and discharge cases only; creating the two latter tables here has some problems, because the number of cases in some cells is very small. However, the overall pattern in those tables is very similar to that in table 12.

56. These figures were obtained by fitting a special logit model (see table 14) containing two parameters: a constant term (estimated as $-.328$) and a dummy term that allowed the one combination to deviate from the constant (estimated as $-.490$). The value of 41.9 reported in the text is converted from the constant, and the value of 30.6 is converted from the sum of the constant and the dummy term.

57. There may be a slightly different pattern for discharge cases, with the minor diagonal constituting the deviant pattern; however, the sample size is too small to determine whether there is some different underlying pattern here or whether this is just sampling variation.

58. The method of analysis used here is again categorical regression on the logits; a model containing only the main effects of union representation, employer representation, and type of case actually technically fits the table with a goodness-of-fit χ^2 of 6.63 ($7\ df,\ p = .4687$). However, this χ^2 hides within it the significant interaction; adding that interaction reduces the goodness-of-fit χ^2 to 2.38 ($6\ df,\ p = .8818$).

59. The two logit parameters for this model are $-.346$ (constant) and .396 (special interaction term); the goodness-of-fit χ^2 for the model is 6.64 ($10\ df,\ p = .7588$), and the χ^2 for the special interaction term is 4.80 ($1\ df,\ p = .0285$).

60. R. Zavoina and W. McElvey, "A Statistical Model for the Analysis of Ordinal Level Dependent Variables," *Journal of Mathematical Sociology* 4 (1975): 103–20.

61. This is the key that is labeled e^x on many hand calculators.

62. Another way to think about this variable is that it is system-specific experience rather than general grievance arbitration experience.

63. The cube root is similar to the square root. The square root of a number is the value which when multiplied by itself yields the original number; the cube root

of a number is the value that when used as a factor three times yields the original number.

64. This statistic is equal to two times the difference between the log likelihood of the fitted model and a model containing only the constant term.

65. This statistic is equal to the model χ^2 divided by 2 times the log likelihood of a model containing only the constant term.

66. The effect on the odds, a multiplier of 3, is from $e^{1.05} = 2.86$ (2.86 is the coefficient for health-care locals in Model 3), which I have rounded to 3 for purposes of discussion.

67. The "2 to 3" figure is from the coefficient for "discipline short of dismissal" in model 4 ($e^{.66} = 1.93$, rounded to 2) and the coefficient for compensation cases from Model 2 ($e^{1.10} = 3.00$).

68. This value is derived by taking the difference between the coefficients for "lawyer versus outside lawyer" and "nonlawyer versus other than an outside lawyer" ($.95 - .23 = .72$) and exponentiating that value: $e^{.72} = 2.05$, which I have rounded to 2 for discussion purposes.

69. Computed as $e^{.95} = 2.58$, rounded to 2.5 for discussion purposes.

70. Computed as $e^{.40} = 1.49$, rounded to 1.5 for discussion purposes.

71. The average appearance ratio was 3.3.

72. Three of these four locals are affiliated with the Teamsters; it was one of the Teamsters locals that used predominantly nonlawyers (15 out of 17 cases).

73. Another indication of this lack of *systematic* difference is that when I fit logistic regression models containing only representative characteristics (type of representatives and log appearance ratios), the resulting coefficients differ little from those when I include type of union and type of issue in the equation. This suggests that type of issue and type of union are not correlated with the characteristics of representation.

74. Note that in this part of the research, I did not distinguish between inside and outside lawyers for employers, or regional and local nonlawyer representatives for unions.

75. The nonstudent samples were drawn from standard directories. While I refer to a distinction between arbitrators and law professors, some of the arbitrators were, in fact, law professors, and some of the law professors had experience serving as arbitrators. My labeling refers only to the type of list from which an individual was drawn.

76. The students participated on a volunteer or extra-credit basis. The lawyers, arbitrators, and law professors were asked to participate with only the promise that I would let each one know how he or she did on the four briefs, and that I would then send each participant a summary of the results.

77. The variation among the five groups was statistically significant: $\chi^2 = 18.93$, $df = 4$, $p < .001$.

78. To evaluate this difference statistically, I applied the categorical regression technique used earlier in this chapter. The results are somewhat ambiguous, but suggest that it is unlikely that the pattern discussed above can be attributed to sampling variations.

79. Kevin M. Clermont and Theodore Eisenberg, "Trial by Jury or Judge: Transcending Empiricism," *Cornell Law Review* 77 (1992): 1124–77.

80. Stewart Macaulay, "Non-Contractual Relations in Business: A Preliminary Study," *American Sociological Review* 28 (1963): 59–76.

Chapter 6

1. In his book on appellate courts, Judge Frank M. Coffin describes an oral argument presented by a highly regarded appellate lawyer (the late Edward Bennett Williams): "Williams had so prepared himself that he was absolute master of the huge record and could respond to any question with a quick reference to the volume and page containing the precise answer." Despite his preparation and skill, Williams lost the case. See *On Appeal: Courts, Lawyering, and Judging* (New York: W. W. Norton, 1994), 145.

2. One of the very best UC advocates I saw (a nonlawyer, who represented employers) told me that he had lost cases on a number of occasions when the claimant was unrepresented or represented by an inexperienced law student.

3. There was nothing in my observations to allow me to distinguish between accountants and other tax specialists.

4. A motion of summary judgment asks the judge to decide the case on the information then available. Typically, a lawyer makes such a motion when he or she believes that the agreed-upon facts clearly dictate a decision favorable to the lawyer's side. For example, in Wisconsin, truth is an absolute defense against libel. If person A sues person B for libel because A had said that B was a drug user, and B then acknowledges that he had in fact used illegal drugs, there is nothing in dispute, given that the truth is an absolute defense, and B's statement about A was true. B can then make a motion for summary judgment.

5. James Podgers, "Legal Profession Faces Rising Tide of Nonlawyer Practice," *ABA Journal* 79, no. 12 (Dec. 1993): 54.

6. This may operate at all levels of the legal spectrum; see Kevin T. McGuire, *The Supreme Court Bar: Legal Elites in the Washington Community* (Charlottesville: University Press of Virginia, 1993), 175–83.

7. One lawyer quoted a judge as saying to his client, "I'm going to give you the benefit of the doubt because of the lawyer you have."

8. I did observe one case of a nonlawyer advocate handling the appeal of a neighbor; in this case it could well have helped that the advocate had seen the appellate in his home and had a personal familiarity with the appellant's disability.

9. I observed several cases involving lawyers handling a set of interrelated matters, such as a wrongful dismissal claim before the state civil service commission along with the UC claim.

10. This is true of the legal profession more generally; see John P. Heinz and Edward O. Laumann, *Chicago Lawyers: The Social Structure of the Bar* (New York: Russell Sage Foundation, 1982); John P. Heinz, "The Power of Lawyers," *Georgia Law Review* 17 (1983): 891–911; and Robert L. Nelson, *Partners with Power: Social Transformation of the Large Law Firm* (Berkeley: University of California Press, 1988).

11. In a broad sense, I would lump in here the "enrolled agents" who are subject to a separate system, but handle the same kinds of cases.

12. I should also note that the law students I observed could have well have benefited from such observation. In the Social Security setting, the nonlawyers who trained to do such hearings did, in fact, use observation as part of their training process (I encountered one nonlawyer observing hearings for precisely this purpose). I suspect that similar procedures are used by law firms training new associates, and perhaps by union regional councils training new representatives. In his study of lawyers who appear before the U.S. Supreme Court, McGuire discovered that many of the lawyers who regularly appear before the Court make a practice of just going and watching cases, and experienced advocates advise newcomers to do the same; see *Supreme Court Bar,* 185.

13. The most vocal has been an organization named HALT (originally this acronym stood for Help Abolish Legal Tyranny); see Deborah Chalfie, "Lawyers Not Only Source of Good Legal Advice," *Milwaukee Journal* (Dec. 23, 1989), sec. A, 9 (this Op-Ed piece appeared in a number of papers around the country).

14. Quoted in *Nonlawyer Practice in the United States: Summary of the Factual Record Before the American Bar Association Commission on Nonlawyer Practice,* discussion draft for comment (Chicago: American Bar Association, Apr. 1994), A.TX-2.

15. See Richard L. Abel, *American Lawyers* (New York: Oxford University Press, 1989).

16. See Herbert M. Kritzer, "Abel and the Professional Project: The Institutional Analysis of the Legal Profession," *Law & Social Inquiry* 16 (1991): 529–52; Richard L. Abel, "The Decline of Professionalism," *Modern Law Review* 49 (1986): 1–41.

17. "ISBA [Illinois State Bar Association] Task Force Warns of 'Inherent Dangers' in ABA Plan to Expand Non-lawyer Practice," *Chicago Daily Law Bulletin* (May 16, 1996), 21.

18. See Judith Citron, *The Citizens' Advice Bureaux: For the Community by the Community* (London: Pluto Press, 1989).

19. See, for example, William H. Simon, *An Innovative Model Providing High Quality Legal Assistance for the Elderly in Wisconsin* (Madison: Center for Public Representation, 1988).

20. Podgers quotes one Iowa lawyer, asked what she thought about the possibility of a nonlawyer opening a practice nearby: "I'd probably freak. Then I'd realize they weren't encroaching. They'd probably screw things up and I could charge double"; Podgers, "Rising Tide of Nonlawyer Practice," 55.

21. See Lori B. Andrews, "Hazardous to Your Health: Medical Error in a Hospital Setting," *Researching the Law: An ABF Update* 6 (winter 1995): 1; *Patients, Doctors, and Lawyers: Medical Injury, Malpractice Litigation, and Patient Compensation in New York,* Report of the Harvard Medical Practice Study to the State of New York (Cambridge: Harvard Medical School, 1990).

22. It should be noted that errors by lawyers are not the primary basis of client dissatisfaction. This dissatisfaction typically turns on misunderstandings about what the lawyer was supposed to do or what the legal fees would be; see

Don Van Natta Jr., "Group Urges More Scrutiny on How Lawyers Treat Clients," *New York Times* (Oct. 10, 1995), sec. A, 14. Interestingly, probably the most common client complaint is that the lawyer fails to return phone calls; see Amy Stevens, "Lawyers' Annoying Misdeeds Targeted," *Wall Street Journal* (Sept. 9, 1994), sec. B, 1; Fern S. Sussman, "Lawyers Have to Take Complaints of Clients More Seriously," *New York Times* (Nov. 26, 1993), sec. A, 18; Randall Samborn, "Anti-Lawyer Attitude Up," *National Law Journal* (Aug. 9, 1993), 22.

23. We do know that many clients feel that their lawyers have not been sufficiently attentive to the client and/or the work the lawyer is doing on the client's behalf; see W. L. F. Felstiner, "Professional Inattention: Origins and Consequences," in *The Human Face of Law: Essays in Honour of Donald Harris,* ed. Keith Hawkins (Oxford: Clarendon Press, 1997), 121–50.

24. David B. Wilkins, "Who Should Regulate Lawyers?" *Harvard Law Review* 105 (1992): 801–87. Wilkins identifies a fourth potential mechanism that some observers have proposed, which he labels "legislative controls." This would involve a wholly independent regulatory agency outside the judicial branch (something like the SEC).

25. See Lawrence C. Marshall, Herbert M. Kritzer, and Frances K. Zemans, "The Use and Impact of Rule 11," *Northwestern Law Review* 86 (1992): 943–86.

26. See Bruce L. Arnold and John Hagan, "Careers of Misconduct: The Structure of Prosecuted Professional Deviance among Lawyers," *American Sociological Review* 57 (1992): 771–80; James Evans, "Lawyers at Risk," *California Lawyer* 9, no. 10 (Oct. 1989): 45–48.

27. See Jacob M. Wolf, "Nonlawyer Practice Before the Social Security Administration," *Administrative Law Review* 37 (1985): 415.

28. See Jonathan Rose, "Nonlawyer Practice Before Federal Administrative Agencies Should Be Encouraged," *Administrative Law Review* 37 (1985): 371; David B. Holmes, "Nonlawyer Practice Before the Immigration Agencies," *Administrative Law Review* 37 (1985): 419; Donald J. Quigg, "Nonlawyer Practice Before the Patent and Trademark Office," *Administrative Law Review* 37 (1985): 410.

29. Wisconsin Administrative Code (*Wis. Adm. Code* ILHR 140.18(2)(a) [1994]) provides for the suspension of advocates who fail to comply with standards of conduct established in the code (*Wis. Adm. Code* ILHR 140.18(1)[1994]).

30. When I asked the head of another state agency which conducts administrative hearings and which permits nonlawyer advocates to appear before it whether the agency had any rules concerning the regulation or disciplining of those advocates, he told me the issue had never come up because the agency had not encountered any advocates who seemed to be particularly problematic.

31. Wolf, "Nonlawyer Practice," 415.

32. Quigg, "Nonlawyer Practice," 410.

33. See NYCRR, chap. 5, §302.

34. *Nonlawyer Activity in Law-Related Situations: A Report with Recommendations* (Chicago: American Bar Association, 1995), 129.

35. For example, in Wisconsin physicians, podiatrists, private detectives, cosmetology schools, and car dealers must be insured or bonded; accountants, archi-

tects, surveyors, chiropractors, funeral directors, dentists, psychologists, and securities brokers have no such requirement.

36. Just looking at phone numbers listed in the Madison telephone book, this department regulates and licenses accountants, acupuncturists, architects, professional engineers, designers, land surveyors, barbers and cosmetologists, chiropractors, funeral directors, pharmacists, physicians, dentists, veterinarians, hearing and speech therapists, physical and occupational therapists, respiratory therapists, marriage and family therapists, nursing home administrators, nurses, optometrists, counselors, social workers, real estate brokers, marriage and family therapists, physicians' assistants, psychologists, professional fund-raisers, and private detectives. Other departments of state government license and regulate teachers, school administrators, insurance brokers, pesticide applicators, and plumbers. In 1996, the Paralegal Association of Wisconsin drafted a statute that would have the Department of Regulation and Licensing assume responsibility for licensure of paralegals; however, the proposal serves more to legitimize the status of paralegals than to make available alternative sources of legal assistance to the general public.

37. See Thomas W. Alpert, "The Inherent Power of the Courts to Regulate the Practice of Law: An Historical Analysis," *Buffalo Law Review* 32 (1983): 525–56. For descriptions and analyses of the workings of these systems, see Jerome E. Carlin, *Lawyer's Ethics: A Survey of the New York City Bar* (New York: Russell Sage, 1966), 150–64; Eric H. Steele and Raymond T. Nimmer, "Lawyers, Clients, and Professional Regulation," *American Bar Foundation Research Journal* (1976): 919–1019; *Lawyer Regulation for a New Century: Report of the Commission on Evaluation of Disciplinary Enforcement* (Chicago: American Bar Association, Center for Professional Responsibility, 1992).

38. While some of the difference in cost of lawyer and nonlawyer services is undoubtedly attributable to the lawyer's licensing and (optional) insurance costs, this is unlikely to account for a significant part of the difference. For example, a paralegal in San Mateo, California, charges $295 to file uncontested divorces and $175 for simple bankruptcies, services for which a local law firm would charge $1,500 and $1,000 respectively; see Mike France, "Bar Chiefs Protect the Guild," *National Law Journal* (Aug. 7, 1995), sec. A, 28. However, it is far-fetched to attribute more than a very small fraction of this difference to malpractice insurance premiums or bar dues (despite the fact that the author of the article in which this is reported seems to do so).

39. See *Nonlawyer Practice,* A.CA-8f; Victoria Slind-Flor, "'No' to Legal Technicians in California," *National Law Journal* (Sept. 9, 1991), 19.

40. See *Nonlawyer Practice.*

41. See France, "Bar Chiefs Protect the Guild."

42. *Nonlawyer Activity,* 11–12.

43. See Deborah Rhode, "Meet Needs with Nonlawyers: It Is Time to Accept Lay Practitioners—and Regulate Them," *ABA Journal* 82, no. 1 (Jan. 1996): 82.

44. Hope Viner Samborn, "Shades of Regulation: State Bills Apply Sundry Standards to Independent Paralegals," *ABA Journal* 83, no. 6 (June 1997): 26.

45. On the increasing role of specialized knowledge, see Philip Lewis, "Knowing the Buzzwords and Clapping for Tinker Bell: The Context, Content and Qual-

ities of Lawyers' Knowledge in a Specialized Industrial Field," in *The Human Face of Law: Essays in Honour of Donald Harris,* ed. Keith Hawkins (Oxford: Clarendon Press, 1997), 151–76; and Richard L. Abel and Philip S. C. Lewis, "Putting Law Back into the Sociology of Lawyers," in *Lawyers in Society: Comparative Theories,* ed. Richard L. Abel and Philip S. C. Lewis (Berkeley: University of California Press, 1989), 509–13.

46. For a history of the debate over specialization, which dates from at least the 1920s, see Michael Ariens, "Know the Law: A History of Legal Specialization," *South Carolina Law Review* 45 (1994): 1003–61.

47. Regarding the history and development of legal education in the United States, see Robert Stevens, *Law School: Legal Education in America from the 1850s to the 1980s* (Chapel Hill: University of North Carolina Press, 1983); William P. LaPiana, *Logic and Experience: The Origin of Modern American Legal Education* (New York: Oxford University Press, 1994).

48. Stewart Macaulay, "Law Schools and the World Outside Their Doors II: Some Notes on the Margins of Heinz and Laumann and Zemans and Rosenblum," *Journal of Legal Education* 32 (1982): 515.

49. See Ronald Pipkin, "Legal Education: The Consumers' Perspective," *American Bar Foundation Research Journal* (1976): 1176; Frances Kahn Zemans and Victor G. Rosenblum, *The Making of a Public Profession* (Chicago: American Bar Foundation, 1981), 140; Bryant Garth and Joanne Martin, "Law Schools and the Construction of Competence," *Journal of Legal Education* 43 (1993): 482–88; Alex M. Johnson, "Think Like a Lawyer, Work Like a Machine: The Dissonance Between Law School and Law Practice," *Southern California Law Review* 64 (1991): 1231–60; Robert Granfield, *Making Elite Lawyers: Visions of Law at Harvard and Beyond* (New York: Routledge, 1992), 160.

50. See, for example, Francis A. Allen, *Law, Intellect, and Education* (Ann Arbor: University of Michigan Press, 1979), 51–92. The conflict between legal training from the academician's viewpoint versus from the practitioner's viewpoint is by no means new; see John Henry Schlegel, "Law and Endangered Species: Is Survival Alone Cause for Celebration?" *Indiana Law Review* 28 (1995): 401–2.

51. Kurt M. Saunders and Linda Levine, "Learning to Think Like a Lawyer," *University of San Francisco Law Review* 29 (1994): 121–95.

52. John J. Costonis, "The MacCrate Report: Of Loaves, Fishes and the Future of American Legal Education," in *The MacCrate Report: Building the Educational Continuum,* ed. Joan S. Howland and William H. Lindberg (St. Paul: West Publishing, 1994), 65; Daniel J. Givelber et al., "Learning Through Work: An Empirical Study of Legal Internship," *Journal of Legal Education* 45 (1995): 1–48.

53. *Legal Education and Professional Development—An Educational Continuum,* report of the Task Force on Law Schools and the Profession: Narrowing the Gap (Chicago: American Bar Association, Section of Legal Education and Admissions to the Bar, 1992).

54. Ibid., 40. The report goes on to recognize that in many if not most practice settings, lawyers have increasingly become specialists.

55. Competence is, of course, not a simple concept. Some of the complexities are nicely captured by Neil Gold: "Competence is not an absolute concept which

exists apart from the specific work in question, the context of the public to be served or the particular needs of an individual client. In practice it is a minimum standard applied to a single context and transaction at a time. As a generalised concept it is the ability to manage one's limits. . . . A profession's concept of competence will be different in different times and different places. It is not a static concept." "Reconceiving Professional Competence," *Journal of Professional Legal Education* 10 (1992): 140.

56. Ibid., 140, 207–12.

57. Ibid., 212, quoting the Model Rules of Professional Conduct.

58. For a bibliography of commentary and other writing on specialization, see Nathan Aaron Rosen, *Lawyer Specialization: A Comprehensive Annotated Bibliography of Articles, Books, Court Decisions and Ethics Opinions* (Chicago: American Bar Association, Standing Committee on Specialization, 1990).

59. See Nelson, *Partners with Power;* Erwin Smigel, *The Wall Street Lawyer: Professional Organization Man?* (New York: Free Press of Glencoe, 1964); Marc Galanter and Thomas Palay, *Tournament of Lawyers: The Transformation of the Big Law Firm* (Chicago: University of Chicago Press, 1991); Edward Laumann and John Heinz, "Specialization and Prestige in the Legal Profession: The Structure of Deference," *American Bar Foundation Research Journal* (1977): 155–56.

60. Lynn M. LoPucki, "The De Facto Pattern of Lawyer Specialization," University of Wisconsin, Institute for Legal Studies, Disputes Processing Research Program Working Paper 9–10 (Apr. 1990), 53.

61. The U.S. Supreme Court provided some impetus to the development of certification plans in its decision in *Peel v. Attorney Registration and Disciplinary Commission of Illinois,* 496 U.S. 91 (1990), in which the court struck down an Illinois ban on the communication (advertising) of certification. For a review of the relevant Court decisions, see James Podgers, "Recent Developments in Specialization: The Relationship between Specialization and Advertising," in American Bar Association Standing Committee on Specialization, *Specialization Desk Book* (Chicago: American Bar Association, 1993).

62. Ibid., 2.

63. 433 U.S. 350 (1977).

64. See Rosen, *Lawyer Specialization,* 3. A revised version of the *Model Standards for Speciality Areas* was published by the ABA Standing Committee on Specialization in 1987 and contained model standards for 25 areas of practice from admiralty to workers' compensation.

65. By 1990, only 14 states had adopted plans (most rather limited), and one state, Georgia, had abandoned its plan; see LoPucki, "De Facto Pattern," 53. By 1993, 18 states had plans in place; see ABA Standing Committee on Specialization, *Specialization State Plan Book* (Chicago: American Bar Association, 1993).

66. LoPucki, "De Facto Pattern," 1–2; see also Terrence M. Gherty and Dean R. Dietrich, "Specialization: Pro and Con," *Wisconsin Lawyer* 64, no. 11 (Nov. 1991): 10–13.

67. There are other dimensions of specialization as well: type of client, type of industry, side represented, size of matter, and geographical area; see Clarance E.

Hagglund and Robert Birnbaum, "Legal Specialization: The Need for Uniformity," *Judicature* 67 (1984): 438; LoPucki, "De Facto Pattern," 11.

68. This approach to specialization, either certified or informal, seems to be the norm within common-law systems; see, for example, David A. A. Stager and Harry W. Arthurs, *Lawyers in Canada* (Toronto: University of Toronto Press, 1990), 199–201. The one exception is the barrister/solicitor division within the English (and part of the Australian) profession.

69. This specialized training and mentoring is the most developed in the large corporate law firm setting. However, competitive and economic pressures are forcing those firms to rethink how they train their associates; see Mike France, "Dilemma: Who Will Teach Associates?" *National Law Journal* (Nov. 20, 1995), sec. A, 1, 22.

70. See Ken Myers, "Students Tapping LL.M. Programs to 'Master' Their Own Fates," *National Law Journal* (July 31, 1995), sec. A, 16.

71. W. Scott Van Alstyne, Joseph R. Julin, and Larry D. Barnett, *The Goals and Missions of Law Schools* (New York: Peter Lang, 1990), 112–25.

72. Interestingly, Judge Richard A. Posner has argued for moving in the opposite direction, reducing the period of study for a law degree to two years; see Chris Klein, "Revolution from Above? A Judge Calls for Two-Year J.D. Program," *National Law Journal* (Oct. 14, 1997), sec. A, 12.

73. Most Canadian provinces require a 12-month clerkship; Manitoba requires 11.5 months, New Brunswick and British Columbia 10 months, and Quebec, which has a different system, 6 months for graduates seeking to become *avocats* (no clerkship is required for those wanting to become *notaires*); see Stager and Arthurs, *Lawyers in Canada,* 127.

74. Marie T. Huxter, "Survey of Employment Opportunities for Articling Students and Graduates of the Bar Admission Course in Ontario," *Law Society of Upper Canada Gazette* 15 (1981): 205.

75. See Stager and Arthurs, *Lawyers in Canada,* 130–32; Frederick H. Zemans, "Articling—A Law School Perspective," *Law Society of Upper Canada Gazette* 22 (1988): 382–91. However, a review of articling by the Legal Education Committee of the Law Society of Upper Canada [Ontario] called for continuing the articling process in a largely unchanged form; see Philip M. Epstein (chairperson), *Proposals for Articling Reform* (Toronto: Law Society of Upper Canada, 1990 [updated 1994]).

76. See Richard L. Abel, *The Legal Profession in England and Wales* (Oxford: Basil Blackwell, 1988), 153–56; David Weisbrot, "The Australian Legal Profession: From Provincial Family Firms to Multinationals," in *Lawyers in Society: The Common Law World,* ed. Richard L. Abel and Philip S. C. Lewis (Berkeley: University of California Press, 1988), 268–69.

77. Clinical training in law is not unique to the United States; see Philip F. Iya, "Educating Lawyers for Practice—Clinical Experience as an Integral Part of Legal Education in the BOLESWA Countries of Southern Africa," *International Journal of the Legal Profession* 1 (1994): 315–41.

78. See Zemans, "Articling," 386.

79. See Stephen R. Alton, "Mandatory Prelicensure Legal Internship: An Idea

Whose Time Has Come Again?" *Kansas Law Review* 41 (1992): 137–67; Givelber et al., "Learning Through Work"; and Arline Jolles Lotman, "Like Doctors, Lawyers Should Serve Residencies," *National Law Journal* (Dec. 9, 1996), sec. A, 18. For a contrasting view see Wallace J. Mlyniec, "Internship: A Nice Idea, But It Wouldn't Work" (Jan. 27, 1997), sec. A, 24.

80. My efforts to locate previous uses of this concept identified only one, a book entitled *Post-Professionalism: Transforming the Information Heartland,* by Blaise Cronin and Elisabeth Davenport (London: Taylor Graham, 1988); this book focuses on developments in the "information professions."

81. This is, of course, a gross oversimplification of Bell's analysis, which is a rich, highly nuanced discussion. Bell identifies a set of five dimensions.

(1) Economic sector: the change from a goods-producing to a service economy;
(2) Occupational distribution: the pre-eminence of the professional and technical class;
(3) Axial principle: the centrality of theoretical knowledge as the source of innovation and of policy formulation for society;
(4) Future orientation: the control of technology and technological assessment;
(5) Decision-making: the creation of a new "intellectual technology" [quotations in the original].

The Coming of Post-Industrial Society: A Venture in Social Forecasting (New York: Basic Books, 1973), 14.

82. Ibid., 37.

83. Carroll Seron, *The Business of Practicing Law: The Work Lives of Solo and Small-Firm Attorneys* (Philadelphia: Temple University Press, 1996), 19–30, 167 n. 4.

84. Ibid., 147; omitted material references the major changes in the gender composition of the legal profession.

85. On the problem of, and importance of, definition, see Eliot Freidson, "The Theory of Professions: State of the Art," in *The Sociology of the Professions: Doctors, Lawyers and Others,* Robert Dingwall and Philip S. C. Lewis, eds. (London: Macmillan, 1983), 19–37.

86. Andrew Abbott, *The System of Professions: An Essay on the Division of Expert Labor* (Chicago: University of Chicago Press, 1988), 8.

87. Richard L. Abel, "The Decline of Professionalism," *Modern Law Review* 49 (1986): 1–41. While this essay specifically focuses on the English legal professions, Abel has made similar arguments about the American profession as well; see his book *American Lawyers* (New York: Oxford University Press, 1989).

88. Richard L. Abel, "The Transformation of the American Legal Profession," *Law & Society Review* 20 (1986): 7.

89. See Herbert M. Kritzer, "Abel and the Professional Project: The Institutional Analysis of the Legal Profession," *Law & Social Inquiry* 16 (1991): 547–50.

90. Bell, *Post-Industrial Society,* 17.

91. Ibid., 20.

92. See Peter T. Kilborn, "Doctors Organize to Fight Corporate Intrusion,"

New York Times (July 1, 1997), sec. A, 12; Milt Freudenheim, "As Nurses Take on Primary Care, Physicians Are Sounding Alarms," *New York Times* (Sept. 30, 1997), sec. A, 1.

93. This distinction is what Heinz and Laumann label the "two hemispheres of the bar"; see *Chicago Lawyers.*

94. Seron, *Business of Practicing Law,* 106–26.

95. See Austin Sarat and William L. F. Felstiner, *Divorce Lawyers and Their Clients: Power and Meaning in the Legal Process* (New York: Oxford University Press, 1995).

Index